SURVIVING CHILDLESSNESS

FAITH AND FURBABIES

'Steph writes, "When God saves us, he does not recruit us into his pyramid scheme", and I feel the same can be said of this book. It is not providing a magic solution or a step by step guide to surviving childlessness and reaching the top of the pyramid. Instead you are encouraged to ask questions and rediscover how you view your own faith; to look at your doubts and insecurities; to feel safe in the knowledge that you don't have to agree with everything the church tells you.

'Steph shares, "A faith without room to question, to explore, to wonder, would lack depth". This book gives you the opportunity to look inwards with a fresh perspective and see how you hold the power to transform your life.'

Stephanie Phillips,
founder of *World Childless Week*

'Steph Penny's latest work is a deeply moving and much needed book that shines a penetrating and much needed spotlight on faith and childlessness. Steph draws on the deep well of her Christianity and personal experience of childlessness-by-forced-choice to offer guidance, succour and comfort. Using a light and revealing touch, Steph explores the real life stories of several similarly childless-by-circumstance and the challenges they faced in their intimate and wider relationships, socially, culturally and matters ecumenical.'

Dr Robin Hadley,
international childlessness
researcher, blogger and author of
Men and Me(n): Researching Men

'In *Surviving Childlessness*, Steph Penny has given the childless Christian community, and all those who minister to them, a powerful and long-overdue gift–an honest voice.

'My organisation, *Gateway Women*, includes many Christian members and followers who have experienced (and are experiencing) considerable exclusion and misunderstanding from their Churches as a result of their childlessness (and often their singleness too) and this book will provide them with comfort and validation. Some of the childless Christians I know are also clergy themselves, doing their best to create change from within, and this book will provide them too with tools and guidance for their mission.

'One of the things I particularly appreciated about this book was its willingness to engage with some of the many hidden reasons for involuntary childlessness such as childhood trauma, domestic violence, chronic illness, abortion and the complexities underpinning the "just adopt" comment. All are handled with a frank sensitivity that the clergy would do well to take heed of– especially if it is to offer a more inclusive experience to the many childless women and couples who find themselves turning away from their Churches after one-too-many experiences of exclusion after yet another "family-focused" service or initiative.

'As Steph points out, the 21st century Christian Church would do well to remember that Jesus was single and childless himself.'

Jody Day,
psychotherapist, author and
founder of *Gateway Women*
www.gateway-women.com

Surviving Childlessness

Copyright © 2021 Steph Penny

Printed by SOS Print + Media
Cover design and internal layout by Book Whispers

ISBN
Paperback: 978-0-6450627-0-0
Ebook: 978-0-6450627-1-7

A catalogue record for this book is available from the National Library of Australia

Scripture quotations taken from The Holy Bible, New International Version® NIV® Copyright © 1973 1978 1984 2011 by Biblica, Inc. TM Used by permission. All rights reserved worldwide.

All quoted scriptures are from the NIV unless otherwise indicated.

Scripture quotations marked MSG are taken from the THE MESSAGE, copyright © 1993, 2002, 2018 by Eugene H. Peterson. Used by permission of NavPress. All rights reserved. Represented by Tyndale House Publishers, Inc.

SURVIVING CHILDLESSNESS

FAITH AND FURBABIES

STEPH PENNY

For Obadiah Lucas
And Reema Grace
The children we never had

CONTENTS

Acknowledgements x
Helpful Terms xii

SECTION ONE: ALL ABOARD 1

Introduction — *My Story, the Springboard for this Book* 3
1: Childless vs Childfree — *What's the Difference?* 9
Marie's Story — *United Kingdom (UK)* 21

SECTION TWO: SETTING SAIL 27

2: Society — *Surviving in a Child-Centric World* 29
Elena's Story — *Australia* 57
John and Rachel's Story — *Australia* 59
3: Church — *I'm the Odd One Out* 64
Sarah's Story — *UK* 88
4: Infertility — *Why is Everyone Else Pregnant?* 97
Philippa's Story — *UK* 121
5: Singledom — *Maybe I Want Kids Too* 125

SECTION THREE: STORM DAMAGE 135

6: Sex — *Procreation is Hot* 137
Anita's Story — *UK* 150

7: Trauma — *Why Can't I Stop Thinking About It?* 154
Maddy's Story — *Australia* 169
8: God — *When Faith and Disappointment Collide* 176
Carmel's Story — *UK* 197
9: Grief — *Living with Broken Dreams* 203
Rosemary's Story — *Australia* 224
Joy's Story — *Australia* 228
10: Ageing — *Do You Have Grandkids?* 234

SECTION FOUR: SURVIVAL 243

11: Friends and Family — *What Not to Say* 245
Fiona's Story — *New Zealand* 261
Melanie's Story — *UK* 265
12: Sanity — *A Survival Smorgasbord* 268
Natasha's Story — *Australia* 297
13: Faith — *The Meaning of it All* 303
14: Inconclusions — *Now What?* 331

Helpful Resources 342
About the Author 343
References 345

ACKNOWLEDGEMENTS

God—my anchor.

Husband—for being who you are.

Editor—Nola Passmore—for wisdom, guidance and enthusiasm for this project.

Beta-readers—Jo-Anne Berthelsen, Juliana Purnell and Richelle Hatton—living proof that one can be both honest and gracious at the same time.

Omega Christian Writers, especially my Sydney chapter—for lovingly spurring me on as a writer.

Interviewees—Marie, Elena, John and Rachel, Sarah, Philippa, Anita, Maddy, Carmel, Rosemary, Joy, Fiona, Melanie and Natasha—for sharing your stories.

*'Perhaps a greater tragedy
than a broken dream is a life
forever defined by it.'*

Sheridan Voysey (2013),
Resurrection Year[1]

HELPFUL TERMS

Childlessness terms:
CNBC—childless-not-by-choice
CBFC—childless-by-forced-choice
DINK—Double Income, No Kids
PANK—Professional Aunt, No Kids
PUNK—Professional Uncle, No Kids

Medical terms:
AMH—anti-mullerian hormone
GIFT—gamete intrafallopian transfer (type of infertility treatment)
ICSI—intracytoplasmic sperm injection (type of infertility treatment)
IUI—intrauterine insemination (type of infertility treatment)
IVF—in vitro fertilisation (type of infertility treatment)
NHS—National Health Service (in the UK)
PCOS—polycystic ovarian syndrome
PTSD—Post-Traumatic Stress Disorder
STI—sexually transmitted infection
ZIFT—zygote intrafallopian transfer (type of infertility treatment)

Places:
ACT—Australian Capital Territory, Australia
NSW—New South Wales, Australia
NT—Northern Territory, Australia
NZ—New Zealand
QLD—Queensland, Australia
SA—South Australia, Australia
TAS—Tasmania, Australia
UK—United Kingdom
USA—United States of America
VIC—Victoria, Australia
WA—Western Australia, Australia

Others:
ACE—adverse childhood experience
DV—domestic violence
EFT—Emotional Freedom Technique
FOMO—fear of missing out
n.d.—no date

SECTION ONE
ALL ABOARD

INTRODUCTION

My Story, the Springboard for this Book

Ten years ago I discovered I was in sin.

The year was 2010. We were engaged to be married. Before the wedding, my fiancé and I attended three months of pre-marital counselling like all good Christian couples. This was largely a positive and educational experience.

There was, however, one conversation that stuck with me.

I did not expect it to end in tears.

Back then, in my pre-marital state, I had no desire to have children. I was not clucky or super-maternal and I thought I would die happy without kids.

(This shifted once I got married. I became open to the idea of having kids with my husband. It made sense, sharing an intimacy so powerful it could create a whole new person. I was still not gooey over other peoples' kids. But giving my husband the gift of children? Absolutely.)

Anyway, I told our pre-marital pastor I had no desire for children.

This was a mistake.

He told me God commands us to have children. He told me I was therefore in sin.

At that moment, the room froze around me. The blood pounded in my ears. I was in shock. Did he really say that? I could not believe what I was hearing from this Christian man, a trained pastor, about my apparent sin.

But the pastor was not finished. He asked me, gently but repeatedly, why I did not want children. I had no defence. I was not prepared for this. He pushed the point so hard I ended up crying.

I wasn't anti-children, I just had no desire for kids of my own—yet. I was neutral. And I did not understand why the pastor could not comprehend this. I could not fathom why he was applying pressure for me to become pro-kids on the spot.

I second-guessed myself afterwards. I felt tossed in an ocean of accusation and confusion. Was he right? Then I got furious. How dare he. How dare he suggest that just because I have a uterus, I am obligated to use it.

Perhaps he was convinced I was actually committing a spiritual crime. Perhaps he believed telling me to have kids would magically make me want kids. I am not sure. I just know it was unhelpful.

(If you believe not having or wanting children is indeed a sin, stick with me. Hopefully we can discuss these issues even if we disagree.)

After that incident, I thought that would be the end of the pro-child pressure.

But no.

Friends and people at church started asking when we would

have kids. Even while we were still engaged. (Why are there so many self-appointed family planners around?)

When I told them I was unsure, because I had not yet experienced that shift towards children, they would stare and say, 'Steph, why is that?' Like I was suffering from some kind of undiagnosed anti-child syndrome.

I got the distinct impression they were looking for an underlying reason for my neutral desire. In their eyes, I was weird. Abnormal. Strange. Inexplicable.

And my neutrality, in their view, was a problem. An illness. A deficiency. Their shocked and puzzled expressions indicated something was dreadfully wrong with me.

These people had a sea of assumptions about me and perhaps about Christian women in general. They assumed I would become a baby-making machine the instant I got married.

Guess I disappointed them.

Since then, my husband and I have made the difficult decision to remain childless due to significant health issues (more on that to come). Interestingly, people are far more accepting of my health-related childlessness than my original alien-like lack of desire.

I wonder why we feel compelled to explain or defend childlessness. It's not just me. Other childless people have experienced incredulity and interrogation when confessing they do not have children. They have told me so. Those people asked me to write about childlessness.

What a fabulous idea.

But I did not want to write about my childless experience

alone. After all, it was the promptings of other childless couples that inspired this book in the first place. I felt it would be appropriate, vital even, to include the stories of other childless folk in this book.

So I decided to interview anyone who would talk to me about their childless experience. I put a tiny advert on social media one night, asking for volunteers. Then I went to bed.

I awoke the next morning to a tsunami of responses.

These volunteers seemed hungry to share their stories. They told me there was painfully little written on this subject. They told me we have to get the word out. They told me the church needs to talk about this.

I did my own search for Christian books on childlessness. I found a few about 'barrenness' (ugh. I mean, why?) and one promising book on childlessness, but upon further reading, it seemed to suggest childlessness is caused by a lack of faith. It claimed if we simply increase our faith, our problems will be solved and—voila!—children will miraculously appear.

I nearly choked.

Why do we think that childlessness is a problem to be fixed? Why do we think childless Christians are somehow less-than or inferior to the rest of the church? And why, oh why do we think faith is a cure-all?

Such are the challenges I take up here.

I have included stories from childless people around the world. Some have used pseudonyms to protect their privacy. All of them were invited to review and make changes to their stories prior to publishing. All of them gave me detailed and at times startling insights into the world of childlessness.

INTRODUCTION

I hope you find their tales as eye-opening and heartwarming as I did.

You may be reading this because you are childless. You may have struggled with this for a long time. Welcome. This book is for you.

Perhaps you are a family member or friend of a childless person and you want to understand them better. I have set aside Chapter 11 just for you.

Perhaps you are a church pastor or leader, seeking to support childless members in your congregation. I speak to pastors and churches throughout this book. Some of my comments may apply to you and your church. Others may not.

Whoever you are, I hope you find something helpful here. In particular, if you are childless, I hope you find connection through the stories of childlessness. I hope you realise you are not alone. You are part of a worldwide childless community. And there are new possibilities your life may yet hold.

I pray God will be near to you as you read. May you find him in these pages and beyond, in our conversations, our collective hope and our indomitable survival.

May we know God's kindness and companionship in the midst of mystery.

May we be inspired to speak more about childlessness in our churches and communities.

May Jesus be our anchor, whether we are in a safe harbour, tossed by a tempest, sinking in a tsunami or lost at sea.

1

CHILDLESS VS CHILDFREE

What's the Difference?

When I first met my husband, I warned him I had chronic pain. That way he knew what he was getting into and could jump ship if he wanted.

He married me anyway.

Awww.

Then, two years into our marriage, after we had started planning for our children, I got diagnosed with lupus.

Lupus is a wildly unpredictable disease, ranging from being a mild nuisance to completely disabling. It has given me, amongst other things, an increased risk of miscarriage and bad pregnancy outcomes. Initially I was not too worried about this. Then I started writing this book.

I didn't know it, but my world was about to be shattered.

The discovery

One day, as I was researching childlessness, I found a marvellous website, *Access Australia* (2020)[2], which has medically-informed fact sheets about childlessness and infertility. I skimmed through these fact sheets with interest.

Until one stopped me in my tracks.

It was about the immune system and infertility (Access Australia n.d.)[3]. It identified several conditions that raise the likelihood of miscarriage. Conditions like lupus and antiphospholipid antibodies, which increase the risk of blood clotting.

A bomb went off in my head.

I have lupus and antiphospholipid antibodies.

The fact sheet said lupus and antiphospholipid antibodies can cause miscarriage. The antibodies in particular are 'reliable predictors' of bad pregnancy outcomes such as pregnancy loss and retardation of the foetus (Access Australia n.d.)[4].

Reliable predictors.

That got my attention. I stopped reading, frozen in breathless horror, staring at the screen. The words 'reliable predictors' were lit up as though by stadium spotlights.

I knew my antibodies carried an increased risk of miscarriage, but I had assumed the risk was low. Maybe I was wrong.

I should check this out, I thought. So my husband and I dug deeper.

We found studies on lupus and antiphospholipid antibodies and their outcomes for pregnancy. We researched fancy medical terms and did some calculations. What we discovered forever changed our lives.

Apparently I have a fifty percent chance of miscarrying or producing a child with significant deformities and lifelong high needs.

Fifty percent.

It hit us like a full-speed semi-trailer. It made up our minds on the spot about having children. The risk was way too high.

I already suffered from chronic pain and fatigue. Caring for myself was a daily challenge. I could not even push shopping trolleys (you know, the uncooperative ones), let alone juggle prams and babies and baby-related baggage. Caring for a healthy child would be difficult, but caring for a high-needs child their whole life? I felt I was unequal to the task.

The decision was clear.

We chose a life of childlessness.

The fallout

Before doing this research, I was holding on to the hope of one day having children. But the research shot this hope to pieces.

I was in shock for a few days afterwards. I had learned the true nature of the risk my body carried. I could not believe it.

I felt sad about it. I felt I had lost something I had not even begun to grasp. A lost opportunity, a missed experience. A hope prematurely aborted. A choice dispossessed. A decision snatched away.

It hit me all over again when I realised the names my husband and I had chosen for our children, names selected with great care, would never be needed. At that moment, my heart hurt and the tears flowed.

It affected my identity as a woman. A woman's body is

supposed to be a safe haven for growing life. It is supposed to be a place of nurturing and protection.

But my body is designed to kill. The combination of lupus and antiphospholipid antibodies is deadly. If I became pregnant, my disease would turn on that which it is supposed to protect. Like a police officer turning rogue and starting to shoot civilians, lupus would identify my baby as an enemy and try to destroy it.

What does that mean about me as a woman?

If anyone has an answer, let me know. I have not worked that out yet.

It hit my husband too. He had wanted children even more than me, so it affected him greatly. I felt an enormous amount of guilt about that. I still do. I had always thought my husband would make a superb father. Not being able to give him this gift was almost more than I could bear.

We discussed how to support each other through this and what might help us to grieve. It was my husband's idea to dedicate this book to the two children we named but never had.

It was a good idea.

So which am I?

Childlessness is common and on the rise. In Australia, one in four women under the age of forty-five are childless. In the United Kingdom (UK), it is one in five. In Germany and Japan, it is as high as one in three (Day 2017)[5].

I could not find equivalent statistics for men in Australia. (Clearly, more research is needed.) But one researcher in the UK, Dr Robin Hadley, drew on a number of studies and concluded one in four men in the UK are childless (cited in Lynch 2018)[6].

Countless men and women have a childlessness story to share.

But my story lives in a grey zone. There is often more to childlessness than being 'able' or 'not able'. This raises a pertinent question.

How should I define myself? Am I childless-by-choice? Or am I childless-not-by-choice? I am both—and neither. I need a spectrum, not a black-and-white box.

So I researched the existing childlessness terms.

First, there is childfreedom. This is where a person or couple freely chooses to remain childfree for social, political, environmental, vocational or spiritual reasons. Clear as day.

Second, there is childlessness-by-circumstance. I believe this refers to childlessness due to not being able to find the right partner with whom to have biological children. For example, a childless-by-circumstance person may marry someone who already has kids from a previous relationship and has no desire to have any more. Childless-by-singledom people also fall under this category.

Third, we have childlessness-not-by-choice (CNBC). This one is about medical issues such as infertility or other conditions that cause problems with falling pregnant or carrying a baby to term.

A fellow childless person told me I was childless-by-circumstance because my health issues could be viewed as a unique circumstance leading to childlessness. They are right, of course.

But I am torn.

> *If you have felt robbed of the choice to have children, or believe your 'choice' was no choice at all, you might be CBFC.*

The 'circumstance' bit infers I had no choice. Did I have absolutely no choice? Am I CNBC because of my medical conditions? After all, I did not choose to get sick, right?

On the other hand, I kinda did have a choice. I chose not to try for a baby. Most CNBC people have at least tried to conceive. I did not even do that. Did I have the right to refer to myself as CNBC?

And yet, there was no real choice involved. Fifty percent likelihood of a bad pregnancy was too steep for me. It was a choice made under a cloud of terrifying medical risk. It was a forced choice.

I have therefore coined a new term: childless-by-forced-choice (CBFC).

If you have felt robbed of the choice to have children, or believe your 'choice' was no choice at all, you might be CBFC. It may fit better for those of us who are not completely disabled by illness but who are limited by it. CBFC recognises our constraints and acknowledges the absence of choice.

We CBFCs now have a name for ourselves.

CBFC

There are other reasons, beyond chronic illness, for being CBFC.

My husband and I married relatively late (relative to all our Christian friends who married by the age of twenty-one), so this meant we would have kids later than most. Which increased the chance of baby complications. Being older can feel like forced childlessness.

Living with a disability or mental health issue might create difficulties with raising children. And the stress of parenting could exacerbate these conditions. At the same time, disabilities, as with mental health issues or chronic illnesses, do not necessarily preclude people from having children. With the right support, people can become effective parents. But some may feel limited by their condition to the degree they feel this choice is taken away from them.

Having undesirable family genes or a history of trauma or abuse in the family may create worries about having one's own children. People may fear repeating history with their own children, or may feel incapacitated by the physical and psychological effects of trauma.

Personally, I inherited a genetic mutation (no, I am not an x-men-style mutant, but thanks for your interest), and I am not super keen on passing this on to any children.

Specific medical conditions can directly affect one's ability to bear children, such as endometriosis or early menopause. In Melanie's story, she experienced early menopause at the age of thirty-eight. These conditions may contribute to difficulties conceiving or make it altogether impossible.

Still others may find themselves in a less-than-ideal situation, like living with substance use or domestic violence (DV) in the home. They may feel the instability or unsafety of their situation effectively takes the choice about children out of their hands.

Infertility is also a major contributor to childlessness, but it gets its own chapter (see Chapter 4).

Living with CBFC brings complications. Speaking for myself, I experience survivor guilt. Survivor guilt is where you have a near-miss while others get hurt. If you and I were on a boat and we both got tossed overboard, and I made it to the lifeboat but you did not, I might experience survivor guilt. Survivor guilt tells us something was unfair—in our favour.

CBFC people can have a vague sense of obligation to have kids just because they have a chance, even if that chance is slim. They can feel guilty for not trying to conceive. As I did.

Guilt can be powerful. Society may tell CBFC people their position is privileged and they are lucky to not be infertile, for example. They may tell you to *carpe diem*.

I am not here to tell you whether you should *carpe* your *diem*. Guilt alone should not dictate your decision. The forced choice to be childless may be influenced by many things, but I encourage you to not let things like guilt or fear rule you.

However, as with me, guilt may be a long-lasting thing.

Endometriosis

I have endometriosis. Yep, they were having a two-for-one sale at the diagnosis store.

Some of my interviewees also have this unenviable condition. Some believed it directly contributed to their infertility. It is a possible explanation for those with problems conceiving, as it messes up the reproductive organs. So it is conceivable. (Pardon the pun.)

In Australia, one in ten women experience endometriosis (*Endometriosis Australia* 2020)[7]. I believe the figure is similar in other countries too. It is common, but interestingly, not talked about a lot.

This delicate feminine matter is incredibly difficult to diagnose. I am told it takes an average of eight years. Mine took twenty. (I always knew I was above average.)

In the space between first symptoms and diagnosis, women suffer pain, discomfort, embarrassment, digestive difficulties and reproductive problems. They may not even know they have this under-diagnosed delight.

I suffered for many teenage years with outrageous period pain, living on painkillers and taking several days off school at a time. But I assumed, as did my doctors, it was typical period pain. How was I to know?

This women's thingy can cause complications such as pain during sex. This makes trying to conceive awkward, if not downright impossible. Sex can become anxiety-provoking if a woman is anticipating pain.

Endometriosis is not necessarily a deal-breaker when it comes to kids. But it might affect the ability to conceive. So it is crucial to get the right diagnosis, treatment and support for it.

The gamble

CBFC is a gamble. If you are CBFC like me, you have probably spent a good deal of time debating the pros and cons. Having children is a chance to bring light and beauty into the world. But it also involves risk. And some risks are costly.

We can worry about having children because of all the things that might go wrong. We might create terrible tragedies in our heads. We might get so caught up in fear of worst-case scenarios that we take the safer route, or never make a decision—which is in itself a form of decision.

While CBFC is usually about mitigating risk and protecting would-be children, it is worth pointing out that CBFC comes with its own risks. We risk grief. We risk missing out on the whole parenthood thing. We risk regretting our choice—even if it felt like a forced choice.

There is risk in childlessness, whatever form it takes. Risk is inevitable. So it is important to accept the risk, whatever pathway we choose. And it is natural to question ourselves, or feel guilty, or wonder about how our lives might have turned out if we had tried to have children. Like the movie *Sliding Doors,* we might always wonder what would have happened if we had made one different decision.

CBFC can be a difficult thing to explain to others. It can be tough to understand it ourselves. (I have spent the better part of this chapter trying to articulate it.) Even with a great CBFC definition, others may not understand us. I think the main thing is to be clear, within ourselves, why we are CBFC and why we feel forced into that position.

And one day you might like to share your CBFC story.

Stories worth telling

We do not have to be defined by our childlessness.

Sure, terms like CBFC can be helpful. But they are not the sum total of our existence. We can define ourselves by who we are, the passions we pursue and the meaning we make of our lives. And the furbabies we love.

I have a furbaby, a pet who provides companionship and comfort. Some of my interviewees have furbabies. My feline furbaby, a rescue cat, gives me great comfort in childlessness. Sure, she is not the same thing as having a child. (Although sometimes I wonder, what with the nighttime crying and leaving little deposits around the house.) But she helps. You may have a comforting furbaby too.

We are not alone in childlessness. You may feel alone at times, but there are thousands of people just like you, all over the world, facing similar challenges of childlessness.

> *One thing that unites us is we each have a unique story to tell.*

You may have felt that you have nowhere to belong. But you do belong. You belong with us. We understand what you are going through. And even if we do not understand, even if our experience of childlessness has been different from yours, your story is worth telling. And we will listen to your story without judgment.

We will not tell you who to be. We will not convince you to live a different way. We will not tell you to grieve, or stop grieving, or feel anything other than what you feel. We will accept you just as you are.

One thing that unites us is we each have a unique story to tell. So I want to encourage you, some day, to share your story. You may not have a free choice about children, but you can choose when and how to share your experience.

Not everyone wants to share their experience and that is OK. You might want to wait. That is fine too. Some people share with friends and family, blog online or write books about their journeys. Like the stories in this book shared by my interviewees, each story shines a unique light on the murky waters of childlessness.

Your tale may encourage someone else. It may enlighten them. It may help them to understand you better. Telling your story may do you the world of good too. It may show you how far you have come.

Guess who else listens and understands without judgment? (Spoiler: God.) God sees your situation and knows every intimate step of your journey. He is well acquainted with your pain. God always listens and he is always there. When I am in difficulty, I can count on him to be right beside me. He loves me no matter what state I am in. He takes me just as I am.

In a world that sets fickle and meaningless standards of belonging, it is a relief to belong to God.

Most days, that is enough.

MARIE'S STORY
United Kingdom (UK)

Marie's gran raised her. Marie was influenced by her gran's Catholic values, so although she wanted kids, she wanted to be married first.

She started dating her now-husband at twenty-five. They both wanted kids and they married when Marie was twenty-nine. They tried conceiving for a couple of years before discovering Marie's husband had a low sperm count. There was no explanation accompanying this life-changing news.

In the back of Marie's mind burned the question: would my husband's sperm count have been higher if we had started trying earlier?

They opted for IVF, by which time the sperm count had dwindled to zero. They used donor sperm. Marie's husband was fine with this but it was disconcerting for her. She wanted their child to be her husband's biological child.

However, there was no alternative.

The National Health Service (NHS) in England decides which postcodes get funding for a specified number of IVF rounds. In one postcode you might get funding for three rounds, but if you move to an adjoining suburb, you might only get one. Some relocate to another suburb or district to access IVF funding.

According to Marie, IVF clinics operate on the premise that you want unlimited rounds. After one attempt fails, they automatically book you in for the next round. This is why many people do multiple rounds of IVF.

In some ways, this is easier than opting out while deciding on another round. If you opt out and then opt back in, the waitlist is astronomical. By staying opted-in, you are kept in the system.

Marie described IVF as 'not for everybody'. She said some see IVF as unnatural or as 'playing God'. She shared the medical details of IVF with a hint of horror in her voice. The medications following embryo implantation are designed to trick your body into thinking it is pregnant. This means you get all the symptoms of pregnancy, including breast tenderness, hot flushes, bloating and the rest. So you are effectively pregnant, according to your body. But you might not end up with a baby.

As was the case with Marie.

She had two rounds of IVF and neither was successful. While ill-prepared for the first round, Marie entered the second round with some idea of what to expect. She thought she was better prepared.

But the second-time devastation was just as bad as the first.

She was unwilling to try a third time. However, she found out why IVF did not work for her. She had low levels of anti-mullerian hormone (AMH). This female hormone gives an indication of the number of eggs remaining in the woman. Every woman gets a certain number of eggs per lifetime and that is it.

Apparently, the AMH does not respond well to IVF medical injections and can lead to early menopause. This might have contributed to Marie's IVF not working. She was told the chance of IVF success was thirty-five to forty percent. For Marie and her husband, with their combined health issues, their chance of success was less than five percent.

Even though Marie did not try a third round, she still finds herself wondering if she will regret not trying again. She can access a third round through the NHS if she wants to. She questions whether she should do everything possible to try for a baby.

On the other hand, Marie is mindful of her own survival. IVF took a toll on her physically and emotionally. At her lowest point, Marie felt suicidal. 'I feel like I have lost two years,' she lamented, now thirty-five. 'I don't want this year to be like the last two years.' She focuses on things she wants to do with her life and things she is grateful for, not things she wants but cannot have.

Marie's husband blames himself for their childlessness. Although she did question their timing early on, she does not want to lose him and she empathises with him. They are determined to solve this issue together, because it belongs to both of them.

Childlessness affected Marie's belief in God. While not 'religious' in the traditional sense, she was brought up Catholic and once believed in God. Now she feels angry with him. She also feels insulted when people say childlessness is God's will, as though God has deemed her an unfit mother. Being a mother was all Marie ever wanted.

Certain things keep her sane. She always wanted to play guitar and learned how to play a couple of years ago. She is now able to immerse herself in guitar-playing and completely let go.

Marie has indulged in figure-skating these past four or five years, which connected her with a community of skaters whom she otherwise would never have known.

When people ask about kids, she is honest. But people do not always know how to respond to her and often give advice. While this is unhelpful, she is compassionate towards them.

'Their advice-giving is unintentional,' she said thoughtfully. 'They do not mean to be unhelpful. People want to give you solutions. It's a natural human reaction to want to help. They want to find their common ground with you, and kids are a useful way to do that. I try to remind myself that people are not out to hurt me. I try to see things from their perspective.'

Even with Marie's empathic response, she finds miracle baby stories hard to hear. And there are plenty of them. She rarely hears stories of baby failure.

The most common advice she receives is about adoption. People tell her she should adopt. She has an opinion on this.

'Just because I cannot have my own kids, it does not mean other kids are my responsibility,' she states emphatically. 'Besides, those kids are often high-needs. I have no experience in child-rearing, let alone the extra skills that would be required in caring for those children.'

Marie is still recovering. The grief is up and down, some days better than others. Like other people, she thought having kids would be a milestone, moving her life into the next chapter. Not having children has left her at a standstill.

She wants people to understand the legitimacy of this invisible yet ongoing grief. 'People expect you to get over it,' she reflected. 'But it is important they understand the intangible. In reality, there is nothing they can say that will help, except for, "I am so sorry, I don't know what you are going through."'

Having close family and friends around, plus counsellors, has been helpful. And Marie is looking for new ways to be happy. 'I try to focus on the day-to-day,' she shared. 'Ultimately, I need to change the dreams and goals I want to live for. I need to focus on what I can change. I try to live in the moment and find things to keep me happy.'

But her happiness is bittersweet. 'I do manage to put grief to the back of my mind most days and have happy moments,' said Marie. 'It will just never be true happiness. There is always this vacancy in my heart that cannot be filled.'

SECTION TWO
SETTING SAIL

2

SOCIETY

Surviving in a Child-Centric World

I have a confession to make.

I don't like avocado.

I know this makes me the most unhipster person to ever roam the reaches of this gentle planet, but it is true.

I have done everything in my power to make myself fall in love with this smashable superfood. I have tried avocado with prawns, with lemon juice, with my nose pinched to see if it improves the flavour.

It does not.

I keep trying it over the years, hoping my taste buds will change and I can join the mainstream throng of avo lovers. But it is no good. I have to face the facts. I simply cannot eat avocado.

It is hard living in a pro-avocado world. When I go out for breakfast, everyone else is tucking into their plates of avocado, looking like adverts for happiness. It is even harder to order from a pro-avocado menu. I find myself ordering the one avocado-free meal, just so I do not have to say 'without avocado, thanks' to the waitperson and squirm under their judgmental stare.

I feel like the odd one out, to say the least.

Just like many childless people feel in our kid-centric world.

Conversion therapy

When I was still single, people seemed genuinely concerned over my lack of desire for kids. They would ask me serious questions about what lay beneath this psychopathic trait. They seemed… worried.

I felt like handing them an avocado.

Some made it their mission to convert me to the religion of child-loving maternals. They argued I 'should' want to have children. Some said I should just have them anyway, regardless of whether or not I want them.

Um, no.

Even when I got engaged and was still undecided about children, people were quick to point me in the direction of child-rearing.

On one occasion I was sitting in church with my fiancé and a friend asked if we would have kids soon. I shrugged non-committally. 'Oh, I dunno. We may not even have kids.' My friend's face changed. She leaned in close and asked, 'Steph, why is that?' She looked like she was bracing herself to hear all about my childhood trauma. Either that or a heinous crime.

I realised I had unknowingly committed an atrocity. I had dared to say I was unsure about having kids.

Such is the case with society. When having children is the socially reinforced mainstream, childlessness is bound to be treated with a certain amount of bewilderment and even concern. It is a by-product of living in a pronatalist society (a fancy term meaning our society is in favour of child-bearing and parenthood).

Thankfully, ever since I developed health issues, my childless status has become much more socially acceptable. No one has judged me or tried to convert me. Childlessness-by-a-medical-condition is apparently OK.

These issues raise important questions about how to function in a child-centric society. I want to know how to answer people's leading questions about having a family. I want to retain my sense of dignity while confessing my apparent crime of childlessness.

And I want to contribute to society without feeling like a sub-species of human.

The nuclear family

In the 1950s the world was recovering from World War II. Women in particular were changing, challenging assumptions about the work they could do. While men went to war, women became nurses, secretaries and all manner of tradeswomen.

After the war, some women did not want to go back to the family home. They wanted to stay at work, thank you very much. They had discovered independence and financial freedom. They had something to offer besides mothering and homemaking.

Governments realised they were losing women to the

workforce. In order to entice women back to the family home, they created the myth of the nuclear family. The nuclear family—comprising of a working husband, stay-at-home wife, two-point-three kids, a white-picket fence and a dog—had never existed before. At least, not as a concept. It existed in practise of course.

Women were urged to return to the 'traditional' nuclear family. They were manipulated into thinking the nuclear family was mainstream and desirable. It was an attempt to restore pre-war equilibrium.

It was very effective propaganda. The myth has stuck. Contemporary society still holds to the image of a nuclear family as the ideal living situation. It is viewed as some kind of mandatory milestone for adulthood.

I have no problem with picket fences and dogs. But it seems social and spiritual debates are argued and won based on who worships at the shrine of nuclear family. I have a problem with that. We argue in favour of whatever maintains the legend of the nuclear family. Families are in the bible, we cry, therefore the nuclear family is biblical.

But it is a myth.

Yes, there are families in the bible and in our churches. There is also war and rape and fraud and witchcraft and murder in the bible. And some of these exist in our churches too.

The nuclear family is only one type of family. There are other types of families: couple families, single-with-furbaby families, extended-relatives families, foster families and it-takes-a-village families.

It is easy to see how the nuclear family myth pervades our

culture. Anything designed for children is inherently more valuable. Apparently. Politics is filled with rhetoric for 'our children, and our children's children'. Politicians are expected to represent the needs of working families. I know one childless politician who was recently grilled about her capacity to be effective. The press claimed she could not represent the average Australian because she was childless. Appalling but true.

Childless people are often asked to defend their circumstances. Society cries 'selfish' and assumes childless people are incapable of understanding parental needs. 'You have no idea what it is like to be a parent,' they shout.

I have been publicly ridiculed for not understanding parenting. Of course I do not understand it like a parent does. I have not lived it. But I am not incapable of understanding someone's experience simply because it is different from mine. I am not a numbskull, nor a psychopath. For such situations, I use empathy.

Hopefully your experience has been different from mine. I hope you have never been questioned, criticised or mocked for being childless. I hope it never happens to you.

Child-centric world

The success of the nuclear family myth has provoked an onrushing of family-centric advertisements, products and services. In Australia, ads frequently target the guilt and fear of parents.

Cleaning products claim to protect children from life-threatening germs and are advertised as being 'parent-approved'. Thank goodness there are parents around to advise us about household cleaners.

Food, vitamin supplements and electronic devices promise to give children a head-start in life because 'nothing is more important'.

Life insurance plays on the guilt of being a burden to your children when you die, and the fear of what will happen to your children when you do.

Children's products emphasise FOMO (fear of missing out). They claim, 'Your child will miss out on this vital developmental stage if you fail to buy our crucial product.' Even though children have survived for thousands of years without this essential product.

Shopping centres and restaurants are focused on child-friendliness. They have supersized LEGO-style children's play-areas with mum-benches and cafes placed strategically nearby. Some restaurants have play areas (for kids, that is) and most have high chairs and kid-friendly menus. Some have 'Kids eat free' days.

There are tangible child-related cues all around us, prams and pram-allocated parking spaces, car seats and baby changing rooms. These can be painful reminders of what childless people do not have. Every pregnant woman, every child, is a reminder of what is 'normal'.

Baby showers and pregnancy announcements on social media can be especially hard to avoid.

The pressure to have kids may be closer to home. Family may expect us to have children or fail to invite us to parties for the other kids in the extended family. Our parents may insist on grandchildren or subtly 'remind' us we are not getting any younger.

Many special events in the calendar year are geared towards the nuclear family, not towards childless people. The obvious ones are Mother's and Father's Days and children's birthdays (industries unto themselves). Major holidays like Christmas and Easter are promoted as being 'family-friendly'.

Christmas carols are crowded with kids' activities like petting zoos and face-painting. (Just once, I would like to see face-painting for adults. If they can do adult jumping castles, they can do adult face-painting.)

These efforts on behalf of children are admirable. But it can leave childless people feeling excluded and invisible.

And do not even get me started on workplace options for parents.

Oh, all right then.

Parents get flexible working options. It is a perk offered by many organisations. Woe betide any company that does not provide these alternatives. And maternity and paternity leave are just the beginning. Parents are privy to special privileges on account of their little ones. They can, for example, reduce from full-time to part-time hours. They can start later and finish earlier. They can excuse themselves from after-hours duties because they need to be home with their kids.

All of which, of course, is completely right and proper. I totally understand parents' needs to be available for their children. I am not about to suggest parents should not be allowed to collect their children from school. I just do not understand why others are not afforded similar flexibility to attend important things and achieve their desired work/life balance.

As an example, a parent-worker can leave early every Tuesday if they need to take their child to soccer. But I do not get that option, even if I have something really important to do every Tuesday, like play soccer myself.

Only kidding. I hate soccer.

If I have something genuinely important to do after work, like visiting a sick family member, taking my furbaby to the vet or plucking my eyebrows, I am not afforded the same flexibility.

OK, so maybe collecting children from school is slightly more important than my browline. But seriously, there are things I want to do outside of work that really matter to me.

I understand parents need a lot of flexibility. But it smarts when I think of what I wanted—what I never had—that my parent-colleague has. If I did not know better, I would think children get prioritised over extended family and pets.

And browlines.

Motives and instincts

Childless people often have their motives microscopically examined, interrogated by others as to the justification of their childlessness. Interestingly, parents are not often put through the same rigours of questioning.

This is curious. And unfair.

Why don't we ask parents their reasons for having children?

I have occasionally explored the motivation for parenthood with parents. The conversation usually consists of me turning the tables on them:

Parent: So, do you have kids?
Me: No, I don't.
Parent: *gasping for air* Wait, what? Why don't you have kids?
Me: Well, why did you have your children?

Parent: ...

Some become parents in order to fulfil God's command to multiply. However, this is not always the case. People have kids for non-spiritual reasons too:

- they have strong parental instincts;
- they think they will be good at it;
- they believe it will give their lives meaning;
- they believe having children is a crucial milestone and life goal;
- they worry life without children will leave a void;
- they do not want to age without children to care for them;
- they think they are missing out on a fundamental human experience if they do not;
- they want to make their partner happy;
- they want to give their parents a grandchild;
- they are fulfilling cultural expectations;
- they think it will fix their relationship problems;
- they think parenthood will bring out the best in them;
- they want to belong to the club of parents; or
- they believe they will regret not having children.

There are some interesting motivations there, like using children as a linchpin to solve certain problems (why should kids be under pressure to solve the problems of adults?) or believing parenthood brings out the best in people. I am not sure that being sleep-deprived brings out the best in me, so perhaps some of these beliefs are somewhat romanticised.

And some of these motives might be driven by selfishness.

But most parents do not disclose the selfish kinds of motivation. At least, not publicly.

However, we should not judge parents. Not at all. (Some of my best friends are parents.) And I do not want to stereotype parent-friends or others in our communities—in just the same way that I do not want to be stereotyped as a childless person.

We should not judge anyone, childless people included. And society should definitely stop accusing childless people of being selfish. Society and parents do not have the monopoly on selfless behaviour.

The other side of the parenthood coin, one seldom discussed in our pronatalist society, is regret. Research is emerging—along with facebook support groups—demonstrating that a growing number of parents regret having children.

I found a frank article about the regrets of some parents (Marsh 2017)[8]. Some parents in this article loved their children but hated the parenting role. They hated the loss of freedom and sleep. And they felt guilty about hating parenthood.

Some parents in the article experienced scathing criticism for voicing their regrets. One parent was told to take their selfish, self-indulgent feelings to psychotherapy to 'sort it out'. It seems society expects parents to love it. Forever. And never regret it.

Regret is seldom anticipated by would-be parents. But apparently it happens. So regret can go both ways.

It might be worth remembering that having children does not guarantee against feelings of regret. Nor does it guarantee that one's parenting instincts will kick in the minute a baby arrives. I have known some non-maternal friends to turn maternal when they have children. But others do not.

The assumptions that all women possess a 'maternal instinct' or that normal men feel paternal are erroneous. Some suggest the whole parental 'instinct' thing is simply a creation of our culture. In other words, any felt instinct is not biological but created by gender stereotypes.

This bears discussion. Some people have a genuine desire to have children. But a lot of this desire is encouraged and reinforced by society.

How many of us were raised to believe we would have children someday? How many of us still get told it will happen, even in our forties or fifties? Yes, it happens. How many women were given baby dolls to play with as girls? I was not a big dolly girl but I do remember feeding and bathing and clothing a few dolls. (Even though I preferred LEGO.)

> I was taught at every turn that childrearing is normal, desirable, yes, even inevitable.

For that matter, how many of us were raised with fairytales and school sex education programs that taught us to expect children? I don't know about you, but I was warned, as a teenager, not to have sex because it would surely lead to pregnancy. Oh, the cruel irony.

I was taught at every turn that childrearing is normal, desirable, yes, even inevitable.

That is social reinforcement.

Wherever you stand on the nature vs nurture debate, it is clear that society expects us to develop parenting instincts at some point. And it expects us to have children, according to the norm.

The stigma of childlessness is real.

The male perspective

Childless men in particular are often stigmatised. Men miss out on much of the attention during their childlessness journey. Doctors and family generally seem to think childlessness affects only the woman.

Not so.

Dr Esmee Hanna, researcher for male infertility, found ninety-three percent of infertile men were negatively impacted by their infertility (Hanna, Gough & Coan 2017)[9]. They felt anxious. They felt emasculated. They felt worthless.

Dr Robin Hadley has researched the male side of childlessness, driven by his own experience of childlessness and lack of support. He could not find any resources for childless men so he created his own.

He concluded (as cited in Gorman 2016)[10] that men want to have children as much as women.

Men are just as impacted by childlessness as women, if not more. Men get more depressed and angrier than their female counterparts. Men feel excluded, like they are on the outside looking in. Especially around fathers.

Men worry about the future. They worry about their name and family legacy coming to an end. They worry about being lonely. Some worry about being perceived as a paedophile. They feel self-conscious in public and worry people will think, 'Why doesn't he have kids?'

Medical and counselling professionals often focus on the woman's experience of grief. But men grieve too. Men get broody.

Men feel despair. And men can feel neglected by the medical profession, friends and family.

That was John's experience. In John and Rachel's story, John felt a stab in the heart watching other men play with their kids. He felt it was thoroughly unfair.

For the men reading this book, I have some things to say to you.

First, I see you. I see all you have done for your partners. I see your supportive efforts over prolonged periods of time. You matter. Your story matters.

Second, you do not have to hide your feelings. I know you want to be strong for your partner. But they need your honesty. They need to know you are grieving too and you feel the same loss they are feeling.

Your partner probably wants to share it with you. You may want to protect them, but it might be better to walk through this together than to hide your true feelings. Hiding creates distance. And this can erode relationships.

Third, get some support. There are online groups just for childless men. You can share your story. You may discover how much you have in common.

There is a myth about men being tough and never crying. But men feel the same emotions as women. Some men grieve more keenly. And some men cry.

It is OK to cry. Grief is OK. Sadness, regret, having worries and doubts about the future are all OK. Whatever you are feeling is OK. You are OK just the way you are.

You are not alone. I see you.

A changing society

An article in the *ABC news* (Corsetti 2017)[11] highlighted the growing number of childless couples in society. According to this article, the childless couple will become the most common family type in Australia between 2023-2029. If true, I wonder how society will accommodate this change. Society will have to adapt to mainstream childlessness.

I can see it now. TV ads, previously sporting the tag line 'As a parent...', will have to switch to 'As a thinking person' or 'As a human being who is alive'.

Restaurants will have special days of the week where couples without kids eat for free. (I hear some places already do this.)

Kids will be charged a surcharge at movies, on planes and in adult-friendly theme parks.

Schools will go bankrupt. Parks will be deserted, with tumbleweed blowing through the empty sandpits as the swings flap and sway freely in the breeze.

Or it might go the other way. Parenting payouts will skyrocket. Mothers will garner special privilege and become super-matriarchs. Parents will become an endangered species, closely guarded, lording it over us.

OK, maybe that is going a tad too far.

Still, it is an interesting prospect. If this article's prediction becomes a reality, we may see dramatic changes in the structure and expectations of our society.

Assumptions about childlessness

There are many reasons for childlessness. This article, *270 reasons why people choose to be childless or childfree* (Adams, Fung, Scheller & Shifflett 2015)[12], lists a few. But despite the rising numbers of childless people, there is an outcry from parents towards them. I have experienced this personally.

And I am not the only one.

One article, *Childfree and OK with it—but still dealing with moral scolding and social disapproval* (Marcotte 2017)[13], demonstrated a moral outrage from parents towards the childless, particularly the childfree. The reasons are unclear, although theories abound.

One theory suggests the less-happy parents project their feelings of unhappiness onto the childless because childless and childfree couples are perceived as happier. It is the 'If I am unhappy, I am going to make you unhappy too' phenomenon.

I have a personal theory about moral and spiritual outrage from Christian parents. Parents locked in the family deification mindset (idolising nuclear families) can find it hard to respect childless people, believing we are 'lesser than' or 'missing out'. This can breed division between parents and non-parents.

Professor Renske Keizer has researched childlessness in Europe, particularly male childlessness, and the consequences, including perceptions of the childless. Keizer, Dykstra and Poortman (2011) found that compared with parents, childless and childfree people are viewed as being less

> *Because childless people are not mainstream, society does not know how to respond to us.*

well-adjusted, less nurturing, more materialistic, more selfish, more individualistic and more career-oriented[14].

It's definitely not just me. There is a common view that childless people are less mature than parents of comparable age. It appears having children gains one entry into real adulthood.

In my work as a psychologist, I am often asked if I have children. Some are genuinely surprised to hear a psychologist does not have children, as though it were one of the selection criteria for the job.

In some professional roles, it can work against you if you are not a parent. Especially when most of your clientele are parents or foster carers. You can lose credibility. And not just with clients. Colleagues of mine have been equally surprised, even outraged, to learn I work in a helping role as a non-mother.

It seems motherhood is a pre-requisite for being a helpful and compassionate listener. Or perhaps helpful and compassionate listeners are automatically maternal in nature. Either way, I missed that memo.

It can be challenging to be a childless woman who works part-time. Many people assume a childless woman must be career-driven, ambitious and workaholic by nature. I am none of those things.

Another assumption I have encountered is that I, as a female, must be a super-maternal person who goes weak at the knees at the sight of babies. I remember being told, as a teenager, that I would develop maternal urges one day. 'Just you wait', older friends would say with knowing smiles.

I never shapeshifted into that super-maternal person. I do not get clucky around other peoples' kids. (Especially when they scream.) Weirdly, people taunt me about being clucky when babies are nearby. It gets old.

My advice to childless people: if you do not want to get labelled 'clucky', do not talk to babies or smile in their general direction. In particular, never hold them. Holding babies is the social point-of-no-return. In fact, it might be easiest to avoid babies altogether. You will dodge that clucky label.

Here are further common assumptions about childless people I have encountered:

- They are not ready.
- They want to be more financially or otherwise stable before having kids.
- They are childfree-by-choice.
- They like to party/get drunk/sleep in.
- They do not want to grow up.
- They are waiting.
- They are not trying hard enough.
- She is a career woman. (Interestingly, men are rarely accused of being 'career men'.)
- She is a feminist. (I did not know feminism precluded one from having kids. Also, I wonder if childless men get accused of being feminists.)
- They forgot to have kids. (Because, yeah, it can just slip your mind.)
- This is only temporary. They will have kids soon enough.
- They are missing out.
- They are selfish.

- They do not care about the future of our society.
- They are freeloaders.
- They do not want to spend the money. (Translation: they are greedy or stingy.)
- She is a crazy cat lady. (Guilty. Any crazy cat men out there?)
- They should adopt. Don't they know how many kids are looking for a home in this country?
- They are weird.
- They are abnormal.

No wonder childless people feel misunderstood.

The eternal optimist in me would like to interject at this point. I believe society does not intentionally set out to be hurtful towards childless people. I believe most of our friends and family hold these assumptions innocently, if not ignorantly. Assumptions are part of life.

Most people who talk to us are genuinely interested in our lives. But because childless people are not mainstream, society does not know how to respond to us. We do not fit the mould (the mythical nuclear family). Anything deviating from the mould can cause surprise. So I get it. I do. I can see where society is coming from.

Nonetheless, these assumptions shame us. They blame. They accuse. They highlight how different we are from the rest of the baby-producing population. We are the social scapegoat.

Worse, there might be a little part of us that says, 'Maybe there is truth to their accusations. Maybe there is something wrong with me.'

That feeling of being 'wrong' is shame. It is that sensation you get, late at night, when all the noise has stopped, and you wonder if you are a mistake.

Shame is debilitating.

One way to fight shame is to find genuine connection and empathy with others. These are powerful tools against shame. That is why it is so vital to share our stories. When we are accepted by others, we no longer believe we are inherently wrong or flawed. We see ourselves through their eyes. We believe we are worthy.

One final assumption we often hold is that our partners will feel the same way we do about having children. This does not always happen. Sometimes our desires are in conflict—which I think warrants its own section.

Desires in conflict

What if your partner wants kids—but you don't?

It might be tempting to try to have children to make the other person happy. There is no guarantee this will work, but it can certainly bring couples closer together. And what begins as an effort to make another person happy can end in genuine affection for one's children. I have seen it happen.

Compromise can help, if one of you is willing to move. Of course, if desires for children are completely opposite and neither person moves on their position, a final decision is still needed. You cannot have half a kid. You either have a child or you don't.

Counselling may be useful at this juncture. It can clarify what each person wants and help both feel heard.

In the event one person does not get what they desire, they may need support. When two people want different things, at least one person will be disappointed. This may involve grief or guilt on one person's part. Such grief could lead to resentment, especially if not aired. And resentment can uglify a beautiful relationship.

So get plenty of support for desires in conflict.

Receiving advice

We all have ways of coping with the well-meaning advice of friends and family.

Some of us smile and nod politely. Some of us go to our happy place. Some of us fantasise about disembowelling our present interlocutor with a pair of secateurs.

But maybe that's just me.

Advice based on unhelpful assumptions is unwelcome. Advice based on clichés can feel hollow, dismissive and isolating. Perhaps the worst advice comes from people who think they know what is best for us. Especially when those people are parents.

Comments like, 'You're lucky you don't have kids' or 'Children are nothing but heartache' may be well-meaning but do little to comfort the childless person. When people tell me I am lucky, I feel like swapping their heartache for mine. I do not feel lucky. Their reassurance comes across as dismissive of my pain.

Some advice can be based on culture. I read an online blog about an African woman who was childless due to infertility (African Feminism 2017)[15]. Childlessness was a big deal in her African culture. Her mother's response to her childlessness was to send her batches of 'magic potions'. Yep, you read that right. Imagine wording a polite response to that one. Her mother was trying to be helpful, but it did not help.

In Elena's story, she experienced cultural pressure to have kids. It was normalised in Catholic-Italian culture for her to produce grandchildren.

When children are normalised using phrases like, 'Children are a gift from God' or 'Your children will carry on the family business', the pressure can be powerful.

I support the notion that children are a gift from God. But when you are told this over and over, you can feel like you are missing out on God's blessings.

There are helpful responses out there too. Some friends and family are super-sensitive and thoughtful with us. They say lovely things like, 'That's awful' and 'I'm here for you'. Such support is a breath of fresh air.

It gives me hope.

'I have a friend...'

This has to be the absolute worst—the mother (no pun intended)—of horrible responses to childlessness.

You have just told your friend you cannot have kids. They respond by telling you about someone's miracle baby, some mother who was childless but then a magic ingredient was introduced, say, garlic or IVF or buddhist chanting, and voila! A child was born.

Sometimes the mother was actually a celebrity your friend read about in a magazine last week. In which case they cannot possibly know the full story. And that celebrity probably has access to resources—like money—that the rest of us do not.

Your friend might be trying to encourage you with the miracle story, but it can be pure agony. Truthfully, miracle baby stories rarely help. It does not help to know others are receiving their miracles while you remain overlooked. It is not easy to be happy for others when you are struggling to come to terms with your own childlessness. And you cannot take comfort in the miracle story when your own narrative says you have failed. And failed. And failed.

It is bewildering that society clings to one-off miracle success stories but does not listen to our countless stories of failure, loss and discouragement. Perhaps it is because we are hopeful creatures. We like to hold on to hope and we like offering hope to others. We want to believe we can accomplish anything, against all odds, if only we try.

Or perhaps it is because miracle-baby stories are rendered newsworthy by their scarcity.

Or perhaps we have bought into the lie, 'If you believe, you can achieve anything'. If so, it can be devastating to discover money, willpower, persistence and desperation are not enough.

In Australia we love the 'Aussie battler', a person fighting against all odds to succeed. We hail battlers as heroes. Australians like to believe a battler can achieve anything purely through 'battling'. How crushing to discover there are some problems no amount of battling can solve.

We do not like those stories so much. They are not popular. Miracle-baby stories are great for magazine sales. That is about all.

You will not find any miracle-baby stories hidden in this book. There are no 'I have a friend...' tales waiting to ambush you. My interviewees are still childless, as am I.

Besides, I do not want to imply having children is the only solution to childlessness. Children are not always a solution to our problems. While children can be a gift, they can also be a source of regret and heartache for some parents. And some kids come with their own problems.

We have romanticised the notion of children. We have romanticised the nuclear family. Even childbirth has been romanticised. You know those movies where the woman goes into labour and the man holds her hand, gazing adoringly at her, saying sickly things like, 'I have never loved you as much as I do right now?'

Ugh. Romanticised.

We know childbirth is disgusting. A miracle, yes, but revolting. I have no idea why we pretend it is otherwise.

Parenthood is the same. (Romanticised. Not revolting. Although it may be that too.) We know parenting is hard yakka (an Aussie phrase meaning what doesn't kill you will make you want to kill yourself—I mean, will make you stronger), yet we get all misty-eyed at the mention of parenting.

It is possible we over-emphasise the positives of parenthood. When we do not or cannot have children, our grief may be, to some degree, attached to our romanticised ideas of parenthood.

It may be helpful to remember the hardship of parenting. I am not suggesting this is a panacea for grief. But it might shift our perspective a little.

Some childless people feel relief and gratitude when they hear the problems of parents. There can be a moment of, 'Thank God we did not have to deal with that'.

This may not fit for you. But it can help shift our perspective around parenthood and the glossy picture society has painted for us. We might appreciate what we have a tiny bit more.

In the absence of a miracle baby, there are opportunities for other miracles. And there are other gifts to be embraced, other ways of making meaning besides having children.

Our value does not lie purely in our capacity to have children.

Coping with society

Questions about childlessness can be tricky. Especially when your reasons behind childlessness pertain to issues of physical and mental health.

One may not, for example, want the entire world knowing about one's family history of schizophrenia, or one's predisposition for Down Syndrome, or how endometriosis is affecting one's sex life.

So what can we say instead? Personally, sarcasm and satire tend to be my default settings. You may have noticed this.

But seriously, we can respond to friends and family with compassion and understanding. We can give them the benefit of the doubt, realising they probably want to help us, not upset us. We can try not to judge them—in just the same way that we do not want to be judged.

You might find it helpful to have a script handy. Here are some suggested responses from my interviewees and me to that infamous question, 'Do you have kids?':

- We do not have kids.
- I would rather not discuss the details.
- I am curious: is it an issue for you that I do not have

children? (Especially useful if they push the point.)
- Sadly, no.
- We tried, but we could not have them.
- Unfortunately we were unable to have kids.
- How about we change the subject?
- We do want kids, but we cannot have them.
- No, and you?
- I am childless.
- My partner already has kids from a previous relationship.
- Do pets count? I have a furbaby...
- No, but we love being an uncle and aunt to our beautiful nieces and nephews.
- I do not talk about my personal life at work.
- We have not managed to have them.
- Nope. *cue awkward pause while they pick up their jaw from the floor.*

See Chapter 12 for my more tongue-in-cheek responses.

Sometimes words are unnecessary. We do not necessarily have to answer questions. We can change the subject or excuse ourselves if needed.

Workplaces are one of the easiest settings to do this as there is always work to be done. My workplace lunchroom is female-dominated, so lunchtime conversations easily drift towards children. Most of the time this is fine, but if it becomes difficult I can slip away with, 'Well, back to the grindstone'. No one can judge me for that.

There are some situations best avoided. Baby showers and

Christmas celebrations seem especially brutal for childless people. If this is you, feel free to say no on the basis of self-care. Special occasions should not be torture. It is understandable we feel sad when trying to celebrate someone else's happiness, but if sadness is truly overwhelming, it may be best to opt out.

Access Australia (n.d.)[16] suggests alternatives for surviving Christmas and other family celebrations. For Christmas, they propose getting together with family a week or two before Christmas rather than on the actual day. You still get to see the people you love and they get to see you, while freeing you to spend the Day quietly or in whatever way you choose.

Family may struggle to understand this. That is OK. They may never fully understand what you are going through. And they do not need to understand. All they need to do is respect your choices. You can ask them to listen, even if they cannot understand. You can tell your family you still love them and you know they love you. You can tell your family you do not want your sadness to interrupt their celebrations.

If you are not sure about attending, you can tell them you will not decide until closer to the day. This may not be easy, depending on your family arrangements, but it may help you. How they respond is their choice. Yes, it might make things a bit awkward. Yes, they might miss you. No, it does not mean you are making the wrong choice.

It comes down to this. Who are you going to put first? If you choose loved ones over your own needs, you will suffer. If you prioritise your needs over theirs, they might suffer.

You are going to let someone down.

Who that might be is up to you.

No 'fix-it'

Our loved ones often want to make us feel better. Part of loving someone is protecting them from harm. It hurts when we see someone we love in pain. So it is natural and understandable our loved ones want to fix our 'problems'.

But some problems cannot be fixed. Some issues have no explanation. Some medical problems have no treatment. Some things like grief never fully go away, though they may shift over time. There is no 'fix-it'.

> We need to get comfortable saying 'I do not need you to fix this'.

Grief is difficult enough without the added pressure of 'fixing' your grief to make others happy. The pressure to get back to normal (whatever that means) can heighten rather than relieve these struggles.

So we need to let people know. We need to get comfortable saying 'I do not need you to fix this'. We can decline their advice. Often we do not even need sympathy.

Sometimes we do not want to talk about it at all. Other times we cannot shut up about it. Grief is a strange beast. One minute it bursts out in uncontrollable verbal diarrhea, the next it leaves you utterly drained.

As much as I am an advocate of talking (hey, I am a counsellor), I am a big fan of just being present. Some things cannot be said. Sometimes there are no words. Troubles do not always need to be verbalised to be shared. Shared silence can convey more empathy, more presence, more understanding than a stream of words. Being there is the important thing—while resisting the temptation to fix it.

And that support, as Elena found in her story, can make the world of difference.

A comforting presence

When my dear little cat had a stroke recently, there was little I could do to help. I couldn't stop it from happening. I couldn't intervene. I watched helplessly as she staggered around the floor, shaking and crying, trying to put one paw in front of the other.

All I could offer, beyond the obvious first aid like ensuring she was still breathing, was to get down on the floor with her and be with her. All I could do was cuddle her and reassure her I was there and I wasn't going anywhere.

Jesus is like that. (Like me, not the cat.) He is a comforting presence to me. When I am hurting, he is silently present with me. Not the echoey, empty kind of silence. The silence of communion. He is not going anywhere. He stays by my side, not because he feels obliged, but because he truly cares. He feels what I feel and shares my unspeakable grief. It is the empathy and compassion of one well acquainted with sorrow.

God hears the whispers of hearts, the turmoil of emotions, the clamour of minds, even when words are not spoken. And in my darkest moments it is his presence, not his words, I need most. He radiates calm through his nearness. He breathes peace until the noise dies down. He bathes me in love until I am soaked through.

That is where I find healing.

I pray you find communion with him too.

ELENA'S STORY
Australia

In Elena's Catholic-Italian culture, children, especially boys, were highly esteemed.

But for Elena, it was not to be.

She and her husband did five rounds of IVF and none of them worked. She even travelled interstate to access IVF. The travel, combined with IVF itself, was physically and emotionally demanding.

Elena did not tell anyone about IVF as she felt they would not understand. IVF was a hard and expensive process for them. Elena's husband in particular became sick of it. After the fifth attempt they reached a point of saying, 'Enough is enough'.

Elena was greatly affected by her inability to have children. She found it hard to listen to other women talk about their children. It was easier to avoid socialising.

It affected her faith in God. At times she wondered why this had happened to her. She baulked one day at Mass when the priest said parenting was the greatest gift one could have. Elena felt inadequate as a woman.

Perhaps the greatest impact came from her cultural background. As she put it, 'In an Italian family, kids are a big deal'. She and her husband were excluded from family events because they did not have kids. Elena was never invited to her relatives' children's parties.

She started to 'hibernate', locked away from the world. She tried to hold her head up and keep going. She found after a while she was able to block it out. Her family does not raise the subject of children anymore.

'I am over it now,' says Elena. 'I still find it hard to watch other people with kids, especially when people use their kids to get money or something they want from grandparents. It is so unfair. My husband and I made it on our own.'

She also noticed her work peers get flexible hours and other work/life balance options she will never have.

Having support has made a big difference. She has one close friend in whom she can confide. 'You need to talk about it,' advised Elena. 'Don't make it just your problem.'

She encourages childless people to believe in themselves. 'Don't believe you are not valuable just because you don't have children. Not having kids doesn't make you a lesser person than people who have kids.'

She and her husband have two dog furbabies who have helped fill the void left by childlessness.

Elena firmly believes that despite the lasting pain no one sees, it is possible to move on from the heartache of childlessness.

JOHN AND RACHEL'S STORY
Australia

John and Rachel were faced with the prospect of invasive surgery after discovering John was infertile. The surgery came with no guarantees.

John and Rachel were against the idea of surgery. Even their surgeon was against it. The surgeon suggested John and Rachel focus on having a strong marriage, rather than having surgery. He said their relationship was more important.

Infertility was not their only medical issue. John also had scoliosis and multiple sclerosis, both of which were hereditary. He was reluctant to bring children into the world and pass on these health issues.

They looked into alternatives. Sperm donors were not an option. John and Rachel definitely wanted their own biological child. So they researched and spoke with couples who had adopted.

They made an interesting discovery. Adoptive couples who had originally wanted their own children found their grief did not resolve once they adopted. Nor did adoption solve their problems of childlessness. In fact, those couples experienced persistent sadness, despite having adopted children.

John and Rachel did not believe the popular opinion that having children is a magic fix for life's problems. They were under no romantic illusions about kids keeping marriages together. They believed, from experience, many proposed 'solutions' only created more problems.

For example, Rachel's sister had children but separated from her husband. Her idyllic family was torn apart. Even though Rachel's sister had children, her separated situation was far from ideal.

Without remaining options, John and Rachel were left childless. This was far from OK. Both John and Rachel were greatly affected.

John felt an unfair stab watching other people have children, especially when they had miracle baby stories or when fellow Christians received prophecies about having children.

He felt the pain of fellow Christians receiving physical healings from God while his chronic illnesses continued. He knew there was no formula for healing and that God was keenly interested in his inner healing as well as outer. Still, it was painful.

For Rachel, the struggle was more existential in nature. She wondered about the meaning of their childlessness and questioned whether she might have been a good mother or not. She struggled to reconcile her belief in God with childlessness. For a while, Rachel was angry with God and blamed him. This affected her prayer and worship. But Rachel also felt drawn to God, magnetically pulled towards prayer. She sought and blamed him all at once.

John and Rachel heard many well-intentioned stories and received much advice from Christians. They are sick of hearing miracle baby stories like Hannah and Sarah from the bible. They are also sick of hearing Christian platitudes such as 'God can do miracles' and 'It's God's plan'. Such clichés long ago lost their novelty.

During the roughest times, Rachel was carried by the faith

of her church. When she had no reserves of faith herself, it was helpful to lean on the faith of others. She and John went to a Christian grief and loss workshop which helped. Reaching out was a strength they shared.

These days, church life still presents difficulties. Baby dedications can catch them emotionally unawares, and they generally avoid Mother's and Father's Day church services.

To preserve some sense of sanity, John and Rachel give themselves permission to skip things as needed. They found this more helpful than struggling through a difficult church service, trying not to cry. They feel no guilt about this and encourage others not to feel guilty.

'You have to give yourself permission to do what you need to do,' they said to me, rather persuasively.

John has issues with men's ministry meetings. 'I went to a men's event once and it turned out to be a fathering talk,' he recalls. 'I felt ambushed.' Even meeting up with other blokes can be difficult. Most local men's gatherings tend to focus on children and grandchildren, making it hard for John to participate. He feels like he is on the outer.

Rachel finds it hard in her job. Working in a female-dominated industry, it is especially challenging for her when all the other women on staff are pregnant.

She finds mothers generally tend to congregate together. While this is understandable, she feels out of step with families. Some of her friendships with parent-friends have drifted apart for this reason.

Family gatherings are difficult for both of them, owing to one-sided conversations about children in the family. There are family expectations that John and Rachel are still pursuing child-rearing. It is hard to talk openly with family about what is going on.

Despite this, or perhaps because of it, John and Rachel actively involve themselves with their nieces and nephews. They find this helpful. It provides them with an alternate response to the usual 'Do you have kids?' question. Instead of simply saying no, they can talk about being a doting uncle and aunt. It gives them funny stories and warm memories.

Much of their grief is hidden. Like other childless couples, John and Rachel found people stopped asking about kids once they reached a certain age. But if anyone does ask, they respond with a deft, 'No, and you?'

Humour helped them survive, as has counselling and anti-depressants. Both musicians, they wanted fewer 'happy-clappy' songs and more lamentations songs. For lament, Rachel chose *Beauty from Pain* by Superchick. Rachel also recommended some books that helped, including *Restoring Hope* by Graham Leo and *When God Says No* by Sheridan Voysey.

While Rachel feels somewhat better these days about being childless, John still struggles with it.

'It has raised broader questions on the nature of healing,' they both reflected. 'We have learned there are no formulas for securing miracles and healing is a mystery. We have also learned God is just as concerned with our spiritual healing as with our physical needs—perhaps more so.'

They can look on the bright side of childlessness and find silver linings.

'We have been able to travel, which is important to us, and we have had opportunities that would have been impossible to pursue had we had children,' says Rachel. 'Besides, having children is not always a happy ending. Some kids end up being high-needs.'

John and Rachel encourage other childless people to look after themselves. 'Seek help. Get the support you need. And give yourself permission to do what you need to do.'

3

CHURCH

I'm the Odd One Out

One fateful day, my husband and I attended our church's morning service. I found a friend who had transitioned from the night to the morning service after having children (as had most of our congregation) and I asked how her children were doing.

A few minutes later, I regretted starting the conversation. It was nothing personal (I want to make that clear, in case my friend reads this book!) and I genuinely cared about her kids. But our entire conversation circled around her kids' health, development and schooling and my friend's coping strategies in the midst of demanding parenting.

And I had nothing to contribute.

I care about my parent-friends and truly want to support them. I love seeing their kids grow up. I love hearing about their successes and their heartaches. I love playing with them. (The kids, that is.) I love it all.

What I do not love is feeling excluded from one-sided conversations because I do not have kids. If I contribute my ideas on parenting, I feel like a fraud. In the absence of parental credibility, I feel reluctant to saying anything.

Normally, if I want to change the subject of conversation, I will do so. But how can I do this in the middle of discussing someone else's child? It feels inappropriate, uncaring and downright rude.

It's a little unfair though. And that is why I feel torn. I cannot comment on their life (because I have no idea what it's like to be a parent) but they can comment on mine. Because every parent can relate to a time when they did not have kids.

Lengthy conversations about other people's kids leave me feeling like an outsider. It starkly reminds me of my childlessness. I feel it in the air, in the moment when my friend stops for breath in her child-driven monologue, asks how I am doing, and my response gets hijacked by their kids.

It is not the fault of my friends or their kids.

It is a consequence of childlessness.

Mission and ministry

Every church has a unique mission that shapes the focus and programs of that church.

Many church missions include growth. This mission requires the church to target children and youth ministries, for therein lies the greatest potential for growth. They must also hold lots of family-focused events throughout the year which naturally draw larger numbers of people.

It is logical for churches to run events that attract families. It is reasonable and necessary for churches to spend time and resources on their children and youth. They are the ones who will be leading the church in the future. I get it. If I were running a church, I would do the same thing.

> But here is the kicker: we also need to cater for childless people.

But.

Have you noticed how much of church life revolves around kids?

We have Sunday school. We have youth group. We have celebrations for Easter and Christmas, often consisting of kiddy plays, carols and fun outdoor activities (for 'fun', read child-friendly).

We have special events on Mother's and Father's Days. We have holiday programs galore. Depending on the denomination, we have dedications, christenings, baptisms, first Holy Communions and confirmations.

The church expends much effort on celebrating and tending these families, as well they should. We should reasonably cater for families so they can engage with church life.

But here is the kicker: we also need to cater for childless people.

Playgroups, mum's groups and dad's breakfasts are all valuable ministries. But in the churches I have attended, women's ministries often focus on motherhood and home-making, while men's ministries often discuss fathering issues.

I encourage churches to at least advertise what your ministries are about. Be clear about who you are targeting. Otherwise childless people can feel ambushed. Like John did when he turned up for a men's meeting—about fathering.

I personally would not attend a women's event if I knew it targeted mothers. But then, I am not all that comfortable with attending women's events that target wives either. (And I am one. Go figure.)

I am not for one instant suggesting we ditch these worthwhile ministries. Perhaps, though, we could think about running events where everyone feels welcome—including childless people.

Social grouping

Similar species gravitate towards one another.

Birds, for example, tend to hang out with their own kind, and definitely do not spend a lot of time with, say, cats. Whereas cats do not care about anyone else. I have one. I should know.

Humans can be the same. (The grouping, not the cat-like arrogance.) People with common interests get together with like-minded people. It makes sense.

The church is not immune to the phenomenon of social grouping. Parents spend time with other parents because of their commonalities. They need other parents. This is healthy. They can share parenting information and tips, normalise the good, bad and ugly of parenting and debrief over a cuppa. Many parents find this support vital. Nothing wrong with this.

But an unintended consequence of the parental grouping effect is the exclusion of childless people. While parents congregate together in the warm glow of mutual experience, childless people can be left out in the cold. This is especially true in those churches where families form the majority.

Sometimes this exclusion is OK. Personally, I love other people's kids, but there are days when I do not want the blow-by-blow narrative of a child's toilet-training. And what is with the endless sharing of videos of children and babies? You are gushy. We get it.

Sorry, had to get that off my chest. I feel better now.

Actually, in the interests of full disclosure, I am not one to talk. I show off pictures of my cat all the time. (Check my social media feed for confirmation.)

On those feeling-less-tolerant-of-your-fiftieth-video-of-your-baby days, I am happy to be excluded from child-centric conversations. But it does not mean I want to be excluded altogether.

It is frankly embarrassing to sit with a bunch of parent-friends at church, hearing them arrange a playdate while I do not get the invite. On and on they chat, unaware of my increasing uncomfortability at being left out. I could attempt to join the conversation, but what would I say?

'Yes, that sounds like such fun for you guys! Please, continue making your exciting plans in front of me.'

As a childless person, I will never get the invite. And I find this strangely curious. Why shouldn't I be invited to a playdate? 'Um, Steph, you do not have kids, so you cannot come and play. Only kids play.' Oh, OK then. Never mind my burning desire to run wildly around the kiddie park and throw myself down the slippery dip. Adulting is hard. *Sigh*

But what do parents do on playdates anyway? They drink cuppas and watch their kids run wild. I can do that. I am not the most coordinated person, but I can drink and watch things at the same time.

I do not know why childless people are excluded from visits with parents. Maybe our parent-friends just need to be around other parents right now. Maybe that is the best thing for them. I am OK with that.

Maybe they have forgotten how to socialise with people whose worlds do not revolve around children. Sometimes my cynical brain wonders. Maybe it is just uncomfortable for them or they worry it will be too uncomfortable for me. They could be trying to protect me.

Maybe they are concerned about sharing parenting insights with non-parents. Maybe I cannot understand the world of parenting. Because (sarcasm alert), unlike parents, I have never had a sleepless night. I have never had to deal with noise, or a loved one's sickness, or the physical limitations of my own body. I could never possibly relate.

Parents: you can invite childless people over. We can handle it, I promise. We can even decline if it is too uncomfortable for us. But being asked once in a while would make a nice change. Childlessness by its nature is isolating. We do not need further isolation from parents who only associate with other parents.

When I got married, I formed a whole new family with my husband. We are a legitimate family comprising of two adults. But this is rarely recognised. Some churches are exclusively geared towards families with little people instead.

This was once highlighted for me at a church dinner event. My husband and I sat at a big round table with three other couples. Those couples proceeded (and I swear this really happened) to bash childless people for about forty minutes.

'They have no idea what it's like to be a parent!' they chorused.

Finally they paused for breath and one of them asked if I had a family. I chose to misunderstand. I put my arm around my man and gushed, 'Yes, I have a wonderful husband!'

'No,' she blundered on, 'Do you have children?'

Breathe, Steph. Just breathe.

How great it would be if we Christians could work together to break down these barriers.

Deification of families

Mike Frost, theologian and author, says the church has 'deified' the nuclear family (2017)[17].

According to Mike, the church prizes and prioritises nuclear families over the family of God. Children especially are afforded special privileges and exemptions. Families are encouraged to isolate and separate from the rest of church. Parents are praised for idolising their kids. The prioritisation of the needs of their family over the needs of the church is constantly reinforced.

Mike argues that if the church took the notion of 'family' seriously, it would promote the inclusion of people in our midst who happened not to be blood-related to us. We, the church, would include non-family in our family get-togethers. We, the church, would raise one another's children. We, the church, would be hospitable and generous to all, not just to our own offspring.

I have watched Christian families drift out of the church because they prioritise their kids' activities over their spiritual family.

I am all for parents staying home from church to look after sick kids. I think illness in the family should take priority. I would certainly stay home to care for my sick husband.

But we have a wider spiritual family to consider. We are not put on this earth solely to look after our small corner of God's family. We are part of a larger, worldwide community.

As a childless person who serves in church ministry, it is infuriating for me to watch people step down from worthy ministry and withdraw from meaningful church relationships because of family activities.

Why are they doing it? Because the kids need to go to sport, or because there is a family lunch happening, or because of some other family activity. These activities are important, I understand that. But I have witnessed families skipping church again and again due to such activities, and when it becomes a pattern, I start to wonder if they really value their church.

It saddens me to watch yet another young person give their apologies to ministry leaders because of soccer practise. It saddens me even more to watch leaders bow to the almighty gods of sport. 'Oh, you cannot get to rehearsal anymore? You have sport? Oh well, case closed. Clearly you must get to sport.'

I am not suggesting families cease such activities. Let's not throw out the baby with the proverbial bathwater. I am suggesting these activities get put on a pedestal because they are family-oriented in nature. And I am suggesting the idolisation of family activities has ramifications.

The wider church family misses out. They miss out on relationships with absent families. They miss out on those children's lives. They miss out on helping parents when the need arises. The church loses out and the absent family loses out.

That is a lose-lose situation.

I may get vilified for refusing to worship the god of family sport. But I am passionate about the local church and involving young people in ministry. I do not want to see local sport thrive while the local church dies.

The deification of families can come between God's people. It can reinforce the message to kids and teenagers that church does not matter or can be skipped when you want to do something else. It tells the next generation the world has more important things to offer than worshiping God, hearing his word and being with church family. It has long-term, intergenerational impact.

This should not be.

Surviving sermons

In Elena's story, she faced not only familial and cultural challenges of being childless, but spiritual hurdles as well.

At Mass one Sunday, Elena's priest preached about the blessings of children. According to the priest, children were the greatest blessing possible and being a parent was the greatest calling on earth. Elena sat in her pew, silently questioning her worth as a person. Mass was difficult for her after that.

She is not the first to feel the sting of 'parenthood is a blessing' sermons. Others, like Sarah in her story, have heard sermons on the joys of parenthood. And mourned.

For some churches, this emphasis on parenthood could be an effect of their traditions. Pope Francis, for example, has previously labelled childless people as being 'selfish' (Kirchgaessner 2015)[18]. (To be clear, his criticism was of people who were childless-by-choice or childfree, rather than those who were CNBC.)

He implied people who chose to live without children were greedy. He suggested they had an easier life without children. He predicted childless people will grow old in solitude and sink into 'the bitterness of loneliness'. Thanks for that. (Wait—aren't priests celibate? Is he self-disclosing?)

Drawing on his own positive experiences with his parents and siblings growing up, the Pope next extolled the virtues of children and parenting.

But then again, he said in the same article it is OK to hit children. (The Vatican promptly followed this up with a statement saying that violence against children is not OK.) Still, I will take his words with a grain of salt.

I have great admiration for Pope Francis. He has done wonderful work in promoting social justice and acts of kindness in the world. I have nothing against him as a person. This does not mean I agree with everything he says.

Especially when he criticises childless people.

Perhaps the Pope's personal experience of childless or childfree people has taught him they are selfish. Perhaps some childless-by-choice or childfree people do indeed live selfish and indulgent lives. It is possible. And Christians certainly need to be on guard about any kind of selfishness in life.

But 'selfish' has not been my experience of childless people.

While the Pope is singing the praises of children and parenthood, I think of those who are struggling in childlessness. Many childless people understand children are a gift. All too well.

> Childlessness and even childfreedom are typically not about avoiding blessings.

Childless people often worry about being perceived as selfish. But in my experience, most have tried everything to have children or made difficult decisions to be childless (as I did). Some choose childfreedom as a way of protecting would-be children from harm. And childlessness and even childfreedom are typically not about avoiding blessings. I do not know anyone who would willingly pass up extra blessings.

The choice to have children (when there is a choice) is made without others knowing the full story. We need to trust each other's decisions and not pass judgment.

And I believe parenthood is a blessing. I believe the church should provide support and resources for parents. I also believe the church should find a way to support parents that does not exclude childless people.

I can believe two things.

How about this: for every sermon, group or resource on parenting, the church matches it with a sermon, group or resource for those who are childless. Not super-creative, I know. Perhaps you can come up with something better.

Churches need to be as mindful of the childless members of their congregations as they are of parents and children.

Mother's and Father's Days

John and Rachel avoid Mother's and Father's Day church services for the sake of their sanity. I personally find these services a little tough, even when they are done well.

However, there are things that can be done to be more inclusive of childless people. Let's start with things that are unhelpful.

Photo booths in the church foyer, where you can have special family pics with mums and dads, can be confronting for childless people. Asking every mum or dad in the congregation to stand up midway through the service to rapturous applause can be embarrassing (and not just for childless people). Presenting mums with flowers can hurt too.

I have no problem with honouring mothers and fathers for all they do. I believe in honouring people and rejoicing in their successes. But it is bittersweet for me. It starkly reminds me of what is missing from my life.

Of course, it is not just childless people who may suffer on such occasions. Those who never knew their parents, who had bad childhood experiences, who have strained relationships with their parents or who have lost parents may find these days similarly painful.

So it is worth mentioning some positive options.

I love it when churches acknowledge the spiritual mums and dads in the congregation. Most of us have, at some point, encouraged someone else in their faith. We have prayed for them, shown them hospitality, mentored them, taught them or otherwise empowered them in their faith. I count that as spiritual parenting.

I am curious about what it will be like when we get to heaven. I wonder if we will meet all the people we have ever mentored.

Cute videos of kids in church are fine—often amusing—in small doses. Last Mother's Day I found that I enjoyed the first five minutes of my church's kids video, but after that, as the kids talked about what their parents had taught them about God, my feelings turned to sadness. I had hoped to talk to my kids about God. That aspect of Mother's Day may always be painful for me.

Sermons that are focused on God rather than earthly mums or dads can be helpful. Messages that highlight God's fatherly and motherly traits can be wonderfully grounding and uplifting. I have heard such sermons delivered with great pastoral sensitivity, and they are reassuring. Churches can do them well.

Pastors can use such scriptural references as John 14:21-23 (God's fatherly love for us), Isaiah 49:13-15 and 66:13 (God's motherly compassion and attention towards us), Luke 12:22-34 (God as a provider and carer), Matthew 7:7-11 (God as a good father), Psalm 23:1-3 (God as our shepherd), James 1:5 (God as a helper and giver of wisdom) and 1 Peter 5:6-7 (God as a watcher over us—beautifully articulated in the Amplified bible).

You can probably think of more. Personally, I have found such sermons far more helpful than speeches about parenting.

Other church messages about parenting can be unhelpful too. Like the message that parenting is the highest spiritual calling.

For the love of parents

Parenthood is not necessarily the highest calling or type of blessing available. And blessings are not a competition.

While parenthood is undeniably a blessing—contrary to the complaints of many parents—parenthood is not the only blessing ever conceived. God's gifts come in many shapes and sizes. And his creativity has not stalled. It did not finish with creation week. God is continually creative and we are continually catching up with his new creations. He keeps creating fresh and imaginative gifts all the time.

Parenthood is simply one of many possible gifts.

Under the umbrella of 'Parenthood is awesome' sermons there is a particularly disturbing kind of anti-childlessness message: 'You will never know God's love until you have a child'.

This is harmful for several reasons.

First, it devalues those who will never have kids. It suggests the love experienced by parents is superior. It implies childless people are inferior in their faith and in their inherent value as human beings.

Second, it dismisses the multifaceted ways in which God reveals his love to us. Yes, he reveals it through the gift of children, but children are only one of thousands of ways in which God demonstrates his great affection for us.

Third, people may not mean it. They may actually mean, 'When I had a child, I gained a whole new appreciation for God's love'. I have no problem with that. If that is what you mean, say that.

Finally, it can hit a raw nerve for childless people. Some childless people have suffered incredible loss and grief around not having a child. Let's not rub salt into the wound.

Plus, Jesus was never a parent. Does that mean he never

understood his Father's love? I think not.

Christ died for us so that we could know God's love first-hand. The stuff about childless people not knowing the fullness of God's love is rubbish. I believe we can be complete, fulfilled, mature Christians without having kids.

Childbearing is not a rite of passage into adulthood and becoming a parent is not a litmus test for spirituality. Children are a blessing, but the absence of children does not mean I am lacking in blessing—or in any other way.

> While some of us may never experience the love of a child, I am thankful all of us can know the horizonless love of God.

Sure, parents experience a unique form of love with their child. That does not make a child's love any better or more profound or transforming than God's love.

Childless people have experienced many forms of non-child love. They have known the love of spouses, family, dear friends and furbabies. These forms of love help us understand God's love too.

I do not believe we, as brothers and sisters in Christ, have anything to gain from comparing these various forms of love. Surely we are all equal in the knowledge of God's perfect love.

While some of us may never experience the love of a child, I am thankful all of us can know the horizonless love of God.

Ephesians 3:17-19 is a good reminder:

> I pray that you, being rooted and established in love, may have the power, together with all the Lord's holy people, to grasp how wide and long and high and deep is the love of Christ, and to

> know this love that surpasses knowledge—that
> you may be filled to the measure of all the
> fullness of God.

There is no special mention of parental privileges in this passage, nor any spiritual backstage pass. We are all children of God. We can all know the fullness of God's love equally.

Now that we have cleared that up, there is the small matter of surviving parenting sermons.

It can be difficult for childless people to sit through irrelevant and painful sermons on the blessings of parenthood. I encourage churches to consider its whole congregation, not just the child-centric majority, in sermon planning. I know some churches do this well, prayerfully and thoughtfully considering the childless and marginalised and hurting people in their congregation. I am greatly comforted by this.

Some childless people have been badly hurt by thoughtless and inappropriate sermons. To those people I would like to speak now.

On behalf of the church, I apologise if a sermon ever made you feel uncomfortable, distressed or less valued than anyone else. That was not from God. And it does not represent all Christians.

I hope you already know how valuable you are, but just in case it has been lost in translation, let me say it here:

You are valued and loved by Christ, just the way you are.

You are welcome in the church as you are.

You have much to contribute, exactly the way you are.

The church needs you. You matter. Your voice matters.

If parenting sermons get on your nerves or cause you to

question your value, hold fast to Christ. He knows your value even if your church does not. He sees everything you are going through. Hold tightly to him.

And look after yourself. Take a breather during such sermons. I am a big fan of not enduring torture. There is no reason to sit through something unhelpful. Pop out of the room while the sermon is going on. Go for a walk, read the bible (I have been distracted from many a sermon by reading the bible), or skip the service altogether. Give yourself permission to do what you need.

Sometimes skipping a sermon can be the best thing for your faith and mental wellbeing.

Church culture

I seldom hear a sermon about childlessness or miscarriage or infertility. Despite how common they are in our society. Even a sermon on barrenness would be desirable at this point, although the very word gives me the heebie-jeebies.

While I'm at it, I can't recall the last time I heard a sermon about sickness, singledom, grief, unresolved circumstances, divorce, or any type of hard-core suffering.

I sincerely hope it is just me.

I know some churches preach on grief and pain. I recently heard about one church doing a sermon series on grief. That is fabulous. And it fills me with hope for the church.

It is difficult when one's church seems silent on the subject of pain. I do not know why some churches do not address these issues. Perhaps it is ignorance or deliberate avoidance. Perhaps no one has voiced the need for such sermons.

CHURCH

Not every church deals with pain publicly. Some churches address painful matters on an individual level rather than a global one. There may be times when it is too painful for a congregation to hear a sermon about suffering. Pastors need to make their own judgment call on this. And they need to know their own congregations.

It is also possible some churches are not great at talking about pain. This strikes me as bizarre. Surely Jesus was well acquainted with grief. Surely if we follow Christ, we will know suffering and sorrow like he did. Surely we can talk about these things.

Some churches appear to focus on positivity at the expense of acknowledging suffering in their congregation. In Sarah's story, she described her church as all 'rainbows and butterflies', leaving no room for more painful subjects like her infertility. She felt she could not discuss her childlessness at church and it further isolated her.

This breaks my heart.

Such loneliness is far from what the church ought to be: a place of belonging for all of us, in our mess and frailty and vulnerability.

I do not know why some churches overly focus on the positives. (My personal theory is it comes from the 'prosperity gospel' and the teaching that Christians should be walking adverts for victorious living all the time. Just a theory.)

In reality, the 'rainbow' culture can hurt and silence those who are suffering. For those people, there may be no miracle, no answer to prayer, no rainbow to mark the end of the storm. Their pain may be lifelong.

I want the church to be a flagship in welcoming pain and suffering in its midst. I want the church to get its metaphorical hands dirty, to get down in the gutter with hurting people, to embrace the grittiness of their suffering.

I am passionate about this. I also realise change happens slowly. I know some people will read this and think, 'Steph, dream on. My church does not get its hands dirty, metaphorically or otherwise. You are living in a fantasy world.'

Why should this be a fantasy?

Why should the church shy away from the realities of pain and suffering?

Why should we lower our expectations of our churches?

It is OK to desire honest expression of our pain in church. It is reasonable to share our difficult stories, ones without happy endings—or any endings at all. It is fitting to bring our deepest hurts to church.

That is the kind of church I want to see. I want to belong to that church.

Some Christians believe they are supposed to be perpetual Jesus-adverts to the rest of the world. They worry that when the church looks less-than-perfect, it might turn people off Jesus.

Falseness and hypocrisy turn people off Jesus. If we are to be Jesus to a hurting world, our tolerance for vulnerability and hard subjects is more important than our appearance.

And when people start talking, we, the church, need to listen. Without offering a quick fix or spiritual cliché.

God does not always heal. Sometimes God does not deliver us from earthly suffering. Sometimes God does not give us what we ask. Sometimes God extends and deepens our suffering, rather than rescuing us from it.

Ongoing pain is not necessarily a sign the church has fallen short, nor that God is any less faithful or capable. It may be because suffering is an inherent part of existence, a part that God can take and transform and beautify. And one day we will be released from that suffering—for good.

Let us join with people's suffering. That is what Christ did.

Making a start

I recently spoke to my new pastor about childlessness. She is a wife and mum. Our conversation went something like this:

Me: I am writing a book about Surviving Childlessness. I believe Christians without children often have a hard time in church.

Pastor: That is great you are writing about childlessness! Church is so full of kids programs, and youth programs, and things for families...

Me: ... I know! Which the church should be running, because those programs are really important...

Pastor: ... But I think we could do better at including people who do not have children.

Me: *hyperventilating* That's what I wrote in my book!

I think I love her.

If you want to shift your church culture, you could start by speaking with your elders or leaders about your concerns. Share your experience of church and the impact—good or bad—on you. Find out if it is possible to have sermons on difficult topics such as childlessness or pain or suffering.

Maybe you could be part of the solution.

Request them. Talk about them. See if anyone else is interested.

Change in church is best led by the leaders. The change needs to be embraced and driven by them, not just by you. If you can recruit someone in leadership to your cause, you will not be alone. Taking up the cause alone will likely lead to exhaustion, disillusionment and burnout. With support from church leadership, you could kick-start the much-needed culture change.

Ask your leaders if they know the childless people in their congregation. Find out if they are being looked after. You could connect with those people. They could be your tribe.

You do not have to be personally responsible for those people. By simply having those conversations, you are raising the profile of childless people in your congregation.

Consider a Childless Day, in addition to Mother's and Father's Days. (See if you can come up with a better name for it.)

Arrange get-togethers with other childless people. Maybe they are looking for connection but do not have the energy or nerve to ask. Maybe you could be part of the solution. The more people on board, the less you have to do yourself. By recruiting others in the cause, you get support in more ways than one.

Being a childless champion might sound like too much work. Just because we do not have kids, it does not mean we have to drive change. We do not have boundless energy to devote to church just because we are childless. Nor are we obliged to do so.

Personally, I need to be kind to myself and set boundaries based on my needs. Sometimes church is difficult. Occasionally, I need to skip uber-family-friendly events.

It is possible you need another church if things do not improve. There is only so much you can do to change your situation. If you feel raw and emotional at present, it may not be the best time to make that decision; perhaps let your emotions settle first. But if you stick it out and your church continues to be painful and depressing, it may be time to find a new church.

I encourage you to choose one that is healthy and supportive.

We humans like to solve problems. It makes us feels useful. But the church first needs compassion for the childless. Anyone in deep pain requires loving-kindness and empathy, not knee-jerk problem-fixing. Real empathy involves willingness to listen and tolerate someone else's pain—indefinitely.

We can learn to sit with other people's pain, hear their difficult stories and tolerate their grief-without-end. Such raw empathy requires vulnerability and willingness to witness another's vulnerability.

Romans 12:15 says, 'Rejoice with those who rejoice, mourn with those who mourn'. There is no need to 'fake good'. Both rejoicing and mourning have a place. I love that. Joy is neither right nor wrong; same goes for grief. They just are.

Our stories are valuable and relevant to the church. They do not need happy endings or profound spiritual revelations. Our stories are vital, even when they question our faith or challenge the church. Especially then.

I hope we can find courage to tell our stories as they are.

A place of belonging

With the challenges of church life, it can be hard to feel we belong there.

It is ironic when church is meant to be a place for everybody. We are equal in Christ and we need a place where we can come as we are.

Sadly, many childless people have struggled to fit into the church mainstream, like Sarah and her church's 'rainbows and butterflies' culture. Even more sadly, churches have not always recognised this but have carried on as usual, perpetuating social divides and isolation.

> Nothing on this earth can compare to the eternal home that awaits me.

(And it is not just childless people who feel on the outside. Singles, divorcees and those with disabilities often feel they do not belong.)

But we still belong to the global church, the real church, the one that thrives no matter what. The real church welcomes mess and vulnerability and raw honesty. In the real church, you and I have a place. We are valued. We have something to offer. We are accepted and loved. We are worthy. Our opinions, our voices, our stories matter.

I once felt like I did not belong in a previous church. I felt like an outsider, a stranger amongst God's people. I was miserable for years. Then I heard the song *Who You Say I Am* by Hillsong.

The chorus seemed to shout at me.

The line about having a place in my Father's house chimed in my ears like a church bell. I realised my not fitting in at church was irrelevant. My fears about not belonging were unfounded.

Because I do belong. In my Father's house. Jesus is preparing a place for me. And that house is my true home.

I had been focused on my local church, the tiny part of God's Kingdom I could see with my physical eyes. I had lost my view of eternity. From an eternal perspective, I am part of the real church, accepted, redeemed, welcomed and a joint heir with Christ.

So if I feel like the odd one out at my local church, it is because I am longing for my heavenly home. Nothing on this earth can compare to the eternal home that awaits me.

And that floods me with relief.

Our churches are temporary stops on the way to our heavenly destination. Let us hold on to that eternal desire, the longing to be with our Father in his house.

For now, I hope you share your story and find a place of belonging in your church. More than that, I hope you never lose sight of your eternal home.

SARAH'S STORY

UK

Sarah and her husband's childlessness journey is marked by endurance and heartache.

When Sarah turned thirty, five years into her marriage, she and her husband started trying—despite not feeling ready, money- or job-wise. They tried for three years. At first they were not concerned over the delay. They believed it would eventually happen. Things were OK.

Until their friends started having babies.

That changed the situation. They wondered why it was not happening for them. They got tested, an intrusive and difficult process, and the results were inconclusive. Sarah and her husband got worried.

The doctor diagnosed them with unexplained infertility, which, unbeknownst to them, gave them a four percent chance of conceiving naturally. The doctor told them to keep trying. So they did. They believed if they gave it time and prayer and held fast to their peace, the issue would resolve.

Sarah drew strength and comfort from her relationship with God during this time. Her faith grew, flourished even, as she trusted God and waited for a child. She leaned on her Christian friends as well.

The years passed. Sarah took hormonal medication to increase her ovulation rate. She experienced practical difficulties and delays with medical appointments. The only follow-up appointment she got was at a menopause clinic, where the nurse was astonished to learn Sarah had not had monitoring or blood tests. The clinic also discovered her hormone medication, prescribed by the NHS, had caused hyper-ovulation. This could have triggered multiple pregnancies (double-figures). It could have endangered Sarah's life. And the lives of any babies.

Sarah was horrified and furious with the NHS. Their failure to arrange appointments and monitor her medication was negligent and had risked her life. Sarah and her husband worried about how her body might react to the hormones. They were also fearful of further medical care under the NHS.

One day they attended a Rhythm of Hope one-day conference for Christians with infertility. There were over one hundred Christian couples there, struggling to conceive, wrestling with difficult medical, moral and ethical dilemmas.

Sarah and her husband realised, for the first time, they were not alone.

The speakers included international broadcasters, male infertility campaigners, doctors, ethics professors, infertility bloggers and people who had adopted, tried IVF, adopted embryos and used donor sperm.

Sarah and her husband were overwhelmed by the wealth of experience, wisdom and love in the room. There were lots of tears. It felt like a safe place.

At this conference, Sarah discovered she could apply for two rounds of IVF. She could take a milder dose of hormones and use

ICSI (injecting a single sperm into each egg, increasing the chance of fertilisation).

They applied and got the funding. But while waiting for the paperwork to come through, they discovered Sarah's husband had fast-growing cancer.

This devastating news led to six agonising weeks of cancer testing. Thankfully, the tests came back benign. Sarah's husband had been wrongly diagnosed.

Looking back, Sarah wished they had responded to their infertility with the same urgency and vigour as they did to the cancer scare. They had patiently waited in infertility for six years.

The cancer scare left Sarah and her husband exhausted. Not the best way to start IVF. But they started the next month. The worst part was the emotional rollercoaster. Waiting for good or bad news every day was horrendous. Each day the number of embryos decreased.

On the outside, Sarah was acting normal. On the inside, her head was a whirlwind of what-ifs, injections, medications, appointments and lists of things to avoid. They told close friends and family and asked them to pray.

And it paid off. Sarah fell pregnant.

She could not believe it. For years she had felt God say she would be a mum to a child of promise. And her miracle had arrived. She was overwhelmed with joy. She felt like Elizabeth from the bible (Luke 1:5-25).

She had no idea what was coming.

At ten weeks, Sarah went for a scan. But the nurse could not get a heartbeat. The baby had stopped growing.

Their world came crashing down. Everything collapsed. Sarah went from jubilation to devastation. 'It felt like the cruellest trick,' she said. 'To be given that gift after so many years, and then for it to go, was beyond words.'

They walked away from that scan without the expected baby pictures, instead holding a list of options for managing the inevitable miscarriage.

Sarah waited two weeks for her baby to miscarry. But it did not happen. She took medication to induce miscarriage. It gave her the agony of actual labour pains as her body rejected her longed-for baby. She was totally unprepared for it.

That same day, Sarah's sister went into labour. If that was not enough, on the second night of miscarriage a friend rang to say she had fallen pregnant. Sarah hung up the phone and screamed.

'I wanted to smash everything in the house,' she recalled. 'I had been trying to hold it together until this point, but I lost it. Something changed in me that night that can never be mended. My sense of justice died. My idea of God, as a loving father, was broken.'

She found a bible verse that described how she felt: 'I have become like broken pottery' (Psalm 31:12). She did not know if she would ever mend.

For round two of IVF, Sarah increased her medication. The process yielded a similar result: a successful embryo transfer, followed by a bleed a few weeks later. 'The devastation hit all over again like a tsunami,' she said. She had expected the second round to succeed and felt naïve.

Doing IVF was like playing the lottery. She felt people only heard the success stories of IVF, not the failures. But she had heard IVF had a failure rate of sixty-five to seventy-five percent. IVF would always be a gamble.

She could not afford any more IVF without NHS support. That was the end of the road.

Or so she thought.

Her workplace gave her a redundancy payout, enough to fund three rounds of IVF through a refund program which gives money back if it does not work. Sarah weighed up the risks and her age (thirty-seven). It would be a lot of money if IVF did not work. But the money would be insignificant if it did work.

They took the gamble. They did three rounds of ICSI.

The gamble did not pay off.

But the process provided answers. The quality of Sarah's eggs was poor. The only way to improve her egg quality was to grow young again. There was no solution. Nothing more they could do.

Childlessness profoundly impacted Sarah. Infertility was lonely and isolating. It brought a complex grief that few have understood. She found few resources and little mental health support, even though infertility can be as stressful as having cancer. She wishes there was more help available, particularly for Christians who may not get moral or ethical support from their church.

She dreads pregnancy announcements from friends and colleagues. She avoids old friends who are 'so far in mumsy-land, they are best left in that world.' She skips aisles in the supermarket.

She avoids child-centric conversations. She feels overwhelmed when in-laws discuss their grandchildren. She grieves with sadness invisible yet relentless.

It helps when friends get Sarah and her husband involved in their lives. Sarah enjoys quality time with her husband and they keep each other's sense of humour alive. They are finding themselves and each other again.

Sarah is filling her world with joy, laughter, community and friendship. She has an army of friends who build her up and support her, including women who understand unanswered prayer, unmet life stages and living an unplanned life. These friendships run deep. She and her friends share a great level of empathy, arising from shared pain and experience.

She is pursuing enjoyable activities. She believes in being kind to oneself and honestly acknowledging one's raw emotions. Her personal motto is, 'Work out what is the kindest thing for Sarah right now.' Often the kindest thing is to avoid conversations about children. At times, she uses a scripted answer for questions about kids. She steers the conversation towards other people's children instead.

If she feels strong, she challenges people on their misconceptions of infertility. She recently challenged a colleague who told her, 'Losing weight will help you get pregnant' and 'Just adopt'. She sent him an article on how to support childless people (Lowrie 2015)[19].

He took it well.

Sarah found helpful blogs and websites such as *Saltwater and Honey* (2020)[20] (many blogs written from a Christian perspective), the *Fertility Network UK* (2020)[21] (for those facing life without hoped-for children) and *Rhythm of Hope* (2020)[22].

She recommends childless couples attend conferences such as

those run by Rhythm of Hope. She encourages them to do anything that gives them the care and healing space they need. She also found unhelpful fertility 'advice' on the internet (how-to-get-pregnant sales pitches) and recommends childless people ignore these.

Childlessness affected Sarah's faith. It used to be her source of hope and strength, but it was poisoned by unanswered prayer, especially considering the babies she lost.

She found church hard, especially when it was full of 'rainbows and butterflies'. She felt her church struggled with the painful realities of life, including childlessness, and was largely ignorant of the pain of infertility. 'I try to go to church,' Sarah journalled. 'But it is hard. I can't trust, believe or pray. I have too many questions... and no easy answers.'

Sermons on the joys of parenting were painful. Given their sensitive nature, a little advance warning would have been helpful. 'People don't know how to handle unanswered prayer or brokenness,' Sarah said frankly. 'To sit with someone's grief and not provide answers, just comfort, is so important.'

Several prophecies about her would-be children failed to come true. One prophecy gave her child-to-be the name Daniel. Another predicted a timeframe within which she would receive her child. She trusted these prophecies and her ability to hear from God.

But when the timeframe came and went, she began to distance herself from God. She questioned herself, her sin, God's memory, God's hearing, her sugar levels, everything. In the end, she hated God.

Sarah wrote a letter to God, part of it saying, 'If you care for us, why did you allow our baby to die? Why give us hope to have it taken? Why not intervene and allow our embryos to carry on forming?... I have formed a life around a promise of a child and now am bereft of that promise. I don't know what to do, or who I am or who you are anymore... Do you have a redemptive purpose for this pain? Did you prevent a disabled child from being born because our genes are bad? Could you have healed this badness? What is your purpose with this suffering?'

She felt she believed too readily and naïvely that God would simply heal them and answer their prayers. But healing was not automatic. And faith has not been that simple.

'We like things neatly parceled with a bow on top,' she told me. 'But what happens when the child God has promised you dies? Our experience in church has left me broken. My belief in a loving friend and faithful father is shattered.'

This has shifted over time. She is now learning to trust God again and no longer feels angry towards him.

Sarah recommends not blaming partners for infertility and not putting life on hold either. She is doing things that bring her joy like swimming and cycling. She and her husband are pursuing creative endeavours including artistic expressions of childlessness which have helped them heal. They are immersing themselves in music, movies, graphic design, reading, painting and sewing.

They spend time with their niece and godson and a surrogate daughter who lives next door. Close friends have walked with them every step of the way and understand what they have been through.

Sarah reflected on how little she knew about infertility and IVF at the start, especially from a Christian perspective.

'Looking back,' Sarah said, 'I wish I had known how long and hard this was going to be. I would have started treatment at a younger age. I regret not getting a second opinion. I was not properly informed.'

She recommends childless people get lots of support from counsellors, close friends and others on the infertility journey.

Sarah found out one in three marriages fail due to infertility and she encourages good communication. 'Be each other's protectors. You will be stronger as a couple if you communicate. Don't let this rob you of each other as well as parenthood.'

They still want to be parents, so they have applied for adoption. They know it will be another rollercoaster journey, but they hope it will have a more encouraging and rewarding end.

INFERTILITY

Why is Everyone Else Pregnant?

OK. *Deep breath*

Let's start with the bad news.

Infertility is widespread. People from all races and cultures have problems falling pregnant. Worldwide, one in six couples have trouble conceiving (Fertility Solutions 2020)[23].

Yet we, as a society, do not often speak about it. There is stigma around infertility due to popular beliefs and assumptions about reproduction. Assumptions like anyone can have kids if they want them badly enough. Or everyone is fertile.

We know differently.

If reproduction is the default position, the healthy norm,

the social expectation, then infertility is the unspeakable, the unthinkable, the elephant in the womb—I mean the room.

This is partly a holdover effect from bygone eras. Contraception did not become effective till the 1960s, therefore if you were married or having sex, you were having children. The only reason to not have children in that era was because of medical problems like infertility. (Or because you were out of God's favour—hence the stigma around childlessness being indicative of sin.)

So how common is infertility?

One in thirty-five Australian men experience infertility issues (Fertility Solutions 2020)[24]. For these men, being infertile can feel like being labelled as less of a man. Men often view their masculinity through the lens of fatherhood and even sperm count. To discover problems or that it is unlikely to happen can be a blow to the self.

Women experience similar stigma. For Australian women over thirty-five, one in three have issues with fertility (Fertility Solutions 2020)[25]. (Other websites report different statistics, so accuracy is hard. But it gives us a ballpark.) These women can feel less valued than other women. Behind curtain number one, we have 'real women'—mothers—and curtain number two rises to reveal the 'others': spinsters, crazy cat ladies (like me), hags. Unfeminine. Not real women.

Regardless of gender, infertility can have a profound effect.

Defining infertility

When a couple under thirty-five has regular unprotected sex for a year but do not fall pregnant, they are deemed infertile. A couple over thirty-five are deemed infertile after six months of trying.

Most couples (eighty-four percent) will fall pregnant naturally within the first year, and almost all (ninety-two percent) within the first two years (Health Engine 2008)[26]. This is why medical professionals recommend fertility testing for people who struggle to fall pregnant within these timeframes. There could be a simple explanation.

(Infertility is different to secondary infertility, which occurs when a couple, having successfully conceived previously, become infertile afterwards and unable to conceive a second time.)

Causes of infertility include low sperm count, low egg production, early ejaculation, abnormalities in the egg or sperm and recurrent miscarriage.

Additional contributing factors, courtesy of *My VMC* (Health Engine 2008)[27], include:

- Age. Women over thirty-five experience a rapid decline in eggs. Even women over the age of twenty-five experience a decline in fertility. And men are not exempt. Men over thirty-five have half the fertility rate than that of twenty-five-year-olds.
- Cancer treatment. Apparently the nasty cancer-killing drugs can impact the reproductive area.
- Sexually Transmitted Infections (STIs). Any damage to the reproductive area from an STI can affect subsequent efforts to conceive.
- Obesity. Being overweight can affect your chances of falling pregnant.
- Exposure to pesticides. Those whose line of work involves

the use of pesticides may have trouble conceiving.
- Smoking. Besides being bad for you, smoking raises the risk of pregnancy going wrong. The good news is quitting smoking, even for two weeks, can do irreversible good to your body.
- Drugs and alcohol. Using illicit drugs or abusing alcohol can potentially damage the reproductive area (not to mention the rest of you).
- Infrequent sex. The recommended amount of sex for conception is every two to three days. This, apparently, is why doctors ask childless couples personal and invasive questions about their sex lives.

Female-specific factors:

- Endometriosis. According to *Endometriosis Australia* (2020)[28], one in ten Australian women have endometriosis. It affects menstrual cycles and can affect conception. It is difficult to get a diagnosis; many women, as well as doctors, play down symptoms or think they are just 'bad periods'.
- Fibroids. These are benign growths inside the uterus. They can develop during childbearing years and, depending on where they grow, can interfere with fertilisation and pregnancy.
- Polycystic Ovarian Syndrome (PCOS). This affects hormone production. It can cause ovarian cysts, irregular periods and problems falling pregnant.

Male-specific factors:

- Testicular infections or blockages. Any issues with

passages in this region or the testes themselves can make it difficult for sperm to travel. Sperm may be fit to travel but unable to reach the exit.
- Y Chromosome abnormalities. Men who carry abnormalities in their Y Chromosomes can have abnormalities in the sperm. Sometimes the sperm can be collected and successfully used in reproductive technology to fall pregnant. (Yes, there is some good news.)
- Heat exposure. Wearing tight underwear or having hot baths can cause the testicles to overheat and sustain damage.

There can be additional factors such as immunological and hormonal issues, early menopause, chronic illness, stress, relational pressures and sexual dysfunction.

This last one presents unique challenges. I imagine it would be extremely difficult to try to conceive if, for example, one could not maintain an erection, or if one experienced significant pain during intercourse that rendered sex impossible. I heard of one situation where a woman who suffered from vaginismus (involuntary vaginal contractions) was completely unable to have sex.

Having children is complex. It would be easier if it happened naturally and effortlessly for everyone every time.

Sadly, this is not the case.

Statistics and impact

According to the *ABC news* website (McArthur 2007)[29], forty percent of infertility problems come down to the man and a further forty percent are attributable to the woman. Ten percent are a combination of both male and female issues. The remaining ten percent are due to 'unknown factors'. Otherwise known as unexplained infertility. (Note: statistics vary across websites.)

This term will be familiar to a lot of childless people. Heart-thumpingly, gut-droppingly familiar. It means you and your partner are normal and healthy and should be able to get pregnant, but for some reason you are not.

While it can be a relief to learn you have no medical problems per se, it can be frustrating and confusing to be told you should have no problem falling pregnant when, clearly, you do. It can be disheartening to hear your doctor say, 'It should have worked by now'. Whether it should have worked or not is irrelevant. Your experience says it has not happened.

Many people want clarity from doctors, not vague reassurance. The unexplained infertility diagnosis does little to comfort an already stressed-out couple who may have sacrificed time, effort, money and privacy in search of answers. Unexplained infertility is no answer at all.

Living with infertility is incredibly stressful. Thank you Captain Obvious. We know this anecdotally but emerging research is now backing up what many have experienced firsthand.

Dr Robin Hadley, drawing on his own and others' experiences, described living with infertility as similar to living with a grave medical condition (2018)[30]. It can be depressing, anxiety-provoking, stressful, isolating, confusing and draining. It can trigger grief.

Despite infertility, some choose to keep trying to conceive naturally, accepting whatever outcome eventuates. Some want to be parents but decide not to try infertility treatment. It cuts deep, but they can come to terms with it.

For others, infertility is a waking nightmare, a personal catastrophe. They have spent their lives hoping, planning and working towards parenthood. They believe they were put on this earth to be a parent. They may be desperate to have children.

> Infertility can trigger an existential crisis.

For such people, infertility can trigger an existential crisis.

'What do I do with my life, if not parenting? What am I here for?' These people cannot give up on the dream. They will do anything to have children.

This brings us to reproductive technologies, the most common being IVF.

In Vitro Fertilisation (IVF)

IVF has changed the face of infertility. It provides options to those otherwise doomed to childlessness. The whole choice thing is a relatively recent development compared with previous generations. We are indeed living in privileged times.

But privilege, it would seem, is a double-edged sword.

IVF has a hefty price tag. And I am talking literally. In Australia, you can pay around $3000 per IVF cycle (McArthur 2007)[31]. And that is not the only cost. Those who have undertaken IVF understand the significant emotional, mental, relational and sexual toll it can take. The woman, in particular, pays a small fortune in physical and emotional hardship in the form of hormonal injections, implantation, pregnancy tests and a myriad of medications to take.

Even the IVF referral can be stressful. Doctors, I am told, can be very quick to move from 'You're infertile' to 'Here's your local IVF clinic'. It can be difficult to process this new information and ask astute questions when you are in a state of shock.

IVF clinics are not the best at warning people of possible risks and side effects of treatment. Apparently they over-state their rate of success. This makes sense from their business perspective. Obviously the clinics want to sell you their products. It is good for their business if you stay in treatment. And the best way to keep you hooked is to feed you their hope-filled sales pitch.

'The more you try, the greater your chance of success.'

'Never mind, there is always next time.'

'Shall we put your name down for another cycle?'

IVF sells.

While IVF certainly raises your chance of falling pregnant, the overall rate of success is still low. IVF is no guarantee.

Some of my interviewees said IVF makes promises it may never fulfil. These IVF veterans warned others to exercise caution. It might be wise, even while hoping for success, to heed their words.

The grain of salt

First, some good news. The success rate of IVF in Australia is apparently improving. The reporting of stats is also increasing. This means we have a clearer picture of how successful IVF really is.

(Stats from other countries may differ, so readers outside of Australia should undertake independent research. And take these stats with a grain of salt. Because different clinics and websites tell different stories.)

In Australia, one percent of yearly births are attributable to IVF (Fertility Solutions 2020)[32]. It does not sound like much when compared to the rest of the population conceiving naturally. And IVF stats within the childless population would be more helpful.

One IVF clinic I read about boasted a success rate of thirty-three percent in the first cycle. It said those who undertake eight cycles (not for the faint-hearted) have an increased success rate of fifty-four to seventy-seven percent (Chambers 2017)[33].

In other words, presuming you are desperate and rich and in all other ways capable of eight IVF cycles, you have a maximum seventy-seven percent shot at taking a child home.

But that is not all. IVF success rates are linked to age. If you begin IVF before the age of thirty, you have a higher success rate than those who commence after thirty. Over-forties have the lowest chance of success.

Furthermore, if you are under thirty-five and can endure three cycles of IVF, you apparently have a two in three chance of success.

Phew. That is a lot of numbers.

I did a quick check of IVF success rates at other websites. This perfunctory search yielded different results. *ABC news* gave an average success rate of twenty percent for each IVF cycle, with allowance for wide variation (McArthur 2007)[34].

And according to the European Society of Human Reproduction and Embryology (EHSRE), IVF has a global failure rate of seventy-two percent (EHSRE 2020)[35].

IVF success depends on who you are, where you live, your age, your resources, and the specific clinic you attend.

So I would echo the sentiment of many IVF survivors and recommend people take advertised success rates with a grain or two of salt. It could be that IVF clinics only report stats most favourable to their business.

Shocking, I know.

While IVF success is certainly linked to starting younger, this is difficult considering most childless couples have already been trying for years. And people seem to be marrying later in life (not in my church, apparently, but certainly in society at large).

It is important to be aware of the risks of ageing, but it is equally important not to judge or dismiss someone's desire for IVF just because of their age. We do not want to make anyone's childless journey harder because of ageism.

If you choose to accept your IVF mission, remember there are no guarantees. It sounds like IVF For Beginners but it can be easy to lose sight of this once IVF begins. And I am not a doctor. So get your own medical advice, do some research and seek second opinions.

IVF promotes a lot of hope. I am all for hope, but not false hope. We could hypothetically attempt many IVF cycles, devote years and thousands of dollars to the endeavour, and wind up with nothing.

As did many childless people I interviewed.

Perhaps the old adage, 'Hope for the best, prepare for the worst', is sage advice.

What are you talking about?

I knew nothing about IVF when I began writing this book. So it is no exaggeration to say my interviewees taught me much about the terminology, technology, psychology and survivology of IVF.

You heard me.

I undertook independent research before the interviews. Still, I was nervous. Would my interviewees think less of me because I was childless-without-IVF? To my great consolation, they were gracious and patient with me. My imposter syndrome was thrown into sharp relief.

When they realised I was an IVF virgin, they showered me with wisdom, relishing the opportunity to share the graphic minutiae of their stories. One person said it was refreshing to talk to someone who knew nothing about the process.

I also unearthed a wealth of information from *ABC news* (McArthur 2007)[36] about different kinds of IVF. It may be useful to those undertaking IVF. (Aside: if a person is undertaking IVF, does that make them an IVF undertaker?)

The reproductive technologies include:

- Ovulation induction. The woman receives hormonal injections to stimulate egg growth. This intervention alone is sometimes sufficient.
- Artificial insemination. The sperm is collected, treated and optimised (I am not sure what this means), and injected into the woman's uterus.
- IVF. For fertility issues and unexplained infertility. IVF begins with ovulation induction. The woman's eggs are collected, fertilised in a dish with the man's sperm (sexy, right?), then the fertilised eggs are implanted into her uterus.
- GIFT (Gamete intrafallopian transfer). For infertility issues not affecting the woman's fallopian tubes. The eggs and

sperm are collected and implanted into the fallopian tubes.
- ZIFT (Zygote intrafallopian transfer). For sperm issues. The fertilised embryo is placed directly into the woman's fallopian tubes.
- ICSI (Intracytoplasmic sperm injection). The eggs and sperm are collected and a single sperm is injected into the egg. The fertilised egg is either implanted into the woman's fallopian tubes or grown externally and then implanted into her uterus.
- Testicular sperm extraction. The sperm is collected directly from the testes with a needle (yikes) and injected into the woman's egg as per ICSI.
- Freezing. Frozen embryos can be stored for future IVF cycles. Sperm can be frozen on its own and stored in sperm banks. Eggs can be frozen, although there may be some scientific issues with this.
- Donations. Eggs, sperm and embryos can be donated. In Australia, each state and territory has different laws regarding the identity of donors and the rights of donor-children. In NSW there is currently no law regarding donors being identified or having rights of access for either the child or the donor. There are recommendations regarding the choice of donor, such as choosing someone you know to facilitate future relationships with the child. If you are considering donorship, please conduct independent research in your state or territory.

The *Manchester Fertility* website (Cuthbert 2017)[37] lists additional terms and meanings that might help.

This information might help friends and family understand what you are going through.

Ethical and spiritual quandaries

Before I started interviewing, I had no idea there were ethical and spiritual issues with IVF. Particularly for Christians. Yes, I was naïve. Now I know a little more, thanks to the patience and generosity of my interviewees.

> *I am not persuaded that medical creativity and ingenuity, gifts of our creative God which can solve reproductive problems, are inherently wrong.*

First, should one even consider assisted reproduction? Some Christians have a hard time with the 'artificial' bit, fearing it may oppose the natural processes God established. And some Christians stereotype and stigmatise those who undertake or even consider IVF.

Dr Megan Best examines this and other dilemmas in *Fearfully and Wonderfully Made* (2012)[38], her book on reproductive ethics. She suggests medical intervention is ethically sound when it corrects a medical problem. So if you have infertility and undertake medical treatment, there's no ethical issue.

This may be more difficult for those with no medical issue to correct. One example is unexplained infertility, where no medical issue can be found. Is it justifiable for one to undertake IVF when all tests are normal and one 'should' be getting pregnant?

I am not sure. I can imagine circumstances where couples with unexplained infertility would certainly want to try IVF. I can see other situations where IVF would be unhelpful.

Some believe doing IVF signifies a lack of faith and we should trust God for healing. They believe attempting IVF denies God the opportunity to bestow this healing.

This argument is yet to convince me. I do not think our actions or medical interventions preclude God's intervention. He is more than capable of stepping in. Furthermore, I am not persuaded that medical creativity and ingenuity, gifts of our creative God which can solve reproductive problems, are inherently wrong.

But you may disagree. You need to decide for yourself your own ethics on these matters.

Second, there are issues surrounding the creation, storage and destruction of embryos. Embryos are formed when the egg and sperm come together and fertilise. Embryos are considered by some to be life forms—human beings.

If so, we should treat embryos as having the rights to which any other human being is entitled.

For example, we would not normally freeze people without their consent, so should we freeze embryos? They do not have a voice in these matters and are unable to consent, so we need to care for them as for fellow human beings.

Destruction of embryos is even more tricky. How do you ethically dispose of a life form, especially if you believe abortion is wrong? You could keep the embryos in storage, but this costs money and can be time-limited.

You can choose to produce only as many embryos as numbers of children you want. This sounds tidy and logical. But embryos do not always follow a tidy and logical path.

You can avoid these complex issues by freezing eggs and sperm rather than embryos. You can also donate 'leftover' embryos to others or to research. These may be ethically preferable options. But I encourage you to ask your doctor specific questions about these options. Because I am not a doctor.

Third, there are differing philosophical and spiritual opinions about in which stage of growth the embryo becomes an actual life form. Many believe the egg and sperm become a life form once they fertilise. Others believe the embryo becomes a life form once it is implanted in an environment where it can develop—where it has the potential to grow into a full human being.

If you believe an embryo is not human until it is implanted in the woman's uterus or fallopian tubes, you will not have any difficulties with storing and destroying frozen embryos. If, however, you take the dominant Christian view that an embryo is a life, IVF becomes more complicated. It does not render IVF impossible, but there will be more questions and decisions involved.

Fourth, IVF is stressful and dehumanising. One may feel it is unethical to put people through so much suffering and difficulty with no guarantee of children.

There is also considerable pressure from IVF doctors and clinics for couples to take up IVF and, once they have, to continue with endless rounds of IVF until a child materialises.

The ethical issue is one of vulnerability. The childless couple are acutely vulnerable because they want a child desperately. They are vulnerable because they are hopeful. A woman completing at least one IVF cycle will undertake hormonal treatment which places her in a heightened state of mental, emotional and physical vulnerability. Once begun, a couple may feel emotionally and financially invested in IVF. They may feel under pressure from themselves and others to see it through.

One wonders about the ethics of IVF clinics offering false hope to vulnerable people in order to keep them engaged in very expensive treatment.

Fifth, using egg and sperm donors raises potential issues around the child's identity. A child who grows up with multiple mums or dads, or without knowing their donor parent, may experience a loss of identity.

It raises questions about including the donor parent in the child's life. The child may have questions about their donor parents or their genetic and cultural inheritance. These questions will require an answer one day.

For Christians, donorship may raise the issue of adultery. Many people believe marriage should consist of two people. Donorship brings a third party into the intimate state of marriage.

Then again, some may view the donated egg or sperm as simply a product, a means to an end. This viewpoint, while appearing cold, avoids some of the ethical dilemmas.

Still others may experience a form of jealousy with donorship. A man may experience sexual jealousy or intimidation at the thought of another man impregnating his wife.

Donorship carries risks for the donor too. I read one story (Campbell 2017)[39] of an egg donor who was permanently affected by the surgical removal of her eggs. It gave her endometriosis and infertility.

This woman was also unable to contact the parents because the donorship agency (the middleman) blocked her contact. She was not in control. And the agency pushed for her anonymity as well.

Sixth, surrogacy raises questions about the involvement of the surrogate mother in the child's life. Some fear the involvement of a third party in their marriage. For others, it raises different worries.

What if the surrogate mum falls in love with the child?

What if the child bonds with the surrogate parents and not the intended parents?

What if someone changes their mind, say, if the baby has a disability?

What if the surrogate mother from overseas is being abused or exploited?

Some fear the surrogacy process will shift the focus from the child, or from the journey of pregnancy, to the 'end product'.

But surrogacy can be a good option if the mother cannot carry a baby to full term. So while surrogacy is complex, requiring careful consideration, it is an option.

Seventh, some Christians believe the only biblical model for parenthood is a biological mother and father. This would rule out the involvement of other parties, such as egg or sperm donors, surrogates or adoptive parents. It would also rule out single parents, foster parents, same-sex parents, extended family carers or a child being raised by a village.

I do not agree this so-called 'biblical model' is the only

Christian model. Imagine if God was only pleased when a child was raised by a mother and a father and no one else. While the mother-and-father combo is common and can work really well, it is not necessarily 'right'. And it does not mean any other combination is sinful.

Plenty of children fare better in a single-parent household once an abusive parent has left the home. Lots of kids do well with the involvement of extended family. Some kids thrive in the care of foster carers or adoptive parents. Many children are involved with their cultural community, effectively raised by non-biological 'aunts' and 'uncles'.

So I do not believe the mother-and-father model is the only option for Christians. And I kinda think God likes it when the welfare of the child, not the logistical make-up of the 'family', comes first.

Get informed. Ask questions. Find support. Make sure you fully understand the process and your options. If you are hesitant, pay attention to that feeling. It is trying to tell you something. Find out what it is.

If you simply cannot reconcile yourself to the ethics of these treatment options, it might be wise to avoid them altogether.

To stop or not to stop?

Living with IVF can be taxing. Injections, intense hormonal changes, sex life interrogations, anxiety and depression, pregnancy test result-waiting and constant uncertainty—while psyching oneself up for the next round, supporting one's spouse and trusting God—amounts to a highly stressful situation.

Several interviewees described IVF as being akin to a

rollercoaster. Given the effort, finances and uncertainty of infertility treatment, it is understandable that people reach a point of saying, 'Enough is enough'.

It can be hard to know when one will reach this point. Some might reach it after a couple of IVF cycles, others might undertake many attempts before they are prepared to stop.

So how do you know when you have reached your limit?

How can you be sure you have tried everything possible to have a child?

Will you regret stopping now?

Can you keep going?

When is enough really enough?

I wish I had an easy answer. I wish I had a formula where *x* time plus *y* IVF attempts = 'You have done enough'. For that matter, I wish we could see into the future and know if IVF attempts and adoption applications were going to be successful. I am sure I am not the only one.

I could patent such formulas. (Hey, isn't that how IVF clinics make money?) Something like this:

*x3 IVF attempts = **BABY!***

*If >35, x10 IVF attempts = **BABY!***

*5 years on adoption waitlist = **BABY!***

For that matter, how about this formula?

BABY = HAPPINESS!

The trouble is, no one knows the magic formula for babies (or happiness). Yes, I know the formula involves an egg and a sperm. Thank you for that.

But clearly, eggs and sperm are not always enough. Plenty of people with eggs and sperm cannot have children. So there must be other factors. Unfortunately, no one knows what they are. They are a mystery. You have to keep on guessing, keep on trying to conceive, keep doing another IVF cycle, keep waiting to hear from the adoption agency. Maybe forever.

I have an opinion on magic formulas.

Insert drumroll here

Formulas are not the answer.

Why? Because formulas cannot tell us how to live. They cannot tell us when we have reached our goals—or not. They are unaware of our energy limits. They cannot read our minds and assess our mental health.

Formulas do not know when we have had enough. They certainly cannot tell us what will make us happy.

This is both freeing and frustrating. Freeing, because no one can lay down the rules for our lives. We choose whether we continue trying or accept our childlessness. But frustrating, because sometimes we want somebody to tell us the answer. We want someone to take responsibility for the ultimate, life-changing decision. We want someone else to do the mental and emotional heavy lifting. Especially when we are exhausted.

What-Ifs can kick in. There will always be some possibility, ever so slight, that things could have been different. But if we are not careful, we end up living in the land of What-If. What-Ifs can keep us stuck, keeping us hooked into unhealthy hope.

I am not against IVF. I am not against adoption. I am definitely not against hope. What I am against is the prolonged suffering of people I care about. (That includes you. In case you were unsure.)

Many childless people feel their identity is deeply connected to being a mother or father. If you have What-Ifs around your identity, you might fear you are missing out on a crucial part of life. FOMO (fear of missing out) is a powerful motivator.

If any of this resonates with you, it might be time to take stock. Give yourself a breather. Take the lid off your feelings. Suppressing feelings does not work long-term. Like holding a kick-board under water, as soon as you let go it whooshes to the surface.

Feelings are not the enemy. They are trying to tell us something is wrong. They are like error messages on our computer, alerting us to a problem in the hardware.

I have never done IVF but I understand fear. I know what it is like to feel trapped, stuck between a costly choice and an even costlier opt-out. We fear losing the dream. We fear making one wrong decision and regretting it for the rest of our lives. There is the mental tug-of-war of hope, keeping us going despite the cost.

Some hopes have use-by dates. Unfulfilled hope can turn into despair. 'What if this never happens? What if we spent money and effort on a child we will never have? What if it was all for nothing?' For some, IVF is no longer about hope but avoiding fear and despair and failure.

So I want to ask you, especially if you are undecided about stopping:

What emotions are driving you right now?

Are you in a good place?

Is your hope alive and healthy?

How strong is the fear factor—a little bit, a lot, overwhelming?

Do you feel free to make your own choice?

Do you feel stuck, trapped, or paralysed?

Only you and your partner know how you are both feeling. You get to choose whether you stay on this train or get off at the next stop. Each station is another chance to choose again.

Some people soldier on, hoping their feelings will go away. But soldiering on does not help anybody, least of all you, if you are suffering. Soldiering on means you are suppressing something. Find out what it is.

Access Australia (n.d.)[40] has a suggestion about stopping. It suggests we weigh up 'giving it a reasonable chance' against the impact on our finances, life goals, relationship and mental health.

Not a bad idea.

When you are sick of putting life on hold—when you are desperate to have a conversation about anything other than children and IVF—when you feel you are losing yourself or the person you love in the process—it might be time to stop.

If you know your answer, the rest is easy. If not, find out what that is about. If you are truly at a loss about what to do, then my last question is for you.

Ask yourself how badly you are suffering right now and if it is still worth it.

Only you can answer that.

Things that matter

A final thought about stopping.

Some interviewees had positive relationships that served as a buffer during IVF. The strength, support and humour of a partner kept them grounded. In Philippa's story, she greatly appreciated the support of her husband during IVF. They were stronger in their relationship after IVF.

Others are not so lucky.

For some, their relationship is the deciding factor for stopping or not doing IVF at all. Their

> Every journey requires faith and trust in God.

relationship is too valuable to put it through the rigmarole of IVF. They prioritise each other over children.

This may not be the best decision for everyone, especially those who are desperate for children. But for some, choosing the relationship over the possibility of children may be right for them. Not an easy decision. Not without its own form of grief. But necessary.

Some choose to trust God over IVF. In Natasha's story, she trusted God in the face of infertility. She and her husband decided against IVF, believing God would give them a child if he really wanted to. Natasha never had a child. Her faith in God is intact, though it had its ups and downs. She still experiences sadness, grief and What-Ifs, but she is confident in God's care and faithfulness.

I am not saying Natasha's decision is right for everybody. But it was right for her.

We need to know what is right for us. Some need to try IVF or they will always wonder what might have happened. Some do not try IVF, and still wonder, but they are OK. Some believe the costs of

IVF outweigh the benefits. Or they do not want to put life on hold. Or they leave it to God.

For the record, trying IVF does not mean one does not trust God. Embarking on an IVF journey requires extraordinary levels of faith. Every journey requires faith and trust in God.

We need to walk our own faith journeys with God, wherever they might lead.

We need to be compassionate towards one another for the choices we make. We need to understand we are not all the same. When it comes to infertility, there is no formula or one-size-fits-all solution.

And I am glad.

PHILIPPA'S STORY

UK

Children were not exactly top priority for Philippa and her husband. They were both high achievers and met at university where they studied architecture together.

Philippa was twenty-seven when she qualified as an architect. She and her husband married when she was thirty-one. For a while, children were not terribly important to them. They were happy to wait.

But then Philippa and her husband discovered ageing is related to reproductivity. Philippa found the number of women's eggs drops off drastically with age. They had not realised that by waiting, they were reducing their odds of having children. And even though Philippa had never been super-maternal, her husband wanted a family. So they started trying.

After one year they visited a fertility clinic where they discovered they were pregnant.

But Philippa lost the baby at ten weeks.

It was a difficult time for both of them. Even though some of Philippa's friends had experienced miscarriages, it seemed no one was talking about them.

During this time, they both discovered they really wanted a family. They had some difficult conversations. Having children, supposedly an easy and natural process, was not happening for them.

In their region of the UK, Philippa and her husband had access to one free round of IVF. At the age of thirty-six, Philippa began her one free round. She began taking Clomid (infertility drug) beforehand, but otherwise received no guidance or support. She was unprepared for the emotional rollercoaster that lay ahead. It was at once 'terrifying and enlightening'.

After one egg had been implanted, Philippa experienced bleeding. It had not worked.

But Philippa wanted another round. Her parents were supportive and they helped to pay for round two. This time, Philippa took the highest level of hormone medication available.

Once again, the implantation did not take.

Tests revealed no answers. There was no family history of infertility, no explanation for why the implantations were not holding. Philippa assumed it was over. But on further reflection, she changed her mind.

Philippa commenced round three. This time she took new hormonal drugs and her cycle was deregulated. The previous attempts had been done through her natural cycles.

But once again, the bleeding started—this time at a work conference.

That was it.

'I thought I was invincible,' explained Philippa. 'But it was difficult enough balancing IVF with the demands of work.' The bleeding at the conference was the clincher. They stopped IVF. 'I had decided, right from the start, I was not going to re-mortgage my house or anything for this,' Philippa recalled.

But even with this decision made, recovery was not easy.

Philippa found counselling helpful. She notified her family and friends of her decision by email. She told them she was going to get on with life.

Philippa's workplace was supportive. There was no pressure to carry any extra workload just because she was childless, which helped.

Now thirty-nine, Philippa still gets asked if she has kids or wants to have them. 'People assume you have kids or want them,' she said. Her response to such questions has shifted over time. 'I used to divert people away from the subject,' she told me. 'Now, I tell them I want kids but can't, or we tried and could not have them. People always seem shocked by that.'

These days, friends approach Philippa for support with their own IVF journeys. She finds it hard to give them advice as everyone is different. But her experience gives her something unique to offer.

Several things helped Philippa recover. She has always been sporty so getting back into things like yoga and trying new sports is helpful. She feels as though she is returning to her normal self. She is attempting things she never thought she would do.

She and her husband realised they have their whole lives ahead of them. They are planning what to do with their lives in future.

A strong and open relationship is important to Philippa. 'Having my husband involved throughout the IVF process was good,' she reflected. 'We have been through the ups and downs together and now we are stronger for it. We are in a good place.'

At the time of interview, Philippa was soon to turn forty which was her self-imposed deadline for having children. Having a deadline helped her come to terms with not having children.

But acceptance is not always easy. Ongoing support is important. 'Emotion can still hit you when you least expect it. So find someone you can talk to,' she encouraged. 'If I had known how helpful counselling was going to be, I would have gone sooner!'

For others facing similar experiences, Philippa suggests they do things they enjoy. 'Be honest about how you feel, but also try to capture the good times,' she says. 'Enjoy the moment. I actually find myself wondering what life would be like if we did have kids. Life without kids can be great!'

5

SINGLEDOM

Maybe I Want Kids Too

A single twenty-something friend told me that even though she wanted to be married, she wanted kids even more. Being childless bothered her so much she looked into adoption. She did this without having a man on the horizon. She wanted to be a mother.

My friend is not the only single person to feel this way. Many childless people are childless-by-circumstance with a backstory of singleness. They are childless because they cannot find the right partner.

People are often surprised to hear singletons want kids. 'Surely you want to find the right partner first?' is the astute response. Sure, the right partner would be neat. But life is not always neat.

Especially in the world of dating.

Surviving Singledom

I wrote a book called *Surviving Singledom* (2016)[41] (shameless plug alert.) In that book I discuss the plight of modern Christian singles and the struggle to find contentment in a romance-saturated world.

What I fail to cover in that book is childlessness. It is a real but seldom spoken-about subject in singledom. I have a theory: when people look at a single person, they see a pre-marriage person. Especially in the church. They assume the single person will eventually get married (because it is the norm) and the single person will be miserable until this happens. They view singleness as a problem to be solved.

This apparently justifies a constant barrage of questions.

'Been on any dates lately?'

'When are you going to settle down?'

'How's your love-life?

Horrifying.

Much attention is paid to the singleton's relationship status. But—and here is the kicker—no one seems interested in their parental status. Society assumes singles are more interested in dating than having kids. Because singles are supposedly obsessed with dating. (Ugh.)

> When people look at a single person, they see a pre-marriage person.

News flash: singles can have a desire for children that supersedes romantic needs.

Some parents exclude their single friends. They avoid discussing parenthood around them. Maybe they think singles cannot cope with talking or hearing about children. (It might make their heads explode or something.) But denying this desire for children does not make it any less real for singles.

It is one more way singles get excluded from the mainstream.

Exclusionary clauses

Singles do not get invited to playdates or couples' nights. Singles feel out of place at marriage courses and parenting seminars. Singles cannot join in with pregnancy war stories or tales of their baby's first whatever.

Some churches I have attended are filled with marriage- and family-focused sermons and events. Singles do not need a preacher to outline ten principles of dating. As though dating is the sum total of the single life.

OK, some singles do need those sermons.

Still, many churches spend more effort and resources on the families and couples in their congregations. I am not saying they should stop. Families and couples need ministry. But so do singles.

Singles endure the double-whammy of being excluded from couples-oriented events (like Valentine's Day) as well as family-oriented ones (like every other holiday on the calendar).

Singles get excluded in the workplace. Many singles work full-time—they have to—and they are often expected to pick up the slack for parents. While parents are allowed to leave early for school pick-ups or special kids' activities. There is often an unwritten expectation that singles can and will do more than their parental counterparts because they do not have a family.

At its worst, this is a kind of reverse discrimination.

Underlying this behaviour is an assumption that singles have more time and energy to burn, simply by virtue of their singleness. It is assumed singles are footloose and fancy-free. And available.

On the other side of the coin, singles are apparently out partying all the time, living it up in selfish revelry. (At least, that is what I read in the media.) Singles are busy endlessly indulging themselves.

This is simply not true for many singles. They are not always obsessed with late-night parties. Many singles actively contribute to society. Many are heavily involved in church or charity work. Some help out with family caring duties and are highly sought after because of their singleness.

In fact, some singles are over-worked and exhausted.

Single-and-childless people cannot join in the baby-related conversations around them. They can feel alone in a crowd. They may be in a female-dominated workplace where child-heavy discussions reign. They may be in a role that requires working with children or parents, work that inherently assumes first-hand knowledge of parenting. They may feel isolated and excluded.

They cannot get flexible working hours because this luxury is only afforded parents—even though single people might have important but non-child-related obligations after work. Some parents get first pickings at holiday leave, especially over Christmas or during school holidays, while singles have to be content with what is left, because they don't have a 'family'.

Those in a relationship can debrief each other after a rough day of baby-story saturation. The single person does not have such a dedicated confidante. They may come home to parents or a roommate with whom they may not wish to discuss such delicate matters. They may come home to a pet (like I did in singledom) or no one.

Some friends make an effort to reach out to single people and include them. This can work well. Some parents ask their single friends to babysit. Oh joy. Not only do they not have their own kids, they get to spend an entire evening with someone else's kids, working, without the pleasure of adult company.

Don't get me wrong. Some singles love babysitting. They do it all the time. But it can get old, and it can push the friendship. Some of my single friends get tired of always being called upon for babysitting duties. Sometimes they would like to get invited to dinner too.

They can feel like their free time is not their own. They can feel obligated to use it because they are single. They might feel pressured by those who are always 'busy' to lend a hand.

Some singles don't get a chance to rest.

Childless-by-circumstance

Jody Day, TED talker and founder of *Gateway Women*[42], has published a list of fifty reasons why people do not have children (Day 2013)[43]. Several reasons relate to being single, divorced or widowed.

This list highlights the plight of many childless people and the difficulty of finding a suitable partner. Many childless-by-circumstance people today, who once thought they had found the right person, have been proven otherwise.

According to Jody's TED talk (Day 2017)[44], in which she

quotes researcher Renske Keizer (2014)[45], a mere ten percent of childless people are childfree, that is, they choose to live happily without children, while another ten percent are childless due to medical conditions.

The remaining eighty percent? Childless-by-circumstance.

Jody was unable to conceive in her marriage due to unexplained fertility. When she divorced in her late thirties, she was unable to find a suitable partner with whom to pursue her dream of motherhood. Single and childless in her forties, she endured the double-whammy of childlessness-by-singledom.

Jody became a psychotherapist, blogger and author. She founded *Gateway Women,* a global friendship and support group for involuntarily childless women, which runs courses, weekend workshops and social gatherings around the world. Jody supports other childless women to find new lives for themselves after the dream of motherhood has died.

Circumstances do not always align the way we want. Finding a partner is more complex than 'getting out there'. But singles are often blamed for their singleness, for being too picky or too introverted or too outspoken or too... something.

When I was single, I got accused of having standards that were 'too high'. (Apparently, my expectations for things like honesty were unrealistic.)

Childlessness due to infertility or medical conditions can make dating problematic as well. Just picture it. You have a first date tonight. You want to make a good impression. But as you prepare, you find yourself wondering how honest you should be.

Should you tell them how old you are? Should you describe the reasons for your past failed relationships? Should you disclose your medical history and fertility worries? If you have previously tried to conceive and been unable, how do you explain this? When should you tell them—the first date, the fourth date, never?

There is no good time to drop the bomb on a new girlfriend or boyfriend.

Problematic.

Then there is the question of hopes and dreams. In every relationship, there comes a time when you share your goals in life. Inevitably, this means discussing children. And not every couple wants the same thing when it comes to children. For some, these differing desires can be negotiated. For others, the differences are insurmountable.

Unresolvable differences in child-rearing desires can cause the dating person to return to singledom—and childlessness.

The 'otherhood'

Single and childless speaker Melanie Notkin has proposed an alternative approach in her TED talk, *Welcome to the Otherhood* (2017)[46].

Melanie claims childless people are treated as a sub-species of normal humankind. She suggests childless women are considered to be 'less of a woman' than those who have children. Similarly, men are being perceived as being 'less manly' because they are not fathers.

Melanie coined a new species of women: PANKs (Professional Aunts, No Kids). This is a new take on the more commonly known

DINKs (Double Income, No Kids). I guess we could also have PUNKs (Professional Uncles, No Kids).

She suggested those who do not have children because of singleness may have alternate ways of 'parenting', such as being an active part of the lives of their nieces, nephews and other children.

> Those who do not have children because of singleness may have alternate ways of 'parenting'.

This sentiment is echoed on social media. Many childless people are pouring their energy and affection into children other than their own. They are 'parents'. They do not pretend this is the same as having their own biological children; nonetheless, it seems to fit for them. They are convinced they have something to offer.

If this resonates with you and you want to find a way of being a childless 'parent', I encourage you to research and brainstorm ways in which you can give back to children in society.

It might make a difference to their lives. And it might meet some of your parental needs too.

Becoming a champion

People have asked me to write about single parenting, but I have not addressed this issue in this book. (It is a topic for another book. And I bags not writing that one. Get someone with single parenting experience to write it.)

There are ways of involving children in your single life without being a parent, such as Melanie's idea of PANKs. Of course, being a PANK or PUNK applies to childless couples as well as singles. But it is good to know some childless-by-singledom people like Melanie are finding creative ways of embracing childlessness.

I want to encourage you to do the same. You may not come up with a new term, but you could find ways of filling that child-shaped void in your life by spending time with other people's children.

In Chapter 12 we explore ways other childless people are meeting this need for children in their lives. But you might not even follow this list. You might come up with something completely original.

I also encourage you to raise the profile of single people, especially those who are childless-by-singledom, in your social circles. If you speak about it with others, you might find others living in similar circumstances.

Many childless people believe this social support is crucial in surviving childlessness. They seek out friends who understand childlessness. They find their tribe. You might find solace in solidarity with other singles. And you might inspire them too. Perhaps they will feel more comfortable sharing about their childlessness because of you.

How amazing it would be to share your story and learn another childless person was inspired by you to share their story in turn.

Be that childless champion.

SECTION THREE
STORM DAMAGE

SEX

Procreation is Hot

Marriage vows are funny things.

When I got married, I found myself noticing the marriage vows. Being together 'for procreation'. Hot stuff. What does that even mean, I wondered. I have noticed the weirdness of marriage vows ever since. It still makes me wonder.

Marrying purely for the sake of procreation has implications. If the only reason to have sex is to produce children, this implies sex cannot be about gratification or serving one another. It certainly cannot be super-duper-hot. And if that is so, it is unequivocally the most depressing thing I have ever heard.

If you have read *Surviving Singledom* (2016)[47], you know

I married relatively late (relative to the rest of my church who married by the age of twenty-one). That meant I could hardly wait to have sex. Yes, I just said that. Sex was really important to me because of its prior absence in my life. And because I was a normal, healthy female. (Can I get an amen?)

So when I heard the sacred-sounding 'procreation' stuff, it sounded like the church did not want me thinking about the pleasure of sex, just the functionality of it. Maybe I was wrong. Hopefully.

Of course, I knew sex can lead to children. It often does. But I had waited twenty-nine years and did not want to hear sex was only about procreation. I told myself if Christian sex was not to be enjoyed, I was outta there!

> *I told myself if Christian sex was not to be enjoyed, I was outta there!*

I was not threatening to leave my marriage. I simply felt averse to the whole 'Marriage is just for childbearing' thing. It did not sit right. Surely there must be more to life than following the expected trajectory of the mainstream married couple of having two-point-three kids, and then waiting for them to leave home?

I have met Christians, men and women alike, who fervently believe women are put on this earth to create babies. I assume most of these beliefs originate with the well-known 'Be fruitful and multiply' reference in Genesis 1:28. This is good teaching. In the context of the beginning of the world, I can certainly understand why God gave this command to Adam and Eve. Without the patter of tiny feet, the human race would have been over quick smart.

Our contemporary society no longer has this problem. We are no longer trying to kick-start the human race. We have succeeded in multiplying. We have been very fruitful. (Although one does not have to multiply in order to be 'fruitful'.)

Here is my question. In the context of today's well-populated planet, does the command to multiply still apply?

Good question, isn't it? I thought so too.

Designed for pleasure

After God gave the multiplication command in Genesis, there were some interesting marital commands that followed. Check out this beauty in Deuteronomy 24:5: 'If a man has recently married, he must not be sent to war or have any other duty laid on him. For one year he is to be free to stay at home and bring happiness to the wife he has married.'

I really like that one.

Then we have 'one flesh' references. This is not just about physical intimacy but complete union, including mental, emotional and spiritual intimacy. It is about serving one another. Sex tends to work best when both parties put the other's gratification first, rather than getting what they want. When each is intent on serving the other, both parties tend to end up happy. Very happy.

The whole of Song of Songs is about sex and pleasure. It is filled with explicit descriptions of passion and sexual arousal. If in any doubt, cast your eyes over this exclamation from the Beloved:

> Let him kiss me with the kisses of his mouth—
> for your love is more delightful than wine.

> Pleasing is the fragrance of your perfumes; your
> name is like perfume poured out.
>
> No wonder the young women love you!
>
> Take me away with you—let us hurry!
>
> Let the king bring me into his chambers
> (Song of Songs 1:1-4).

Bet you did not know that little gem was hidden away in the bible.

Clearly, the couple in Song of Songs were caught up in the pleasure of their love, swept away by passion.

But let us imagine an agenda of procreation is thrust upon this intimate scene. How would that change things? The Beloved might have said something like this:

> Let him kiss me with the kisses of his mouth—
> for kissing often leads to procreation.
>
> Pleasing is the process of pregnancy; my labour
> will be like agony poured out.
>
> No wonder people love having children!
>
> Take me away with you—let us produce offspring!
>
> Let the king and I be fruitful and multiply
> (Steph's Satirical Version).

I am sure God meant for sex to be more than procreational.

I believe this because of Song of Songs. God does not appear to need to intervene and hastily pour cold water on the demonstrative lovers. I also believe in sex for pleasure because of God's design. He built our bodies in a certain way to maximise pleasure. He gave us many anatomical opportunities to enjoy sex. Not enjoying something as enjoyable as sex is like following road signs to Sydney and not taking the exit to Sydney. All the signs are pointing us there.

Humour me for a second.

Imagine God saying, 'Hmm, let's have a think about this sex stuff. Let's make kissing and touching and nakedness feel good. Let's give them some pretty powerful desires so they follow through with sex. Let's make the climax so freaking unbelievable they will want to keep doing it over and over. But no wait, it's all about procreation, isn't it? Oh darn, I made it too pleasurable.'

Said God never.

(I do not know if God uses the word darn. If he ever says it to you, let me know.)

God gave us many things in life to enjoy. Sex is one of them. Sure, he gave us some parameters for those enjoyable things so we do not get hurt in the process. But as long as we are playing within those boundaries, we are free to um, play.

And make things as pleasurable as we want.

Saved by what now?

Women are apparently saved by childbearing.

This belief is drawn from 1 Timothy 2:15: 'But women will be saved through childbearing—if they continue in faith, love and holiness with propriety.'

Yes, some have taken this verse out of context of the bible—

which teaches that salvation is by grace, not works—and taught that Christian women are saved by having children. Some ministers make allowances for childless women and apply a broader interpretation, saying women are saved by embracing their God-given role as a domestic in the home.

As a what now?

According to this teaching, I am doomed because I am a professional worker, not a homemaker. Any woman who works is neglecting their God-given home-based role in life. They are eternally doomed. (I don't know about women who work from home. Interesting loophole.)

We Christians are good at guilt trips, aren't we? Teach women to stay at home and accuse working women of rebellious or neglectful behaviour. That is a pretty good recipe for all types of abuses of power to be exercised against women.

Yes, I am a feminist.

Some Christians truly believe independent and professional women are a bad influence on the church. Some are also convinced a lack of children is a sin. I cannot believe this is so. I cannot agree that those unable to have children are somehow lesser Christians than the more fertile mainstream.

Whenever Christians posit arguments that split groups of God's people into those who are more Christian and those who are less acceptable or worthy or saved, I am immediately skeptical.

No, not because I am a cynic. Not just because of that.

Because everything Jesus said is about equality. Jesus' teaching is about raising up the marginalised and downtrodden and socially outcast. He is all about empowering beggars, women, children and even the dead. I do not believe this same Jesus rejects me because of my capacity—or, more accurately, my incapacity—to bear children.

I found one alternate view on this controversial verse in 1 Timothy, proposed by John Piper who quotes Henry Alford saying,

> The curse on the woman for her 'transgression' was, 'in pains you will bear children' (Genesis 3:16). Her 'childbearing' is that in which the curse finds its operation. What then is here promised her? Not only exemption from that curse in its worst and heaviest effects: not merely that she shall safely bear children: but the Apostle uses the word 'will be saved' purposely for its higher meaning [eternal salvation], and the construction of the sentence is precisely as [in] 1 Corinthians 3:15—'he will be saved, yet though as through fire.'
>
> Just as that man will be saved through, as passing through, fire which is his trial, his hindrance in his way, in spite of which he escapes—so she shall be saved, through, as passing through, her childbearing (2014)[48]...

In other words, women are not saved via childbearing, but in spite of it, just as any one of us is saved in spite of sin or illness or grief or any other form of suffering.

And here's more food for thought. The Message version of 1

Timothy 2:15 says: 'On the other hand, [Eve's] childbearing brought about salvation, reversing Eve. But this salvation only comes to those who continue in faith, love, and holiness, gathering it all into maturity.' That version highlights the role Eve played in bringing about the birth of our Saviour, Jesus Christ.

Jesus continues to be the first and last word in the story of our salvation. Not childbearing. And not childlessness.

When things get trying

Trying for a baby can be very—well, trying. Over a prolonged and unsuccessful period of trying, hope can wane. It can affect one's sex life when the focus shifts from enjoyment to the pressure of making a baby.

Some choose to stop trying in order to preserve a happy relationship and healthy sex life. Yep, some actually choose childlessness over the stress of trying to conceive.

I did an internet search on the impact of trying to conceive on sex. Yep, I went there. I entered 'trying for a baby sex life' and got a gazillion results.

One was an online forum for childlessness where lots of people had problems in their sex life during and after trying. They felt like failures. They felt like less of a man or woman because they could not have a baby.

So if you feel like things are not the same since you started trying and you are wondering what is wrong with you, you are not the only one. And you are not going insane.

One article, *Make trying to get pregnant more fun* (Eagleson 2013)[49], shows how the pressure of performance can overtake the pleasure of sex for both men and women. Men can feel like their role in life is a sperm donor. And women can feel they have to 'achieve' conception, like it is proof of femininity or an estrogen-driven race to the finish line.

Another article, *How to keep sex smoking when trying to conceive* (Pepper 2008)[50], acknowledges that trying to conceive can take the joy and spontaneity out of sex. When a host of medical professionals are watching your every sexual move, you can feel pressured into having daily sex and producing a result (that's a baby, folks).

Nothing kills your fire quicker than having your sex life coldly dissected by strangers.

Access Australia acknowledges the pain of publicising one's sex life in their fact sheet *Infertility and Sexuality* (n.d.)[51]. They acknowledge the un-sexiness of temperature charts and sex records. It turns love-making into a process of medical compliance.

Many feel degraded by the process. Men can feel pressured to perform on cue. Stage fright can exacerbate the stress of an already tense situation. Failure to ejaculate may heighten men's sense of diminishing manhood.

For women, the arrival of the monthly period can feel like the female equivalent of failure. Women may feel pressured to instigate sex during their ovulation time. They may feel ovulatory sex is the only worthwhile kind.

It is absurd to expect a couple to want sex according to an ovulation cycle. It is even more absurd to expect such a high-pressure situation will not have an impact.

If you have been trying for a while, you might have lost the joy and intimacy of sex. Maybe you have come to associate sex with failure or disappointment. Maybe you are depressed about the whole thing.

Our moods can affect our sex drives.

This does not mean your amazing sex life is over. It might require adjustment. It might mean you change where, when or how you have sex.

You could allow build-up periods between trying, or conversely, indulge in non-baby-making sex just for the fun of it. Throw the chart out the window for a change. Be a rebel.

You could have sex somewhere different, like the couch, the rug, the kitchen benchtop. You could try showering or bathing together. Introduce food into the mix. Try a toy. They are not illegal.

Plenty of online resources have ideas for spicing up your sex life. (No, I am not endorsing porn.) Consider trying some. Hey, what's the worst that could happen?

You can also remind each other of what you have. In Anita's story, she highly valued the support of her husband during the trying, testing and IVF process. His strength was vital for her.

Holding on to gratitude can help restore your affection for one another. It might highlight how you have supported one another and how you have grown stronger and more resilient because of it.

It might remind you why you fell in love with each other in the first place.

Self-esteem and sex

Even with a spicy sex life, we can get down when it doesn't produce a baby. And the way we feel about ourselves directly affects our capacity to engage in, enjoy and climax during sex.

If you cannot have children, your grief can affect everything. If you feel less of a man or woman, it is only natural this will affect how you see yourself as a sexual being.

It can be hard not to blame someone if you discover, say, one of you is infertile. It can be just as hard not to blame yourself if you are infertile. It can be even harder to know who to blame in the case of 'unexplained infertility'.

It may not even matter whose fault it is. The situation just sucks. Grief, combined with frustration, despair and lack of closure, can sap your interest in sex. And everything else you once enjoyed.

In the mind of the infertility doctor, sex = quest for baby. We can be influenced by this. When sex becomes all about a destination, the pleasure of the journey can get lost. Rediscovering your sex life might involve reconnecting with pure pleasure and the joy of being together.

I cannot tell you exactly what will work for you, because we are all unique in what tickles our fancy. (Hey, tickling might help things

> The way we feel about ourselves directly affects our capacity to engage in, enjoy and climax during sex.

along.) But a good rule of thumb might be to simply relax with each other. Enjoy each other's company as an end in itself, rather than a means to an end. Make enjoyment the goal.

Revisit things that originally brought you together. Laugh with each other, especially if something funny happens in the bedroom. (This can happen. Apparently.) Help each other unwind without agendas.

Improvement in mood usually leads to increased interest in sex. Perhaps it is a good idea just to focus on things that make you happy. Sometimes thinking less about sex takes the pressure off.

The road to recovery might be long, but relaxing and enjoying each other can get you back on track.

God cares about your sex life

At the risk of sounding clichéd, pray for your partner. Just like you would if they were sick. Pray for your marriage and sex life. Pray for God's healing and restoration.

God designed us for enjoyment. I think he smiles when he sees us enjoying something he created just for us. He took pleasure in creating us and continues to take pleasure in our pleasure. In a non-creepy way.

> Prayer is not a job interview. It is a living, breathing relationship with our Heavenly Father.

At the same time, God is deeply concerned with things that deeply concern us. He is not floating on a cloud in a galaxy far away, unable to relate to us. He sees everything that happens to us. And he cares.

God has emotions. He feels compassion towards us. He does not enjoy our suffering. God wants to heal us thoroughly, inside and out. This includes our relationships.

I am a big fan of open and transparent talk with God. I can be chatty, quiet, boisterous, solemn, comedic and reverent. As long as it is true. I tell God everything that is going on, sex or otherwise, everything I think and feel. Even if that means admitting things that do not cast me in the best light.

Prayer is not a job interview. It is a living, breathing relationship with our Heavenly Father. He knows everything about us and his love for us is robust and inexhaustible. No matter how great our thirst, his love never runs dry.

So talk to him.

Maybe you are not a big praying person or have never prayed before. That is OK. Sometimes it is better that way. God knows about it. There is no need to explain yourself. Just be you. Tell God your worries. Tell him your hopes. Tell him about your sex life. Tell him the struggles, the devastation and despair. Hold nothing back. Give God the good, the bad and the ugly. He can handle it.

Praying for and with your partner can bring you closer together. It can rekindle a sense of shared spiritual intimacy. And it can bring you closer to God.

ANITA'S STORY

UK

Anita's dream of having kids before thirty got complicated fast. First her mother died of cancer. Then she and her husband renovated their home. She was unemployed for a year. And they moved house.

By the time Anita came off the pill, she was thirty-one.

They tried for nearly a year, then got tests done. Everything came back normal. But after starting her new job, Anita experienced pain. Medical investigations revealed she had endometriosis.

This set off a chain of surgeries. Initially she had two surgeries to remove the scar tissue and then, after waiting six months for IVF, she found the endometriosis had returned. So she had a third round of surgery.

The procedures were painful, especially the second one. In fact, it was agonising. Anita felt anxious afterwards and she worried about having future operations.

They commenced IVF immediately after the third surgery, despite her reluctance to do it so soon. The hormonal injections were stressful. They hoped it was going to pay off, but the news was bad. When it came time to retrieve the eggs, there were no eggs to retrieve. The follicle was empty.

It hit Anita hard. 'It felt like someone had died,' she told me.

And it was not only Anita who was feeling it. Her husband was affected too. They were both depressed for a few months, trying to come to terms with it. Anita felt like she didn't want to be here anymore.

In the meantime, they considered donors. They were under pressure from family to pursue egg donorship. In the end they tried other things—homeopathy, acupuncture, holistic fertility specialists. The alternative therapies were supposed to help Anita get healthy and prepare for future treatment. But it was only after three months of counselling that she started feeling better again.

They decided on a second round of IVF. But before they could, Anita needed a fourth surgery to remove more endometriosis. While the recovery was painful, it seemed to be successful.

In round two of IVF they found and implanted two eggs. When the much-awaited pregnancy test came back positive, Anita was elated.

Until the nausea and spotting started.

She thought the pregnancy had not held, but blood tests showed she was still pregnant. When she got worse, she went to hospital where they found Anita had an ectopic pregnancy at risk of rupturing.

(She explained an ectopic pregnancy is where the fertilised egg grows outside the uterus. She also explained endometriosis is a risk factor in ectopic pregnancies.)

They operated that same day.

'I will never forget that day,' Anita said, pausing to remember. 'It really affected me. I was off work afterwards for five or six weeks. I was in a bad place, physically and mentally.'

Homeopathy and counselling helped her to cope during this

time. She and her husband decided to take a break from IVF and try to conceive naturally for a while. But Anita was still in a bad place. She felt under a lot of pressure.

She talked herself into a third round of IVF. She was averse to it and felt quite anxious, unable to relax. She found meditation helpful but it was far from a cure.

In hindsight, Anita realised the reason she had been so anxious was because the ectopic pregnancy had triggered Post-Traumatic Stress Disorder (PTSD), one symptom of which is persistent anxiety.

The third round of IVF went well until she fainted the night before the pregnancy test result. After she came to, she collapsed again. She was taken to hospital, where everything looked normal. But no pregnancy test was done at the time. She did one herself later that morning. The result was negative.

Anita hit rock bottom. 'That experience scared me,' she shared. 'I cannot think about IVF anymore.'

She thought about doing another round or two of IVF, but she still worries about the endometriosis coming back. She is certain about one thing: she wants her own biological children. She does not want any alternatives.

Meanwhile, Anita finds questions about children awkward. She says she plans to have kids 'God willing' or 'when it happens'. But she believes it is no one else's business. 'Having kids or not having kids will not affect anyone's life but my own,' she told me emphatically.

Anita avoids baby showers when needed and allows herself to feel whatever she is feeling. She reached out to a support group and found a friend there who understands what she is going through.

She encourages others to be informed about IVF before leaping in. 'IVF is not for everyone,' she cautions. 'If you do it, then strap in. But if there is any doubt, do not do it. Know what to expect. Be true to yourself.'

While IVF support is important, Anita also believes in having a life outside the IVF world. She says a good relationship is vital, packed with plenty of resilience. Her husband supported her through IVF and surgeries for endometriosis. 'He was amazing,' she recalled.

Anita enjoys getting out, keeping busy and connecting with people with whom she can be honest.

Being in IVF limbo presents unique difficulties. It is hard to make long-term plans. Holidays are especially tricky. She is trying not to let the possibility of further IVF run her life, but it is challenging. IVF is always lurking in the back of her mind.

'I just try to go with the flow and enjoy things while I can,' she said. 'I have no concrete plans at this stage. I might travel or work abroad. It is hard, but I am trying not to put my life on hold.'

She advises others to avoid unhelpful things as needed. 'Your feelings are valid, so allow yourself to feel what you are feeling,' she urged. 'And know yourself. Know what to expect from your own reactions.'

TRAUMA

Why Can't I Stop Thinking About It?

A friend once told me about her bad miscarriage experience. She lost so much blood during the miscarriage that she nearly died. She needed several blood transfusions to stay alive.

She was so traumatised that she vowed never to get pregnant again.

She told her doctor who replied, 'What are you so upset about? You survived, didn't you?'

I think that doctor needs sensitivity training.

For many childless people, trauma is part of their story. So we are going to talk about it.

May I encourage you, before we dive in, to look after yourself as you read. We will discuss traumatic stories and they may be triggering. While I have done my best to minimise the traumatic content, please feel free to take breaks, skip segments or turn to another chapter as needed. Get some air. Cuddle your furbaby. Do whatever you need to look after yourself.

I highly recommend chocolate. For self-care purposes.

What is trauma?

Trauma is severe stress from the past that continues to affect you in the present. It happens when you are exposed to some kind of danger or threat, be it physical, emotional, mental or spiritual.

Trauma is a normal, understandable reaction to an abnormal event. It is not everyday stress but unusual, out-of-the-ordinary stress. It does not mean you are 'crazy'. Its very nature is overwhelming.

Trauma invades thoughts and feelings at random, without warning, with omnipotent force. A person living with trauma cannot simply 'forget it' or 'move on', because the trauma is in charge of the body and mind. Trauma is a fundamental loss of control.

Consider the example of a man who experiences a head-on car collision. This man may have trauma symptoms afterwards.

He may have dreams of the car crash or near-misses, awakening drenched in sweat. He may have nightmares involving themes of violence, being chased, watching graphic scenes unfold or featuring feelings of fear or powerlessness. He may have flashbacks during the day or suddenly break out in a cold sweat at the sound of screeching brakes. He may find it hard to concentrate; he may feel irritable; he may jump through the roof when someone taps him on the shoulder; he may have trouble eating or sleeping.

In particular, he may avoid the place where the accident happened or avoid driving altogether. He may avoid talking about the accident and may even avoid thinking about it.

These are signs of trauma. The car accident was an out-of-the-ordinary event and it was extremely stressful for our guy. His brain was overwhelmed and could not cope with it. His mind continually rehearses what happened in an effort to assimilate the out-of-the-ordinary experience. While his brain churns, his body stays in a constant state of alarm in case it happens again.

It is normal, expected even, to feel traumatised after a severely stressful event like a car accident. I would not be surprised to hear our guy had trouble recovering from it. I would be more surprised if he was not affected at all.

After such an accident, most of us would feel bad for a few days and then begin to settle down. After a few weeks we would probably feel like our normal selves again. This is a normal recovery.

But some do not return to normal. They feel worse instead of better as the weeks go on. The trauma increasingly takes over their lives. They lose a sense of their identity. They might forget who they are.

That is trauma.

Trauma can happen straight away or develop years later. For those traumatised by childhood experiences, problems might emerge later in life.

Childhood trauma

Childhood abuse is, unfortunately, common.

Accurate statistics are hard to find because children do not always report abuse. They do not always understand they have been abused. And even when they do, they are not always believed.

The Australian Bureau of Statistics suggests at least thirteen percent of children experience physical and/or sexual abuse before the age of fifteen (2017)[52].

These statistics do not include other forms of abuse such as emotional mistreatment, neglect and exposure to domestic violence. The statistics on these types of abuse, especially emotional, would be much higher, but they are much harder to collect.

Some kids experience repeated, ongoing abuse. This can cause complex or developmental trauma, where the trauma affects brain and body development during a child's formative years. These kids learn to live in fear. It becomes a permanent state.

Some kids get moved to a safe environment where they can heal from the trauma. But other kids never get the chance. And some never recover. Some adapt by taking on the adult role in the family because the parents are not able. Other kids never grow up and run from themselves and others.

Some adults with childhood trauma worry it will affect their parenting. They worry about 'passing on' the trauma to their children. They believe they are just like their parents and will therefore be a bad parent to their children. Being raised by parents who did nothing but complain about us can influence our desire to become parents.

Perhaps there is something to this.

Some parents pass on elements of their childhood trauma to

their own children by mimicking the abuse they experienced as a child. These children experience 'intergenerational trauma' in an ongoing cycle of abuse.

Some adults want to break this cycle. They may break it with good conscious parenting choices or counselling. They may become excellent parents. Even though they have experienced bad parenting, there may be good moments of parenting they can pass on. They may have good parenting qualities of their own.

Others break the cycle by not having children at all.

The impact

The impact of trauma can be lifelong. And it may lead to childlessness-by-forced-choice (CBFC). Some may feel backed into a corner by their childhood trauma. They may feel the trauma has forcibly removed any parenting capacity they otherwise may have had.

Some have witnessed horrible manifestations of anger and may be frightened by their own angry feelings. They may worry about passing on undesirable genes in terms of physical illness, mental health issues or personality traits.

Some are terrified of failure, even if they themselves possess admirable parenting qualities. They may worry about turning out just like their father or mother. They may feel the risk is simply too great.

A childhood abuse study (Felitti, Anda, Nordenberg, Edwards, Koss & Marks 1998)[53] explored the link between adverse childhood experiences (ACEs) and poorer health outcomes in adulthood. Those with more ACEs were more likely to have poorer long-term outcomes, including chronic illness, mental health issues, risky behaviours, lower quality of life and earlier death.

In the ACE study, those who experienced four or more ACEs were at increased risk of heart disease, lung disease, autoimmune disease (including diabetes, multiple sclerosis, lupus and rheumatoid arthritis), cancer, liver disease and bone fractures. They were also four to twelve times more likely to develop depression and drug and alcohol issues and to attempt suicide (twelve times more likely for that one).

Dr Nadine Bourke Harris has an excellent summary of the ACE study and its findings in her TED talk (2014)[54].

For those affected by ACEs and their long-term consequences, the prospect of having children may be truly terrifying. They may find themselves on the path of CBFC.

Domestic violence (DV)

DV is more than a bad relationship experience.

DV occurs when one person in a relationship exerts power and control over the other, causing that person to live in fear. It typically happens in intimate relationships but can happen between family members as well.

People often use 'DV' to mean physical abuse like hitting, but it is not limited to this. It encompasses many tactics of abuse, including:

- Verbal abuse—yelling, swearing, name-calling, put-downs;
- Emotional abuse—rejecting you or making you feel worthless or unlovable. Emotional abuse occurs whenever these other abuse tactics are used, because any form of

abuse always has an emotional impact;
- Psychological abuse—threats, intimidation, manipulation that makes you question yourself or feel unsafe, threats to harm you or family members or pets;
- Financial abuse—controlling the money, giving you an allowance insufficient for living, withholding money for essentials;
- Spiritual abuse—preventing you from accessing a place of worship or friends from your religion, ridiculing spiritual beliefs and practises;
- Sexual abuse—forced or coerced sexual activities, rape, sexual put-downs, being forced to enter the sex trade;
- Legal abuse—using courts and legal proceedings to have abusive contact with you, making false accusations about you to police, delaying court proceedings as a means of control, using subpoenas to access privileged or confidential information about you;
- Abuse of male privilege—over ninety percent of DV abusers are male (Kimmel 2002)[55] and they may use their male gender to justify abusive actions or warp Christian teachings about 'male headship' to exert control;
- Denial, blame, manipulation—being blamed for all problems in the relationship, denial of things they have said or done, being made to feel you imagined it or are going crazy;
- Control—phone monitoring, calling incessantly to see where you are and who you are with, stalking, signs of jealousy towards other supportive people in your life, telling you

what to wear, sleep deprivation from interrogations, being prevented from working, being prevented from having friends, being isolated from all support, being locked in a room, being denied access to food or a toilet, being force-fed drugs, being forced into slave labour; and
- Physical abuse–hitting, spitting, hair-pulling, shoving, strangling, restraining, damaging property, standing over you.

DV is a conscious, deliberate, systematic effort to control another person.

And it is common. In Australia, one in three women and one in sixteen men experience DV. One woman every week and one male every month are killed by DV (Australian Institute of Health and Welfare 2020)[56]. It is often cyclical, marked by periods of peace interspersed with times of tension leading to volcanic-like eruptions.

Often people do not realise they are living with DV. Perhaps they live with no physical abuse but constant verbal, emotional and psychological abuse instead. This counts as DV when it causes fear and exerts power and control over another person.

Telltale signs of emotional abuse include the person being abused saying, 'I am walking on eggshells', 'I never know what mood they are going to be in', or 'When they pull up in the driveway, I hold my breath'. Walking on eggshells is a pretty good sign they are living in an emotionally abusive and unsafe situation.

DV is traumatising. It is the systematic destruction of another human being. Many people who live with DV feel altered by it, even to the point of losing their sense of self.

For the person being abused, DV impacts their parenting capacity (how can you possibly parent while feeling physically or emotionally unsafe?) and it poses a risk of harm to children. Imagine, as a kid, living with a parent who feels unsafe. Imagine the atmosphere in the home. Imagine hearing DV tactics from the next room. Imagine witnessing DV as a child or witnessing the after-effects, like bruises or crying spells.

Childlessness may be forced or insisted upon by the person using DV tactics. They may insist that a pregnancy be terminated. The woman may also lose a pregnancy through physical abuse, like being kicked in the stomach while pregnant. Being pregnant increases the risk of DV.

A person using DV tactics is not a safe parent. Those who use DV tactics tend to use children as part of their tactics, like turning kids against the other parent or using children to deliver hate messages to the other parent.

Also, adults who abuse their partners (and males in particular) are statistically more likely to abuse children (Huecker & Smock 2020)[57]. In NSW, the Department of Communities and Justice (our child protection service) classifies DV in the home as a risk of harm to children (2019)[58].

Forced choice in DV can work the other way. Pregnancy may be forced as part of sexual abuse or marital rape.

If you or someone you know is in a DV situation, you can call the DV Line in Australia on 1800 65 64 63. (Also on the resource page at the end of this book.)

One more thing. There is a myth about abusive people being

good parents. It goes something like this: 'They treat me badly, but they would never harm our child'.

Umm, no.

What makes a great parent is an adult who role-models respect, love and safety towards all people, including their partner.

Pregnancy dramas

A bad pregnancy can be traumatising in many ways.

Take my friend at the start of this chapter who nearly died. She was adamant she would never get pregnant again.

Pregnancy can make some women unwell or trigger illness or flare-ups they otherwise would not have had.

IVF, often sold as the gold standard of infertility treatment, can go wrong too and can cause lasting issues. Not to mention the physical, emotional and financial strain of IVF.

These things can leave trauma scars, affecting both men and women for years. It can be equally hard to stop trying with pregnancy. It can feel like giving up on a lifelong, dearly held dream. It might feel like quitting or failing. But it is reasonable to have a limit. Especially if the experience has been traumatic.

Many childless women suffer from endometriosis and, while surgery can help, it can be painful and complicated. And the endometriosis can come back (like it did for Anita). Many unfortunate women like Anita have undergone the surgery, only to discover the endometriosis later grows back and requires more surgery. Anita developed Post-Traumatic Stress Disorder (PTSD) after an ectopic pregnancy, and she became anxious about future endometriosis surgeries.

It is worth recognising the potentially traumatic effect of painful fertility-related surgeries and medical conditions. They can make us fearful of similarly bad medical events in the future. This kind of traumatic impact can leave a lingering effect, like an aftershock following an earthquake.

> It is ok to make up your own mind about how far you will go for a child.

It may be helpful, at this point, to remember we have a choice about this. We get to decide how far to push our bodies. We get to set boundaries around the stressors of trying to conceive. We get to say no. Regardless of what our families, churches or doctors think. (Doctors do not have the monopoly on what is right for our bodies.)

It is OK to make up your own mind about how far you will go for a child. It is OK to acknowledge the physical and mental trauma. It is OK to put an end to that. No one else knows what you have been through. No one else can stand inside your skin or crawl into your mind. So you are the resident expert on yourself.

And you get to decide when you have had enough.

A note on healing

Can God heal us of physical and psychological maladies?

Yes and no.

Yes, God can heal us. No, he does not always heal us when we ask.

This is a tough area, one that warrants an entire book dedicated to the subject. (In fact, I may write a Surviving Chronic Illness book next. You've been warned.)

It can be frustrating when God does not heal us of things like endometriosis and infertility, and this can fester into bitterness.

Illnesses that do not get better can be wearying and confusing. Prolonged suffering can erode one's faith, not to mention one's sense of humour.

The absence of healing inevitably raises questions. If God can heal but he doesn't, what does that mean? Does it mean God is incapable? Does it mean he doesn't care? Does it mean God is not faithful?

Some Christians turn the blame gun on themselves. If God does not heal me, is it my fault? Should I pray harder? Do I not have enough faith? Is there some kind of secret sin I need to eradicate before I will get healed?

The crux of this problem is this: Why does a benevolent, all-knowing, all-powerful God not heal me?

I do not understand this mystery. I only know that while God is fully capable of healing me and is compassionate towards my suffering, he does not always give me everything I ask.

I wish he would. I wish God would heal me of lupus. It would be easier than listening to my body and rolling with the medical punches. It would be simpler than exercising self-care and good boundaries all the time. It would be easier for me to be healed than to trust God afresh every single day.

We can—and should—continue to ask God for healing. It is good to give and receive prayer. I have seen God heal and I have experienced his healing power firsthand. Sometimes God heals.

However, the absence of healing is not proof of God's malevolence or forgetfulness. God's non-healing does not mean he is no longer capable or faithful or caring. I don't know what non-healing means, but it does not mean that.

Learning to trust God, regardless of healing, is the pertinent point. Living with childlike trust in the Father is at the heart of suffering.

Maybe that is why God does not heal me. Maybe my illness is too useful to him. Maybe it drives me deeper into my relationship with God. Maybe that is too precious for God to give up.

Illness can teach us more about trust and adaptability and self-acceptance than we could ever learn from instant healing. I wonder if God, in his grace, sometimes delays our healing so we can pay attention to what God is saying to us.

Maybe, when I have prayed for healing, I have prayed a misguided thing. Maybe it would do me more good to pray for God to deepen my trust in him, rather than praying for healing.

> *It would be easier for me to be healed than to trust God afresh every single day.*

Maybe I could pray not that God will deliver me from this trial but that he will strengthen my fortitude and capacity to withstand it.

Perhaps, in the past, I have asked to be delivered too quickly from difficulty, denying him the chance to mature me. Perhaps I could simply pray for his will to be done, over and above my genuine needs. Perhaps that complete surrender is exactly what God has been waiting for. Perhaps that will bring him greater glory than healing ever could.

There is another silver lining here. Suffering forces us to depend on others and can activate the church's helping responses, bringing forth great generosity and acts of mercy.

We can learn to receive the gifts others want to give us. We can learn to take a turn at being blessed by others. For some of us, that may be the hardest thing we ever do. And God may use our relationships with others to bring about gradual healing over many years.

When we are not healed, we have to rely on God for everything we need. Maybe this is what delights him. Not the pain and suffering, but the faith and childlike trust that results.

We can pray for spiritual healing. Some childless Christians have suffered terrible loss of confidence in God (like Maddy in her story). We can pray that God will restore our faith in him. We can pray for reconciliation with God. He is just as concerned with our spiritual wellness as with our physical being, and he wants us restored into good relationship with him.

Maybe God will use our childless circumstances to bring us closer to him.

Maybe this is the closest to God we will get in this lifetime.

Maybe that closeness is worth it.

The other side of the coin

There is another side to the trauma coin.

Some people with bad childhoods have kids precisely because of their history. They want to change the cycle of harmful parenting. They want to show their children how to use the strengths of a personality quirk rather than the weaknesses. They want to demonstrate a life of faith and trust in God in the midst of struggle or illness or disability.

There is redemptive potential in parenting. God can use it to heal your bad childhood experiences. And he can help break the cycle of intergenerational bad parenting.

Christ offers redemption from the traumas of life. He went

through incredible trauma when he was living on earth. He was betrayed, hurt by others, even abandoned by his own disciples. He understands trauma. He really gets it. He can help. He can bring healing to past memories and bad feelings. He can bring peace to the mental clamour of unanswered questions.

He cares about you. And he can meet with you today.

If you want to let Jesus into the bad places of your life, the traumatic times and messy childhood, ask him to reveal himself to you. Invite him into your living room. Talk to him in the knowledge that he understands and cares about every detail of your life.

Trauma does not mean you cannot have children. With God's help, good support and a safe place in which to heal, you might reconsider.

You might want to try parenting.

You might be great at it.

MADDY'S STORY
Australia

Maddy had no idea how rapidly her chances of having children were dropping.

When she married her husband at thirty-six, she was in no hurry to have kids. They started trying after one year, but not seriously until Maddy was thirty-nine.

After trying for a couple of years without result, they considered IVF. At first they had ethical and spiritual concerns. They delayed taking it up. But after discovering they would have more control over the process than originally thought, they went ahead.

By that time, Maddy was over forty.

One article she read afterwards estimated the chance of successful IVF over forty is less than one percent. If only she had known. Her IVF clinic didn't tell her either. She later discovered IVF clinics are generally not upfront about their success statistics, particularly with older folk.

Maddy was forty-three when she first looked into assisted reproductive technologies. She and her husband tried a few rounds of artificial insemination which were not successful. So they commenced IVF proper.

Maddy was now forty-five years old.

She began IVF armed with biblical inspiration. She felt connected to the story of Elisha in 2 Kings 13:14-19, where Elisha tells the King of Israel to beat the ground with an arrow, symbolising victory in battle. The King responds to Elisha by beating the ground three times. Elisha tells him off, saying the King should have beat the ground five or six times to secure lasting victory.

Maddy felt the numbers in this story were significant for her. She initially felt she was being led by God to undertake three rounds of IVF. On further reflection, she decided five or six rounds was what God wanted her to do.

This number was confirmed through a specific prophecy given to Maddy by a Christian friend. She took this on board and believed God for success. She was hopeful when IVF started.

Maddy explained IVF in detail. First, the woman takes drugs for seven weeks to increase the number of eggs in her ovaries. Then she has a scan to check the progress. The woman gives herself nighttime injections into her stomach for ten to twelve days. According to Maddy, these were not quite as bad as they sound, but not fun either.

The eggs are harvested and fertilised with the man's sperm to form embryos, which are left overnight to grow. If they thrive, they are implanted into the woman's uterus two days later. This is followed by two weeks of more drugs, a teeth-grinding wait and finally a pregnancy test. All being well, a baby forms and grows to full-term.

Maddy's first two IVF attempts got as far as being implanted with embryos which did not survive. Attempts three and four consisted of egg and sperm combinations that did not produce viable embryos for implantation. But Maddy remained hopeful about attempt number five, especially when she received a prophetic confirmation beforehand.

Perhaps this is why it hit Maddy so hard when the fifth attempt failed.

'The wind was knocked out of my sails,' she said. 'I could not understand it. I remember praying, "God, what is going on?"'

Maddy was forty-nine for her sixth and final attempt. She felt some trepidation going into it, knowing about the risks of late pregnancies. She went ahead with the final round.

It did not work.

Maddy was unable to process it right away. She was under pressure at work at the time. She did not have room to feel what she was feeling. She only knew she felt devastated. She walked around numb.

When the news finally sank in, Maddy doubted her decisions and her capacity to hear from God. She questioned whether she had done something wrong or changed something God had wanted to do. It affected her relationship with God for a long time afterwards.

Maddy experienced strong reactions to parents. Stories of child abuse made her angry. She watched as mothers took their kids for granted, even abusing and mistreating them. She could not understand it. She felt like she and her husband had been passed over.

She prayed, 'Lord, we are two Christians with a stable and loving home, but we can't get pregnant. Yet these other women can have scores of children?' She wondered if God saw the unfairness of their situation or if he really saw them at all.

Maddy looked into adoption. An adoptee herself, she ideally wanted her own biological children. She loved her adoptive parents but never had that biological connection with them. She wanted that connection with her own biological child. However, after IVF, she considered adoption.

There were not many kids available for adoption in Australia. She explored overseas options but because of restrictive age criteria, she and her husband were already too old to adopt from most countries. Countries that did allow older parents to adopt had low numbers of children adopted, meaning her chances were slim.

Maddy and her husband did not want to put themselves through further heartache. They decided against adoption.

The turning point came when she went to counselling. The counsellor suggested Maddy consider her original reasons for wanting to be a mother. She invited her to pursue these desires in other ways.

This prompted Maddy to become a Pyjama Angel through the *Pyjama Foundation* (2018)[59], an Australian organisation that provides adult mentoring to foster kids. She feels grateful for this.

She is now pursuing writing in a professional capacity, running a home business and caring for two dogs. Like others, she believes she would not have had these opportunities if she had raised children.

The impact on Maddy's relationship with God has been profound. Her faith is stronger now, but her confidence in God can still be shaken. In those moments, she tries to remember God has answered hundreds of prayers in her lifetime. She tries to focus on this rather than the couple of big prayers that seem to have gone unanswered. She remembers God is still good.

Based on these hopeful moments, Maddy attempts to build herself a life from a house of cards and carry on.

But the cards are precariously balanced.

Sometimes she wonders if God was simply giving her impressions of what to do without actually promising to give her children. She wonders whether the outcome might have been in the best interests of the would-be children.

Maybe the children would have been unhealthy. Maybe it was for the best they did not come. Maybe it would have been hard for their children to grow up with ageing parents. Maybe, maybe, maybe.

These thoughts do not sit quite right with her. She questions them too. 'If God is for families, why would he not give us kids?' Maddy wonders if the purpose of six IVF attempts was so she would know she had done everything possible to have children.

The mental gymnastics are insanity-making.

While she normally feels fine around children, her emotions can be unexpectedly triggered by something random like seeing a teenage mum at the shops. On these days, the carefully constructed house of cards comes tumbling down.

She found space to reflect on her faith and how it has changed through IVF. She found it helpful, even crucial, to admit how she really feels about God. One book that helped was Phillip Yancey's *Disappointment With God*. Being honest about doubts, disappointments, questions and frustrations has been healthy for Maddy.

She tries to trust that God is still good and works all things for good.

There was one more prophecy given to her: it was time to let go of her dream of motherhood. The prophecy referenced the story of baby Moses, hidden by his mother in a basket and sent down the river (Exodus 2:1-3).

'I had to say goodbye to the dream,' Maddy recalled, shivering as she spoke. 'It gives me goosebumps just thinking about it.' (I had goosebumps crawling up my arms too.) It took her another two years, but letting go became easier and more settled for her.

Maddy found well-meaning Christians were generally unhelpful. Prayers for miracles or 'deliverance' were administered to her in a knee-jerk fashion and were presumed to be helpful and wanted. Miracle baby stories were unhelpful, promoting false hope like the IVF clinics.

Another helpful book was *365 Thank Yous* by John Kralik. It helped Maddy shift away from introspection towards things and people for whom she was grateful. In fact, she got motivated to actively express her gratitude. She set herself the task of writing one hundred thank-you notes to other writers. It took her a couple of years, but she did it.

When Maddy finds herself in a child-centred conversation or event such as Christmas carols, she prefers not to make a fuss. She finds it simpler to avoid such situations altogether. But the emotions can still hit home.

'It's a journey,' she reflected. 'It's not over in the first six months. Even after a long time, it can creep up on you.'

For others on similar journeys, Maddy recommends getting information about IVF beforehand and finding good support. 'It is good to have someone to talk to,' she advises. 'And don't be afraid to get counselling if you need to.'

She has particular advice for Christians. 'In terms of your relationship with God, keep up with your quiet time. Stay honest with God.'

Maddy believes that while early family experiences can partly shape us, as can childlessness, our identity is not just found in family. She firmly believes we ultimately find our identity in God.

8

GOD

When Faith and Disappointment Collide

It is easy to trust God when things are going well. It is easy to worship him when we are safe and warm and comfortable. It is easy to praise him when he answers our prayers.

It is not easy to trust God when things go wrong. It is even harder to trust him when life gets worse instead of better.

We are taught God is faithful, he will never forsake us and will protect us from harm. We are taught God will reward faithfulness with blessings in abundance.

But what if he doesn't?

What if God 'fails' us?

What about those times God has not protected us as we thought he would?

What if God seems absent?

How do we make sense of unfulfilled promises and prophecies from God?

These questions will be unpacked in this chapter. But in order to do that, it is necessary to introduce you to my Christian upbringing. It demonstrates how my expectations of God were formed—and destroyed.

And it demonstrates why it is so important to ask these questions in the first place.

What I grew up believing

I was taught, like most Christian kids, that God loves us and listens to our prayers. I prayed a lot. I grew up knowing God was my Father. I trusted him absolutely.

In my early twenties, I got into a toxic relationship that turned my brain inside out. It took everything I knew about God and smashed it to smithereens. (Maybe one day I will write a book about spiritual abuse.)

It took me years to recover. During that time, my relationship with God went out the window. I could not pray. I could not worship. I could not hear from God. Whenever I mustered the courage to talk to God, I experienced flashbacks. I could not even trust myself to pray. Being in church was especially triggering.

I wanted to be close to God again, to hear him speak, to worship him. But my faith was in tatters. God seemed no longer trustworthy.

During that hellish time apart from God, I had it out with him.

> 'I trusted you and you betrayed me.'

'Why did you let me get hurt? You said you would protect me. You said you would keep me from harm. But you didn't. In fact, I feel like you deliberately led me into a deeply harmful place. I trusted you and you betrayed me.'

I blamed God. I took it out on him. (I am not saying I was right to do this. I am only telling you what happened.)

God did not answer my questions. But he told me he wanted to heal me. He told me gently, over and over and over. Oh, how I wanted our relationship to heal. But I felt so vulnerable, so raw, so battered and brittle, his slightest touch made me wince. I held God at arm's length.

I thought he would leave. I thought he would get frustrated and walk out on me. I did not think his grace would extend that far. But for some reason, he stuck it out. He waited for me.

One day I finally sat down and had a real conversation with God. We still had a long way to go, but his patience had won me over.

The healing took years. I had believed my faith in God could not be shaken. Having my faith shattered was a shock.

I learned three important lessons:

1. Safety is an illusion. We are 'safe' only in that we belong to God. Nothing can take us away from him or keep us from his love (not even us). This does not mean, however, we are impervious to harm. We have vulnerabilities, and faith is not an inoculation against these.

2. God is deeply concerned with the state of our relationship with him. Our reconciliation with God is more important to him than ministry, church attendance or any religious effort.

3. God has grace enough to stretch all the way around the world for us. He is more patient than we dare believe. If our faith is a tightrope walk, God's grace is the safety net beneath us. And when we ask him for grace, it is music to his ears.

Healthy questioning

It is OK and even healthy to question God.

My trauma was a test of faith—not a test of my strength per se, but a test of the foundation upon which my faith was constructed.

I thought my faith was based on sound biblical teaching about God. I thought it was indestructible. Going through a bad experience forced me to find out what I really believed about God. It took me beyond what I had read it in the bible, beyond what others had told me about God, beyond what the songs at church said. In the fire of that devastation, I forged my own experience of God.

I needed to learn in a hands-on way that God was faithful. Not a distant-but-benevolent kind of faithful. Not a never-gets-his-hands-dirty kind of faithful. The kind of faithful that gets up in the middle of the night just to hold me and sing me to sleep. The kind of faithful that listens to the same story over and over again without interrupting or judging. The kind of faithful that stays with me in the trenches, holding pressure on my wounds, while bullets fly overhead.

He never left me. Even when I thought he would. His kindness caught me completely by surprise. I learned God is patient and kind, more so than my own idea of patient and kind which is resisting the urge to tap my foot while waiting in the supermarket queue. That kind of patience is pretty heroic.

But God is even more patient than that.

I learned, even though God loved me, he was not going to prevent bad things from happening. I learned God will allow pain in order to shatter my illusions about him.

I learned, while God does not plan or enjoy our suffering, he can appear beside us in the middle of it. I learned if we do get harmed, God is committed to our healing. Like a doctor at a MASH unit, he will not often rush out to the battlefield to stop me getting hit by bullets, but when I come into his hospital, he will give me unparallelled care and attention.

Sometimes God gives us companions for the healing journey, like comrades-in-arms.

> *His kindness caught me completely by surprise.*

They can be supportive friends who are willing to sit in the trenches with us. They can be a childless community. They can even be a furbaby. They can support us, holding our faith for a time, while we question what is going on.

Questioning my own faith had its merits. I worked out what I really believed and why. Like a detective, I pieced together clues of who God really was, not who I had imagined him to be.

I still question things today.

We may never get our answers. But for me, if I ever find myself again in that terrifying place where my faith is smashed to smithereens, I know he is faithful. He is near. I know he can handle my anger and doubt and frank, unfiltered prayer.

His love can scale any wall. Even the ones we might build.

Vulnerability

We do not like uncertainty. We do not like waiting for exam results or medical tests. We hate uncertainty about jobs, money and relationships.

We like spiritual uncertainty even less.

We do not like questioning our faith or wondering if we are wrong. We want to be right. Always. Faith and mystery and the unknown get under our skin.

In our inability to tolerate this essence of mystery, which is the heart of faith, we try to turn the mysterious into something tangible and certain. We see this manifest when people give pat answers to complex problems. I have certainly seen this happen in past churches:

If you are single, don't worry, you will find someone. Boom. Certainty.

If you are childless, don't worry, kids will come along. Boom. Certainty.

If you are struggling in your faith, don't worry, just pray more. Boom. Certainty.

Horrible stuff.

Such statements are dismissive, insensitive and unhelpful. (And I hope these things have never been said to you.)

I have even said such things myself. It is because of vulnerability. We fear being found out as an imposter, a fake, a fraud. We are so worried about coming across as not good enough or unworthy that we make up certainty as we go along. Even if that certainty is only skin-deep.

Brené Brown, TED talker and shame researcher, talks about this vulnerability (2010)[60]. She suggests true courage is found in the place of vulnerability, not outside of it. She recommends we embrace our authentic weakness together, because it is connection that truly heals us. We need to be vulnerable with each other and risk being truly seen in order to truly connect. Avoiding it leaves us feeling disconnected and alone.

Brené's definition of courage is embracing our imperfection.

I wonder what would happen if we stopped faking it. If we breathed instead of jumping in with an answer. If we leaned into the mystery. If we, as Christians, accepted Christians do not have all the answers. And we don't have to.

I wonder if we would really meet God in that place. Maybe we would meet our true selves as well. Maybe entering our greatest fears and extreme vulnerability frees us to be truly ourselves with God.

Christians have an apparent aversion to showing weakness. Some churches teach us others are always watching, judging our Christian performance like we are some kind of walking advert for God. Besides sounding rather paranoid, this teaching is unhelpful and untrue.

There, I said it.

When God saves us, he does not recruit us into his pyramid scheme. We are not his sales reps. I have no idea where this pressure came from, the obligation to 'Be the perfect Christian or you are letting God down'. This kind of pressure does not come from the patient and kind God I have come to know.

Yes, we are Christ's representatives. That is what Christian means. But it does not mean fakery. Being authentically ourselves, while trying to follow Christ, is important.

> *Maybe entering our greatest fears and extreme vulnerability frees us to be truly ourselves with God.*

Vulnerability is a gift—though not always wrapped in pretty paper with a bow on top. Sometimes it looks and smells more like a cowpat. It is not always appealing. But maybe God allows vulnerability into our lives so we can embrace our true selves.

Maybe God knows us better than we know ourselves and he wants us to know ourselves too. Maybe vulnerability is God's grace and kindness to us, a chance for us to bravely concede our questions and doubts and shortcomings.

Maybe vulnerability is where our true beauty lies.

Prophecy minefields

What, you may ask, does all this have to do with childlessness? Good question.

In the story about my bad relationship, I felt let down by God. And this is how many childless Christians feel. Especially those who received prophecies about children.

They feel God should have answered their prayers for children. They feel disappointed and betrayed by God. God apparently promised to give them children—and then pulled the rug out from under their feet.

Several interviewees told me they received specific prophecies from God, confirmed by other Christians. Some were given specific timeframes within which the child would arrive; others, a specific number of IVF attempts to try. They really believed God.

And then... nothing.

Their disappointment was profound. They had trusted God completely, put all their eggs (excuse the pun) in one divine basket, taken the prophecies at face value. When the prophecies were not fulfilled, the loss of faith was devastating.

It raised deeply troubling questions:

Did God really say I would have children?

Did I get it wrong?

Did I pray enough?

Did I lack faith?

Have I sinned somehow and God is punishing me?

How could God do this, leading me up the garden path?

Does God think I am unfit to be a parent?

Was God protecting me, or my would-be children, against some horrible tragedy?

Does God even care?

I do not understand the mysteries of prophecy. What I do know is how hurt these people are. They are disappointed. They are questioning themselves and God. They are looking for someone to blame, looking for answers.

Some want to ditch their faith altogether.

If you have been hurt, it almost does not matter what the answers are. What matters is the impact it has on you. It hurts.

The disappointment has created a rift between you and God. We can argue over prophecy all day, but until you are reconciled with God, I do not give a fig about prophecy. Your peace with God is of supreme importance.

Sadly, but fortunately, you are not alone. If you are living with unfulfilled prophecy about children, you are not the first. There are scores of childless Christians saying, 'What about us, God? Do you see us? Do you know what we are going through? You promised us children! What gives?'

It breaks my heart.

Maddy's story gives rise to my own heartache. When she told me her story, I found myself becoming emotional as I listened to her. I was so moved I wrote a song about it afterwards. I wrote about good and bad weather and walking with God through it all. I called it *Weather*. (Perhaps one day I will record it.)

When faith disappears, sometimes all we can do is cling to hope. Hope that God is still there. Hope that he has not abandoned us. Hope that he has seen us through hard times before and he can do it again.

Solidarity is paramount. We are not alone. We need to stand together against isolation and encourage one another amidst our doubts. Community can save our lives. Community can even bring us back to God.

One final word about prophecy. I believe in prophecy. I have seen it encourage and uplift people. I have seen it bring clarity to dark and murky situations. Timely prophecy is a beautiful gift. But it must be used with wisdom.

Givers of prophecy need to be extremely careful about what they are saying. We must deliver God's message without adding to it or colouring it with our own interpretation. Easier said than done.

And we, as receivers of prophecy, need to test everything we hear, even when it comes from other Christians. We need to discern as best as we can whether the words are from God. And the best test is the fulfilment of prophecy. Until the prophecy is fulfilled, it might be wise to proceed with caution.

Taking prophecy with a grain of salt does not mean you lack faith. It means you are being wise and testing the prophecy like the bible says (1 Thessalonians 5:19-20). It means you are applying wisdom and maturity gleaned from experience.

Even bad experiences can be used for good.

Surviving faith clichés

If you have been around church longer than three seconds, you have probably encountered clichés about faith.

We often throw these statements around as pat answers to profound mysteries of faith. Mysteries such as loss, unanswered prayer, unfulfilled prophecy and childlessness.

Let's look at examples of common clichés. *Cracks knuckles*
Warning: sarcasm alert.

1. 'God is in control.' Well, yes, he is. I can't argue with that. But that is what is so annoying, isn't it? We can't get annoyed with God or question him. But when we say, 'God is in control,' we often mean, 'God is keeping secrets from me which is really frustrating, and I have a bunch of

questions for him but am afraid to ask, so I will just keep on pretending to trust him because, apparently, that's what good Christians do.'

2. 'Everything happens for a reason.' This truism (used by some Christians I know) can infer God knows the mysterious 'reason' and we should therefore feel OK about it, but it offers little comfort to those not privy to said reasons. It would be great if God accompanied every major problem with a briefing on the reason behind it. That would be just super. Instead, we have to follow God, sometimes blindly.

3. 'God wants you to have children.' That is reassuring, except for the evidence to the contrary. By the way, how do you know what God wants for our lives? Are you privy to information that we are not?

4. 'We will pray for you.' Thanks. No really, I do appreciate your prayers. I would appreciate answers to prayers even more, but prayer is good. Actually, I will just take one of your kids home with me, if that is OK.

5. 'Have you tried praying?' No, it had not even crossed the borders of my mind as a lifelong Christian, but thanks very much. I'll try that now.

6. 'Children are a gift from God.' I agree. So, any idea why we are not worthy of this particular gift? Also, why do thousands of bad parents get their kid-gifts while we remain childless?

7. 'You will never know real love until you become a parent.' Guess I am doomed then. And forget the love I have known from my parents, friends, spouse and God. They are obviously inferior.

8. 'You need deliverance from childlessness.' What the? Deliverance? I can't even...

Yep, I found a book about being delivered from childlessness. Believe it. I could hardly believe it myself. It was a deeply concerning book. Perhaps I read it wrong. Perhaps I misinterpreted it. Hopefully I misinterpreted it.

Because if I read it right, it claimed the absence of children signified a lack of faith. It said childlessness is a problem that needs solving. It said Christians should solve this problem by having more faith. And more faith will result in miraculous children.

Where do I begin with dissecting this twaddle?

OK, let me hop up onto my hobbyhorse. Here goes.

First and foremost, there are various reasons why people are childless, Christians included. Many of these are physical or practical reasons. There may be spiritual reasons (and such people may benefit from deliverance ministry), but to assert that childlessness equates to poor faith is presumptive and harmful.

Second, childlessness is not inherently a problem. It may lead to other difficulties such as relational conflict and long-lasting grief. But to say childlessness is inherently problematic is in turn problematic.

Many childless people do identify childlessness as a problem.

> Formulas are to faith what cookbooks are to cake artists. Completely irrelevant.

But we cannot make that assumption. Some are accepting of their childlessness. Making a blanket statement denies the nuances of the childlessness journey. And it denies childless people the right to tell their childless story in their own way.

Finally, the proposition that childlessness (or any problem) can be resolved with more faith is over-simplistic and formulaic. I am wary of simplistic solutions to so-called 'problems'. When it comes to matters of faith, I am wary of formulas in general. Formulas are to faith what cookbooks are to cake artists. Completely irrelevant.

Many Christians readily apply faith to their circumstances, firmly believing in God's ability to provide them with children, only to be let down. Trusting God is not the issue. If it was, every Christian who ever trusted God would have answers to their prayers. All. The. Time.

I wish our problems could be solved by having more faith. Faith, however, does not guarantee answers. Nor does it inoculate against problems or suffering. In some cases, faith actually increases our suffering.

Jesus warned us this might be so. (Yay!)

I have a problem with Christians—or anyone—asserting the answer to problem *x* is solution *y*. This world is full of formulas and religion doubly so. I saw it at my Catholic high school. 'You swore at your parents? Say ten Hail Marys and ten Our Fathers.' I have witnessed it in church. 'Read your bible more' or 'You need more spiritual discipline' (whatever that means).

It has seeped into our culture. 'If you believe in yourself, you can accomplish anything.' Like this:

> **SELF-BELIEF** = *Success. That is a formula!*
> **PRAYER** = *Answers. Formula!*
> **FAITH** = *Baby. Formula!*

Reality check: all our hoping, praying and best efforts may not be enough. It does not mean we are inadequate. Some things in life are gigantic mysteries we will never fully understand. Applying the formula 'More faith = babies' is a mistake. It has the potential to blame innocent people and further confuse and dishearten vulnerable Christians.

If you have been subjected to this 'more faith' cliché, please take it with a grain of salt. And remember you are not alone. We are your family in Christ, your brothers and sisters. We will join you in working out this faith stuff on the fly.

Perhaps we can pray for one another—and for fellow believers still stuck in cliché-land.

The miracle-worker

Now for the elephant in the room.

God is a miracle-working God. There are many examples of God working miracles. There are miracle baby stories in the bible. I have friends with miracle baby stories. So it can be tough when well-meaning Christians share miracle-baby stories with us, encouraging us to hold on to hope based on the miracle-working capacity of God.

On the one hand, we cannot refute them. If we say, 'Yeah, so where is my miracle?', it might sound like we have no faith at all. And that would look bad. (Oh, the horror.)

On the other, we believe God can do miracles. (I certainly do. I have seen them firsthand.) We praise God for the miracles he has done. But God has not done this particular miracle for us at this particular time.

Friends probably tell us about miracles to raise our hopes. Raising hope can indeed be helpful in difficult times. But in childlessness, hope reaches a point where it is no longer useful. Hope can stop us letting go when we really should. Hope needs a resolution, otherwise it can turn into despair.

Sometimes the best thing to do is let go of hope.

Sounds simple. But it is hard. There are mental gymnastics required in letting go. Because other couples, Christian and non-Christian alike, get pregnant without trying. They get pregnant on the pill. They complain to us about it. They tell us how lucky we are to not have kids.

Some parents are not suitable parents. At all. Yet they have children.

It is not fair. At all.

Faith is not a pre-requisite for having kids, or else only Christians would get pregnant. People have children irrespective of their faith, maturity, preparedness or suitability. Being childless is not necessarily a measure of one's spirituality.

Yet some childless people get blamed for that, like in the book I mentioned above where childlessness was blamed on a lack of faith. And some childless people blame themselves.

Childlessness confronts us with the mystery of an all-powerful God who chooses not to cure us. We may pray, fast, read the bible, tick all the right spiritual boxes, and still—no children.

We may apply all the faith formulas without result. We may blame ourselves. We may seek unfindable answers.

Or we may blame the miracle-worker.

Here comes the frank prayer bit.

'Come on, God! Why will you not do this one miracle? If you are capable, why are you not willing? This is the one thing I want! If you will not do this, will you at least tell me why?'

Sound of crickets

We can interpret unanswered prayer as a sign that we are inadequate, or worse, that God has stopped caring. And that has an impact on us. I do not know if it has an impact on God. Sometimes I wonder if he is far less offendable than we think. But it affects us. We may wonder if God is unfaithful.

'You have answered my prayers before. You gave me that parking spot I needed, for Pete's sake. Why not answer the most important prayer of all?'

Here is the kicker. Unanswered prayer does not mean God is unfaithful. Answered prayer does not mean he is. His faithfulness is not about answers. His faithfulness is about his commitment to us. His presence, companionship and steadfast love in the midst of suffering proves his faithfulness, more than answers ever could.

I do not know why God says no to our prayers, especially those nearest and dearest to our hearts. I do not know why God seems silent. I do not know why he sometimes does not heal or save or intervene.

But I know him. I know his love. It is a real, gritty, down-in-the-trenches-with-me kind of love.

When nothing else is certain, his love is rock-solid sure.

Reconciliation

Some childless people, like Carmel, grew up believing in God but the impact of childlessness has killed this belief. Carmel's story highlights the reality of lost faith. If you have become distant from God because of hurt or betrayal, you are not alone.

When I have absolutely no idea what is going on in God's head (told you I would have no answers), I return to my spiritual roots of prayer and worship. I go back to first principles. I simplify. I go home.

I dwell on passages like Matthew 6 where Jesus exhorts us to pray as simply and honestly as we can manage. I remind myself God does not need a religious show from me. I remember he is my Father.

Here is a refresher (I particularly like the Message version):

> When you come before God, don't turn that into a theatrical production either. All these people making a regular show of their prayers, hoping for stardom! Do you think God sits in a box seat?
>
> Here's what I want you to do: find a quiet, secluded place so you won't be tempted to role-play before God. Just be there as simply and honestly as you can manage. The focus will shift from you to God, and you will begin to sense his grace (Matthew 6:5-6 MSG).

With that in mind, I can tell him exactly how I feel. So I tell him what I am thinking about. I share my questions, my pain and yes, my temptation to blame him. I do not hold anything back. I tell him frankly about the fear, the grief, the anger, the despair. I tell him about the loneliness. I tell him about my dreams and hopes for the future. He gets to see the good, the bad and the ugly from me.

Once I have spilled my guts, I settle down to wait. This is the important bit. I have to do the spilling before I can do the settling, but once I have spilled, I can settle. I wait for him to respond.

He does not always use words. Sometimes he just smiles as we sit together. Sometimes he cries with me. Sometimes he pours his love over me until I am swimming in it. He seems to know what I need.

> *Once I have spilled, I can settle.*

Reconciliation may not happen all at once. It may take years. But honesty gives us a place to start.

Sometimes we are so hell-bent on getting our questions answered, we miss what matters most to God. Yes, our questions matter to him. Of course they do. Very much. But God is more concerned with our spiritual wellbeing than with our needs and wants. Sometimes he will let us suffer—even to the point of death—in order to bring our spiritual selves to maturity.

God is more concerned about your relationship with him than you are. He knows what it takes for you to consider trusting him again. He knows about your questions and needs.

When I am stuck with questions that will not go away, I go to this passage:

> It's a good thing to quietly hope,
> Quietly hope for help from God...
> When life is heavy and hard to take,

> Go off by yourself. Enter the silence.
> Bow in prayer. Don't ask questions:
> Wait for hope to appear
> (Lamentations 3:26, 28-29).

I love that. I love the image of bowing in prayer, shelving my incessant questions, and waiting quietly for hope to appear. Surely this is the place where God is present with us: in quiet trust, in silent hope.

And hope is a beginning.

Finding that quiet place can help us reconcile with him again.

When life stinks

In my darkest moments, it is God the comforter who is with me. This is a mystery, one of the paradoxes of faith, that God is often nearer to us in our troubles than in our triumphs.

The persecuted church reportedly enjoys a powerful and intimate relationship with Jesus, not in spite of persecution but precisely because of it. (Try getting your head around that one.) Apparently, struggles and pain bring out the best in us.

Jesus understood suffering. Isaiah describes Jesus as 'a man who suffered, who knew pain firsthand' (Isaiah 53:3 MSG). Jesus endured physical pain (beatings, crucifixion), emotional pain (losing friends, betrayal), psychological pain (soldiers insulting him) and spiritual pain (separation from God).

He experienced fear. He dreaded the cross. He got angry and frustrated with his disciples. He grieved the loss of friends. He was scorned, harassed, belittled and rejected in every way.

Plus, he was childless. Just saying.

> This is a mystery, one of the paradoxes of faith, that God is often nearer to us in our troubles than in our triumphs.

This Jesus has enormous love and compassion for us. We can trust Jesus with our troubles. He is well acquainted with grief. He understands heartache and loss. His empathy is not empty but sincere. He is not detached from our pain but joins in with our suffering.

Jesus is ever waiting for us to cast our cares upon him. He is not looking for prayer that is pretty. He is longing for real, grubby, fumbling, authentic conversation with us. He wants to be there when life stinks. He wants to be our comforter. He does not want us to hide from him. He wants all of us.

That is the kind of relationship I want with God.

CARMEL'S STORY

UK

Carmel had the name of her daughter picked out since she was nine.

Lydia Megan was the carefully chosen name. Lydia was after a friend at school. Megan was a Welsh version of Carmel's mother's name. Her mother held an important place in her life.

Carmel knew she would have four kids. That was certain. She was one of three siblings and decided four would be better so they could play together. She did not want them to feel left out. The four were expected, anticipated, assumed.

It was totally unthinkable that it would never happen.

She grew up surrounded by family. Her mum was one of nine children and Carmel had nineteen cousins on her mum's side. In her teens she cared for these cousins, feeding them, changing them, playing with them. The dreams of her own family were nurtured by these years of caring.

After ending a serious relationship with a man who did not want kids, she went travelling for a year. She had the time of her life. She fell in love with places she had never seen before.

Soon after returning home, she met her now-husband. He already had two children from a previous relationship but wanted a family with her. They got married and started trying.

It didn't happen. Carmel was concerned. She knew the NHS had a two-year timeframe of trying before you could access IVF, and she knew pre-IVF testing could take up to a year. So she started the process and got tested.

The tests came back normal. Carmel had unexplained infertility.

This was not good news. It was more frustrating than not, because if everything was normal she ought to be pregnant. She wanted to know what was wrong so she could fight and win.

She and her husband opted for IVF via IUI (intrauterine insemination). During the first round, she became pregnant with twins. She was ecstatic—until she started bleeding. At first it looked like the babies were OK. But she lost them. First one, then the other.

The second twin died on her wedding anniversary. She cried with a grief inconsolable. The miscarriage pains that followed were terrible. She felt like her stomach was being ripped apart for twenty-four agonising hours.

They did two more rounds of IUI, neither of which worked. They proceeded to IVF proper. While fertilisation appeared to work, the bleeding re-appeared as it had during IUI.

They tried to keep the baby. Carmel did everything right: eating healthy, going for walks, relaxing. But nothing worked. They lost the baby's heartbeat at seven-and-a-half weeks.

She was given options for ending the pregnancy and she chose surgical removal, as she could not stand the thought of going through that miscarriage pain again. At least with surgery, she would be able to control the timing.

The surgery went well. Carmel assumed her body would go back to having regular periods. But six weeks later, her body went into pseudo-miscarriage with painful contractions and bleeding.

It hit hard. She was already feeling down about losing her baby. She managed to pick herself up again. They had one more chance with IVF, so they gave it their last shot, positive and determined it would work.

When it did not, Carmel crumbled completely. Her dream of being a mum was over. She was utterly devastated. 'It was dark,' she remembered. 'How could I ever live again? What was the point?'

Counselling helped, as did her lifelong natural positivity. She had fought illness all her life and knew how to stay positive.

In a desperate last effort, they moved to another area which entitled them to one more round of IVF. It failed. That really was the end of it. No more IVF. No more chances.

It was a bleak time for Carmel. Every parent she knew lived for their families. She could not see the point of living without children.

She wondered if her health conditions were a factor. She might have passed her health issues to her children, so perhaps childlessness had stopped that from happening. But she was unsatisfied. Others with health problems got to have children. Carmel went on a mental merry-go-round, wondering what was wrong with her.

She thought about her efforts during IVF. She remembered the support of family and friends through the darkest times. Mostly she thought of the life she had intended to lead, each step marked with the milestones of her children.

She journalled her thoughts at the time. 'I feel like I'm at the edge of a cliff, looking down. Where before, there was water beneath, and it was blue and calm... now it is just an abyss, just a black hole. The option to bathe in the waters of motherhood is gone. I've gone through stormy seas, paddled in shallow waters, but now there is nothing. I can't go forward and I can't go back. But I must keep moving.'

Raised a Catholic, she ditched her religion. She had prayed for a baby and her prayers went unanswered. She still believes in a higher power. But she no longer believes the 'Everything happens for a reason' cliché.

She kept writing. One day she journalled for twelve hours. It gave her permission to feel everything she was feeling. It gave her perspective. Now she occasionally writes poetry for others.

Carmel decided she and her husband ought to live with enjoyment. It is how they would have wanted their children to live. The current enjoyment project for Carmel, recently forty, is 'Forty things to do in your forties', a suggestion from her counsellor. She and other women in their forties are doing this together.

Travel is on the forties list. She has taken several holidays and has actually enjoyed herself. 'Holidays give me something to look forward to,' she said. 'Sometimes I enjoy myself so much I don't know how I would fit children in!'

Turning forty was a good way to draw a line in the sand about having kids. She knows with certainty it will never happen.

She considers herself quite resilient, a quality she attributes to living with long-term illness. Diagnosed with diabetes at nine, she was told she would never do certain things. But she was undeterred. Determined to prove the doctors wrong, she went abseiling the following week. Perhaps it was the right thing to tell a tenacious nine-year-old girl.

Carmel has a scripted answer for questions about children: 'No, but I have had three rounds of IVF and lost three babies.' Alternatively, she uses shorter versions:

'We have tried.'

'We have not managed to.'

'My husband has two.'

She still grieves the dream. 'You are grieving for a person you never met,' she shared. 'There is a piece of my heart that is broken, and it will never be fixed.'

One current challenge is watching her step-daughter get infertility treatment. It reminds her of what she went through and it stirs envy and guilt. Those are hard days.

Advice and sympathy are not helpful. Carmel is not interested in whether others think they can understand her journey. No one knows what she has gone through. What is more helpful is when her friends want to know how to support her. And friends have helped, especially those who have gone through miscarriage and IVF like her.

Her mother has been her rock. But there are times when her mum still prays for Carmel to fall pregnant. This can be upsetting.

While she envies those with kids, she is determined not to wallow. 'We only get one life,' she counsels. 'Talk to your partner. And do not stop yourself from living the life you want.' She draws from one of her nan's sayings:

'If ifs and buts were pots and pans, you would be endlessly washing up.'

She has things worth living for other than children. She is still very much in love with her husband. She is grateful for this, as she knows the stress of IVF splits up many couples.

'What-Ifs' are no longer part of Carmel's life. She has a new dream: travelling in a campervan for six months. She took out a second mortgage to do so.

'It's all right to get on with life and not feel guilty about it,' she says. She encourages others to do the same.

GRIEF

Living with Broken Dreams

Many childless people are plagued by unanswered and unanswerable questions that flood their minds and sink their souls.

How do I recover from a miscarriage?

Will I ever find out why I lost my baby?

Why can't they explain my infertility?

When, if ever, do I try again?

How do I make sense of life without children?

Will I ever 'get over' this?

Childlessness brings a unique sense of grief: the grief of lost children, the grief of never conceiving, the grief of never trying, the grief of miscarriage.

We are going to look grief in the eye—and try to work out how we can stay afloat in an ocean of sadness.

Miscarriage

What a terrible word. What a terrible thing.

A child started growing and it was a living, breathing being. Then one day, quietly, inexplicably, it slipped away.

How do we make sense of this?

Even the biology of miscarriage is difficult. Many miscarriages cannot be explained because a cause cannot be found. Some miscarriages have clear medical reasons. Others have risk factors which 'probably' led to the miscarriage (and even that tiny morsel of uncertainty is enough to drive one crazy).

But for many, miscarriage remains a complete mystery.

Miscarriage is common. One in four Australian pregnancies end in miscarriage for women under twenty-five. Between twenty-five and thirty-five, the rate of miscarriage increases to one in three. For women in their forties, the rate of miscarriage is nearly one in two (Franks 2018)[61]. And some women have multiple miscarriages.

These statistics are incomplete because a lot of women conceive without realising it. Some may miscarry without knowing they were pregnant.

Unexplained miscarriage in particular has significant implications. Not knowing the cause of the last miscarriage puts one in a difficult and vulnerable position when it comes to 'next time'. One usually wants to know what went wrong so one can do things differently next time. It is difficult to actively put right what is unexplained.

This unknowing can cause considerable grief.

Blame and shame

Blame and shame in miscarriage is a thing.

When life goes bad, we tend to look for someone to blame, especially if we got hurt in the process. We want to fix it, make it better, prevent the bad thing from happening again.

Many would-be parents blame themselves when a pregnancy ends prematurely such as in miscarriage or stillbirth. Women interrogate themselves endlessly, analysing their diet, exercise and stress levels. They wonder 'What-If' and 'If-Only'.

'If only I had not eaten that take-away food.'

'What if I had done more yoga?'

'If only I had slowed down a little.'

'What if I had a less stressful job?'

They might never know why they miscarried. Maybe they did everything right. Maybe it would not have made any difference anyway. The maybes are hard to live with.

The good news is stress is apparently not a factor in miscarriage. It is an old wives' tale. Good thing too, as many women find the mere experience of pregnancy stressful. And yet, would-be mums often blame themselves.

Would-be dads blame themselves too, watching their partners struggle through the physical and emotional pain of miscarriage. It can be hard for men to carry their own pain as well as their partner's grief. Some men feel guilty for not doing more or for grieving in the first place.

Men often want to fix things and make their partners feel OK again. This is admirable. But not all problems can be solved. When men cannot solve the problem, they might blame themselves.

'If only I had been there when it happened.'

'What if I had taken more time off work?'

'If only I had been more supportive.'

Childless people get blamed by medical professionals. Sometimes doctors have to ask about the details of the miscarriage, but at such a painful time it can come across as an assessment of competence.

'What were you doing at the time of the miscarriage?'

'Did you go to the hospital?'

'Why didn't you ring us earlier?'

This reminds me of my friend in Chapter 7 who was shamed by her doctor after a horrendous miscarriage. She was accused of complaining. She decided never to have children. Trauma is real. And it can change the course of someone's life.

I hope no one reading this book has been told off for having a miscarriage. I hope you never receive inappropriate and unprofessional treatment as a result. I hope you get nothing but support and respect.

Telling someone they are wrong for feeling the way they feel is shaming. Telling someone to show gratitude after immense loss is shaming. Labelling someone's honesty and trauma as 'complaining' is an act of shaming.

Many feel shame about miscarriage. They blame themselves and feel like failures. Shame goes beyond wondering if you did the wrong thing. It is a constant drip of depressing water about your value as a person. It seeps into the under-layers of your soul and stains your identity.

Drip. Unworthy.
Drip. Unworthy.
Drip. Unworthy.

On online miscarriage forums (there are some wonderful forums for non-mums-who-have-nearly-been-mums), many women are utterly convinced there is something wrong with them. Miscarriages have devastated their sense of self. Some women ask out loud if they are still legitimate women.

You heard me.

They have suffered under the weight of blame and shame. Women believe they should be able to bear a child. This is, apparently, what defines a woman. Any woman who cannot have a child is therefore less of a woman. They are sub-women.

I have seen a similar response from men. Many men believe fertility is a core aspect of manhood, which means failing to produce offspring draws their manhood into question. They can feel like failures as men.

Masculinity and femininity

We begin forming a sense of identity at a young age, and as we grow we develop ideas about who we are. We experiment, testing what we can do, discovering what we genuinely enjoy. Feedback from others can help cement our sense of self. By adulthood most of us have a pretty good sense of who we are.

One of the many ingredients for identity is masculinity or femininity. You can hear this identity stuff in how people describe themselves.

'I feel girly in this outfit.'

'I am not a blokey-bloke.'

'I have always been a bit of a tomboy.'

Our reproductive capacity feeds our masculine and feminine identity. As a woman in early menopause might feel she has missed out on womanhood, or a man with a low sperm count might feel inferior, so can miscarriage drastically affect the way we see ourselves as men and women.

Society reinforces these gender stereotypes. We have clichés about pregnant women who supposedly 'glow' and men as stand-by chauffeurs and roadies for the big moment of labour.

Reminders of children (which are everywhere) can influence our concept of what it means to be a complete man or woman. These notions of completeness directly feed into our ideas of failure. Society promotes traditional ideas of manhood and womanhood: parenthood is normal, childlessness is abnormal.

No wonder childless people feel like failures.

Fortunately, we are going to turn the tables on failure.

There is no failure in loss. There is no failure in living with unspeakable tragedy. There is no failure in expressing how we feel. There is definitely no failure in sharing our stories.

Connecting with each other and telling our stories can help us fight shame (see Shame Resilience Theory in Chapter 12). Love and support turns failure on its head. Facing our grief throws failure into sharp relief. Re-inventing ourselves, re-discovering meaning, awakening ourselves to new possibilities is far from failure.

Grief does not mean we have failed. It means we have loved

and lost. It means we feel.

Disenfranchised grief

Kenneth Doka (1989) identified a lesser-known type of grief, 'disenfranchised grief', and defined it as 'the grief that persons experience when they incur a loss that is not or cannot be openly acknowledged, publicly mourned, or socially supported'[62].

> *Their grief is as raw and powerful as it is for those who have lost a living person.*

The death of a pet or ex-partner may trigger disenfranchised grief.

Losing a new job you never started is disenfranchised grief.

Having your plans fall through is disenfranchised grief.

Losing a future you hoped and dreamed about is disenfranchised grief.

Mourning a planned-for family is disenfranchised grief.

Society largely does not understand the disenfranchised grief of childlessness. Friends struggle to empathise. They cannot imagine the magnitude of our broken dreams. They may say we have no right to grieve for what we never had. And we may believe them.

Disenfranchised grief is as real as the loss of a loved one or job or material possession. Society may find miscarriage or stillborn grief easier to understand, where a physical body dies. For the childless person who cannot conceive, there is no physical death. Technically they are not bereaved. But their grief is as raw and powerful as it is for those who have lost a living person.

Friends might say things like, 'But no one has died'. Or 'At least you didn't have a child and then lose them.' Or the clincher, 'Can't you be grateful for what you have?'

This further disenfranchises the grief. There is blame in these comments. You can hear the dismissal. If you pour your heart out to someone and they respond with 'But' or 'At least', you know they are not really listening. They are avoiding or minimising your pain.

Many friends are well-meaning. They might believe they are helping by cheering you up or highlighting your silver linings. Perhaps they want to be supportive but do not know what to say. They might be lost for words.

This is common with grief. People often say nothing for fear of saying the 'wrong thing'. Even though it would be simple for them to say something empathic like, 'Wow, that really sucks.'

(If you are a friend or loved one of a childless person and want to know what to say, see Chapter 11. I wrote it especially for you.)

When our friends are not compassionate towards our grief, we can be compassionate towards our friends, especially if they have other stuff going on for them. Our understanding may go a long way.

Hold on to those friends if you can. You might get a chance to grieve with them later on.

Loss of friends

Some friendships are not elastic enough to stretch around the pain of childlessness. Some long-standing friends simply cannot understand how we feel, regardless of our attempts to express it.

This can be especially true of friends who are parents. They might not relate to the struggles of falling and staying pregnant. Especially if they fell pregnant at the drop of a hat. This can create distance between friends.

Sometimes this distance is practical. Even the most sympathetic parent-friends cannot always be available. In juggling kids and friendships, their family will take priority. Some parent-friends drift apart because they are too busy or, in the case of being sleep-deprived, sleep gets the priority.

I understand this. I would make the same decision in their shoes.

Some childless people find they no longer have anything in common with their parent-friends or cannot have a conversation without talking about their parent-friends' kids. Sometimes I want to say to my parent-friends, 'I love you, and I love your kids, but can we not spend the entire time talking about them?!'

Naturally, I understand their position. They are enamoured with their kids. I get it. While I fully support them, I also find such conversations can become one-sided. Before I know it, we have spent three hours talking about toilet-training.

I am also interested in other topics. Just saying.

Perhaps we can make an arrangement. For every story you give me about your baby's diarrhoea, I give you a story about my furbaby's poo. It's only fair.

Some parent-friends prefer to socialise with other parents. This is completely understandable. They should have friends they can talk to about parenting.

But it is hard when good friends become distant. Losing friends who have previously been supportive is especially difficult. This loss is part of childless grief. Many childless people grieve not only for their lost child, but also for lost friendships, lost social circles, lost churches and lost support.

Some friends may come back after a while. Pray about it. God is sometimes gracious with these things. One day he may reunite you with the friends you lost.

What about abortion?

Abortion is one of those highly controversial areas. Many people, including Christians, hold firm views on this subject. But this book is not a theological text in which I will examine the arguments for and against abortion. Better minds than mine are doing that.

I simply want to acknowledge that some of you may be childless due to abortion, and you may be experiencing disenfranchised grief as a result.

Abortion can be tricky to define in the world of childlessness. Are women who had an abortion childless-by-choice? What about those women who had no choice, or felt it was forced choice? What about women who terminate a pregnancy originating from a sexual assault? What about women in abusive relationships who are ordered to have an abortion?

These cases do exist, just in case you are wondering. I know women who have had abortions because they were threatened with death if they did not.

If I had to choose between an abortion or both me and my baby being murdered...

What would you do?

If you've had an abortion, you may be grieving. Regardless of whether you had a choice or not, the grief is real. And just because you had an abortion, it does not mean you do not want children.

Your grief may be complicated by feelings of guilt. Not

everyone feels guilty about abortion, but some do. Some become increasingly guilt-ridden as life goes on.

If you are a person of faith, you may worry about the spiritual implications. Some Christians worry about their reputation in church or Christian circles. You might fear reprisal or judgment from fellow Christians if you speak openly about your abortion, especially if you hold a position of responsibility in your church. If your church believes abortion is a sin, your standing and position in that church might be jeapordised by your disclosure. You might feel safer talking to someone outside your church.

No one seems to be talking about abortion. Especially in the church—or not in the churches I have attended. Hey church! We need to talk about it. Abortion is happening in our communities, families and congregations. The pain is there, hidden in plain sight. It will fester unless we give it some air.

We need to break the taboo around abortion. I am not talking about classifying abortion as a sin or not. I am talking about talking about it.

Grief after abortion is as real as any other grief. The loss is tangible. If you had an abortion and feel affected by it, I encourage you to consider marking the memory of the baby (we will get to that later).

I also encourage you to get support. It might be a counsellor or a trusted friend. You do not have to do this alone.

You are just as deserving of support as anyone else.

The grief of almost-forty

As I neared forty, my grief shifted.

In my thirties, I felt like having children was still a possibility, albeit a remote one. But I have just hit the big four-oh. And my grief is leveling up.

The age of forty is commonly treated as a having-children deadline. Some of my interviewees and people I met online said so. There is something about forty and the biological clock that seems significant.

I experienced the grief of almost-forty and now the grief of the forties.

Forty brings certainty that children are highly unlikely. Not impossible, but near enough. Grief lies in the death of likelihood, the end of probability, the loss of chance. It is the death of hope.

Makes me wonder what turning fifty will be like. (I hear it is fabulous.)

Turning sixty can bring grief around lost grandchild dreams. With ageing comes loss of a life for which we hoped. The grief shifts as our friends' kids achieve milestones we hoped our kids would achieve.

This is the grief of lost baby showers, empty nurseries and car seat research that will never be needed. The grief of anticipated yelling matches with teenagers. Of agonising first dates our children will never have. Of possible grandchildren.

Grief is unending. It never really goes away. It keeps reappearing, shifting and re-inventing itself over the lifespan.

It might always be there.

Grief without end

Many childless people experience grief without end,

particularly in IVF. After a failed round of IVF, the grief of losing a future child may be compounded by effectively putting life on hold to decide or attempt the next round. The grief carries on.

Grief is, by nature, unpredictable. You feel just fine until it pops up out of nowhere. Grief might be triggered by little things like seeing a pregnant woman at the shops or a pregnancy announcement on social media. Big things like birthdays and anniversaries can bring a fresh wave of grief. Discussions of children and childlessness can be almost intolerable.

Grief may chop and change, one minute making you furious with the world, the next leaving you in a sobbing mess. You might feel tossed about in the waves of grief, dizzy and disoriented. You might think you are going insane.

You might even want to die. Bereaved people often think about their own death, not necessarily because they want life to end but because they want to be with their loved one. For such people, suicide may become a real and desirable option.

If you are grieving right now, I want to acknowledge that suicide may be in your thoughts. Suicide and grief are directly connected. If you do not want to actually die but just want to end the grief or be with the baby you lost, this is probably a part of grief. If, however, you are thinking of dying for reasons other than grief or reconciliation with your baby, something else could be going on for you.

Either way, I encourage you to tell someone and get support. The key with suicidal thoughts is to talk about them with a safe person. It will not help to ignore them and hope they will go away. It is not helpful to keep them a secret.

Most people who think about dying and suicide believe they are the only ones feeling this way. They feel isolated and alone. They believe they cannot tell anybody because no one will understand. I encourage you to try anyway.

You might be surprised how compassionate and understanding people are when they realise how bad you are feeling. You might be surprised to learn others have had suicidal thoughts too. It is a common experience.

So reach out. Talk to someone you trust. Ring a helpline (that's what they are there for). Go see a professional. Join an online childlessness or miscarriage forum. Get support. You do not have to do this alone. And I suggest you don't.

In Australia, you can call Lifeline, a 24/7 helpline, and talk to a counsellor trained in responding to suicide. The number is 13 1114. You can also text *Lifeline* (n.d.)[63] between 12pm-12am on 0477 13 1114.

You can talk to *BeyondBlue* on 1300 22 4636, chat with them online (2020)[64], or download their app BeyondNow, which puts together a personalised safety plan for when you feel suicidal.

It can be overwhelming just thinking about who to tell. So pick one person and start with them. You do not have to tell the whole world. Just one person. Their support may kick-start your process of feeling better.

Lots of interviewees recommended counselling and said they wished they had done it sooner. Counsellors are good people to tell. Their job is to listen to hard things. They will not be shocked by your story.

Doctors and medication might help as well. Chat to your doctor about it. Medication is not necessarily forever; it might just help you through a rough spot.

There are organisations in Australia that support those who have lost children through miscarriage and stillbirth. One is called *Sands* and you can find them online (2020)[65]. Another, the *Pink Elephants Support Network* (2020)[66], has online support and facebook groups as well as support for loved ones.

Grief is a significant experience. It can feel like an insurmountable wall. Support, medication and counselling can give you a leg-up over the wall of grief when you cannot quite negotiate the climb.

Marking the memory

There are powerful ways to mark the memory of a lost child or lost hope of a child. In reading online miscarriage forums, I was moved by the tangible ways childless people have remembered their miscarried babies and marked their intangible losses.

Some childless people were able to bury a body. They marked the grave with stones or planted a new sapling on the spot. Some held a funeral or memorial service with close family members and friends.

Some bought a piece of jewellery to symbolise their lost baby. Some, who had chosen names, had these names engraved on the jewellery.

Some built shrines in their homes or re-decorated their would-be nurseries.

Some wrote letters to their babies and kept them in boxes along with ultrasound photographs.

Some held a moment of remembrance on each anniversary of the baby's death.

There are beautiful and touching ways to remember someone. You can use these ideas or create something unique for your lost child or children. There is no right or wrong way to mark the memory. As long as it is meaningful for you.

My husband and I wanted to remember the children we had named but never conceived. In fact, we had never tried to conceive them. Our grief felt slightly strange for us, like we were losing something we had not started. And yet the names existed, lovingly and carefully selected.

Did we have the right to memorialise a journey we never began?

Of course we did.

We were closing a chapter of a book we had not read, not even picked up from the shelf, a book everyone else was raving about and telling us we simply must read.

We have the right to grieve for that missed experience.

We have the right to grieve for the two names chosen but never used.

We have the right to grieve a future lost.

It was my husband's idea to dedicate this book to our two unconceived children. The moment he suggested it to me, my heart sang. I knew right then we would put those two names at the beginning of this book, dedicating it to their memory.

Our two children will be forever remembered.

Finding meaning

Many people cope with grief through finding meaning.

If grief is about losing control or the illusion of control, coping with grief is often about confronting this illusion and regaining a sense of control.

Finding meaning can reacquaint us with this sense of control. It can restore our sense of who we are. It can inspire us with a sense of purpose in our day-to-day living. It can make us feel valued and valuable.

You know the thing that gets you out of bed in the morning? The thing that keeps you going when you are tired, fed up and disillusioned? The thing you look back on at the end of your day with pride?

That is meaning.

Meaning-making is unique to each person. What I hold as being meaningful may mean diddly-squat to you. That is OK. Meaning is not about applying a formula for happiness but a process of discovering a new way of living.

The absence of a formula can be both freeing and frustrating. Sometimes it would be nice if someone just gave us the answer. But I think it gives us more ownership if we re-discover a sense of meaning for ourselves. And it makes meaning even more meaningful.

Here are some examples of how others have found meaning in childlessness. These ideas may spark something for you.

In Fiona's story, she turned her suffering into a cause. She used her childlessness to reach out to other childless women, helping them discover their passions. Her pain is serving as her major driving force.

Carmel created a forty-item bucket list. Her old dream was to be a mother, and the loss of that dream was heartbreaking. Now she is pursuing new dreams.

Marie indulged in figure-skating and, in doing so, she discovered a whole new community of friends.

Philippa took up sports completely foreign to her, taking new risks.

Maddy became a mentor for young children, something she finds immensely satisfying.

Childless people are using grief to re-connect with their identity. They are returning to old interests, resurrecting forsaken passions, doing wild things they have always wanted to do. They are discovering who they are.

I can relate to this. I am using my childlessness experiences to write a book for other childless people. I wanted to build solidarity. My passion is a powerful motivation.

Maybe you have a book inside you too.

It can be hard to know where to start with making meaning. When you are ready to think about life without children, try some of these reflective questions:

What did I previously enjoy doing before grief hit me?

What did I like doing as a kid?

What things give me a sense of satisfaction?

When am I most proud of myself?

If money were no obstacle, what would I do with my life?

What is the wildest thing I can think of doing?

Your answers might give you a hint about where to start.

The death of hope

The beauty of grief (if I may be so bold as to describe grief as beautiful) is it allows us to re-connect with old desires.

Those who have tried to conceive have often lived in a holding pattern, avoiding making major plans or decisions in order to accommodate the potential much-wanted child. Other things like study, travel, hobbies, ministry and career changes have been placed on hold out of necessity. When things have been put off again and again, it is easy to lose touch with them.

> It is a time of risk and courage and adventure.

Indecision is a difficult place to live. Final decisions can be gutting. They acknowledge the end of a chapter, the snuffing out of a candle, the vanishing of a dream. Hope gives us a reason to live.

And yet, in the death of hope we can rediscover those old desires. In this death resides the promise of an entirely new life. The final crushing blow to hope gives space for something new to live. Like digging up an old withered tree in order to plant something even more beautiful, saying goodbye to hope—while painful—can be liberating.

We can dip our toes into new waters, try without knowing, fail without judgment. It is an opportunity to unlock doors previously untried, to sit in rooms unfamiliar and see if we feel at home. It is a time of risk and courage and adventure.

Re-birth often follows death. In Australia, we are familiar with the devastation of bushfires. We are accustomed to the smell of smoke in summer. We are taught about fire danger as children.

We know, from experience, that bushfires generate new growth. We know this instinctively and irrefutably. When we see smoke on the horizon, we know a fresh landscape will emerge soon.

When the fire has burned itself out, we mourn what has been lost but we also look with expectation for the regeneration. We understand the pain has been necessary and even healthy for the circle of life.

And we look eagerly for those first green signs of promise, nature's reassurance that all is well, life will continue again. There is nothing quite so hopeful as a flash of green amidst the charred, blackened remains of bush.

We had a bushfire not too long ago in Sydney as I write this. The bushfire ravaged the local bushland near my route to work. Every day I smelled the acrid stench of the fire. Every day I saw the black and barren landscape.

And every day I looked for the first signs of green.

I knew the green was coming. I felt it. Everything in my body yearned for the new growth. And sure enough, sooner than expected, the green appeared, vivid against the charcoal backdrop. The re-birthing had begun.

One day as I was driving along this road, admiring the contrast of lush green against the black, I felt God whisper to my heart:

'Look at the re-growth.'

Instinctively I knew what he meant. He was not just talking about the visual landscape, which was indeed becoming a beautiful vista. He was pointing out that resurrection is always possible.

I needed to hear it that day.

New things are possible. Life after death is possible. When our lives are ravaged by grief, we need to know something new and good and beautiful can still grow. Rosemary's story tells of life after not having kids. Rosemary discovered new life is possible.

Jesus was resurrected after the most horrendous death imaginable. The Romans physically tore him apart. And he rose from the dead. He is living and undeniable proof that new things are possible, even when the worst thing in the world has happened. When we are in despair, he is standing near with holes in his hands and feet, saying:

> *'Trust me, we will get through this together.'*

'Beloved, I know. I know things look blacker than death. I know you cannot see a way forward right now. But do not fear. I have something new in store for you. It will come, as sure as the dawn, as sure as my love for you. Trust me, we will get through this together.'

Jesus walks with us in our troubles. I encourage you to let him near. In the silence of night, in the space where you hold your breath, let him quiet your mind and lay your fears to rest.

May new hope flicker in your heart like a candle flaring in the darkness, chasing the shadows away.

ROSEMARY'S STORY

Australia

Divorce was highly controversial in the seventies but Rosemary had no choice. After marrying young, she discovered several years into her marriage that her husband was homosexual. And he had contracted AIDS.

Rosemary separated at the age of twenty-five. They were divorced three years later. She had wanted children but the divorce put a full stop at the end of that chapter. Her desire for children was effectively shelved. She came to believe in her singledom and accepted children were never going to happen.

Then she met her second husband.

She was thirty-eight when she married her thirty-year-old husband, a teacher like herself. Her husband was keen to have children. But Rosemary believed it was too late for her. She had shut down her desire for children. However, they agreed to try.

They tried for six months without success. Rosemary did some research and discovered the chance of becoming naturally pregnant drops drastically after the age of thirty-five. She also discovered an increased risk of miscarriage, Down Syndrome and having twins after thirty-five. Plus, she had endometriosis which can cause infertility. So they began IVF.

Maybe it was the effect of the hormonal injections—Rosemary could not be sure—but upon starting IVF, her old maternal feelings began resurfacing. She could not stop trying IVF.

They had seven IVF attempts in four years.

Rosemary was on the maximum injection dose. While her eggs successfully fertilised, they never thrived. After seven attempts, there was still no baby.

Trying for four years took a toll on her. She cried and slept all the time. Her energy dwindled. She was upset by the arrival of every monthly period. She felt anxious and depressed and lost all her confidence.

Rosemary kept her faith in God through those years but drifted away from the church. She did not have the energy. She kept hold of hope, spurred on by every good news baby story she heard. Ultimately, this hope turned to desperation, like medicine turning to poison. She felt like a failure.

At the end of four years she thought, 'I can't do this anymore.' Rosemary and her husband accepted they would never have kids.

It was difficult to speak about her experience. She did not talk about it for another five years. She found respite from grief in going to new places and travelling overseas. As a teacher, she poured her parental instincts into her students, as did her husband, and into their friends' children.

Now in her sixties, Rosemary has bravely decided to return to church. She felt there was a hole in her life and hoped church would help her reconnect with her faith. It has.

Grief is still evident. She tears up when someone has a baby. Mother's Day is an annual challenge. Some things are OK, such as holding babies and talking to friends about their grandkids.

Her maternal instincts have now worn off, a silver lining of ageing. She has gradually returned to a place of contentment in her life. Her husband has been like a rock for her and she has lots of social support.

When meeting new people, Rosemary is upfront about not having kids. She feels a freedom to speak about it now. She has lots of resilience, gleaned from a difficult childhood of having a father who drank. She believes childlessness has further developed her resilience.

She is grateful for the blessings of childlessness, including travel, doing her own thing, being part of other families' lives and helping other infertile couples with wisdom from her own experience. In fact, she has seen other couples become pregnant through her advice. This has been incredibly rewarding.

I asked Rosemary how she turned things around. 'I did not want to waste years fretting about being a mum,' she told me. 'I knew the odds were against me to start with. I did not want this experience to define me.'

Yet her childlessness journey has partly shaped her too. 'My story has made me who I am today,' she acknowledged. 'I do not take anything for granted.'

Rosemary reflected on how life might have been. 'We have not had the joys of children, but we also have not had the heartache. Friends have teenagers going off the rails, and we did not have to deal with that. We feel relieved about it. We are just making the most of wherever we land.'

Rosemary gave advice for others with similar experiences.

'Do not try to conceive for four years if you are thirty-eight, like I did,' Rosemary cautioned. 'That is something I regret. If you want to have kids and you are under thirty-five, think about it now. And remember, there is life after not having kids.'

JOY'S STORY

Australia

Joy believes God uses our pain and trials to help others. This belief comes from personal experience.

She always wanted children. But when she married her husband at age thirty, he was undecided. He had chronic depression and thought he could not be a father. He eventually agreed to try for Joy's sake, knowing how strongly she desired children. But it was not that simple. They were unable to conceive naturally.

Testing revealed Joy's husband had a zero sperm count, an effect of mercury poisoning originating from teething gel used on him more than forty years ago. This type of poisoning (Pink's disease) can also cause depression and other health issues.

The doctor told them the facts straight out, without a trace of empathy or care: 'You will never be parents.' The news of infertility was beyond devastating. Joy's dreams came crashing down. She became depressed and at times suicidal. Fortunately, this was resolved with medication.

Despite the bad news, they were determined to become parents anyway. So they turned to IVF. It was a stressful time. IVF was physically, emotionally and financially demanding. And it wasn't working. They kept trying, round after round, driven by the desire to live without regrets.

Ironically, Joy's husband developed a desire for children during

IVF. His desire became stronger with each round. However, after eleven rounds and no children, they were both distraught.

They stopped because they were utterly exhausted.

They considered other options including adoption, but this was not viable. The adoption rules in NSW require the oldest adoptive parent to be no more than forty years older than the child. They were too old to adopt a baby. Adopting an older child from overseas was not feasible either.

They felt unable to share their experiences with anyone, including other Christians. They believed their church did not understand infertility and as a result Joy felt excluded and isolated. 'Everyone formed cliques around their kids, like school groups,' she recalled. 'I felt I was never really accepted by them.'

They decided to involve kids in their lives through hospitality. They invited nieces and friends with children over regularly and enjoyed getting to know them. 'It never made up for not having our own kids,' said Joy, 'but it was important for us to have children in our lives.'

She found comfort through writing poetry. She wanted her poems to connect with other childless people. She also uses poetry to tell parents what childlessness is like. She has put some of her poems into print, first published in Australia then later translated into Italian and published in Italy. Poetry, and sharing her poetry, has been an important part of healing, enabling her to move on after IVF.

Sadly, Joy's husband died a year before I met Joy. She shared about the healing work God had done in both of their lives before her husband's death and since.

Joy's husband was diagnosed with stage four bowel cancer and given two weeks to live. Friends came one day and prayed for healing and the next day Joy's husband started eating again. He got better and better each day.

In the three months leading up to her husband's death, Joy said her husband had never looked or been better. He was dying from bowel cancer, yet becoming well from the inside out. She said he became whole both spiritually and emotionally. God was restoring him.

Then the cancer returned and he was released from his pain to be with Jesus.

Since her husband's death, Joy has struggled to re-connect with people. But God has been at work, restoring some special friendships from her past.

As part of her healing, Joy undertook significant renovations on the house. This has been a beautiful gift of healing from God. Joy's face visibly lit up as she pointed out to me the highlights of the restored house.

I sat on Joy's couch as I listened, and I looked around her spacious new living room. My gaze was drawn through the expansive windows to nearby trees running along the National Park, hemmed in by a river. There was a distinct sense of quiet serenity about the place. It truly felt like a place of healing.

Joy sometimes struggles when people talk about kids. 'People tell me, "You are so lucky you don't have kids!"' she grimaced. 'I just smile and nod.'

The newest challenge is when similar-aged peers talk about their grandkids. Now in her sixties, Joy finds it hard to identify with this and it can be difficult when friends exchange grandchildren stories. No one is aware of how painful this can be. But most days this is OK. She has learned to rejoice with others and to show interest in their grandchildren, just as she oohed and aahed over her friends' children a generation ago.

There is still a sense of isolation in her life. Joy is now retired, as well as widowed and childless. There are days when she feels invisible. 'Mothers are hard-wired to focus totally on their children. Family and friends without children become invisible,' she said.

In some ways, she feels she is starting a new life, without work, a husband, children or grandchildren. Just a blank slate on which to carve a new identity.

Joy emphasised the importance of solidarity. 'Get with people who understand you,' she exhorted. She has put this into practise, rekindling old friendships. Her closest friends are two couples who are also childless.

She values her feelings and encourages other childless people to do the same. 'Find some way of expressing your feelings,' she suggested. 'Listen to how you are feeling. Take care of yourself.'

While many mothers find their identity in their children and grandchildren, Joy has learned (the hard way) to find her identity as a child of God. Her security, self-esteem and significance are in Jesus, not in other relationships. She encourages others to 'find some way of expressing who you are, and claim your identity in Christ'.

I was curious about one more thing. I asked Joy if she has seen God at work through her childlessness. Her face broke into a smile, and it was like the sun had risen in the room.

'Oh yes,' she murmured, her voice filled with quiet certainty. 'God has been present the whole time. He has used my pain and suffering and now I am able to help others, through hospitality in this house and through writing, mentoring and encouraging others. God has been in everything. Underneath all the pain in my life have been his everlasting arms.'

Joy gave me permission to use her poems. Below is an excerpt from this particularly moving poem, *Never to be a mother* (1995)[67].

Never to be a mother

The counsellor asked
'What would you miss out on
In life
If you were never a mother?'
Facing reality painfully
Yet honestly
Is good for the soul, she said

I thought long and hard
And time and again
Tears welled up
And dripped down my face
Wearing away the barriers of stone
I had built around my heart
To keep me from touching the pain
Of my childlessness
But there
Under the surface

JOY'S STORY

Feelings and thoughts
Writhed in turmoil
Shattered dreams
Exploding powerfully
Yet never understood
By every woman who is a mother.

10

AGEING

Do You Have Grandkids?

People assume I am past the age of having children.

This has both advantages and disadvantages. Hard as it is to endure the 'When are you going to have kids' questions, it can be even harder to face the silence of people not asking.

This is the problem with ageing. You finally work out your childlessness script for coping with questions about kids, and they stop harassing you. And then the questions begin again, this time about grandchildren.

'How many grandkids do you have?'

'Did you see the grandchildren over the weekend?'

'How're you doing, grandpa?'

Discussions about grandchildren can be difficult. The gushing, the photos, the constant in-jokes about 'giving them back' at the end of the visit.

These are the challenges of childlessness across the lifespan.

Ageing childlessly

Some find their parental instincts settle down over time, providing some relief from the grief of childlessness. Others find there is no diminishing of the heartache. Being asked about grandkids can open old wounds. Peers regaling you with tales of their grandchildren can be painful.

In Dr Robin Hadley's article, *I'm missing out and I think I have something to give* (2018)[68], he described how involuntarily childless older men feel like outsiders and believe they are missing out. Contrary to popular opinion, they do not 'get over it' with age. And distress levels in infertile people are high for both men and women.

This highlights how the impact of childlessness is significant and continues across the lifespan. People may assume you are 'over it' now because you are older. But the reverse is often true. If you find your childlessness grief persists over time, you are definitely not alone.

It is a grief without end.

Social situations

Just as society assumes most people have kids, it assumes older people have grandkids. This can be awkward when chatting with peers your age. Not to mention the embarrassment of being called 'granny' or 'pops' by some unsuspecting stranger and deciding whether to correct them.

It can be hard to listen to stories of other people's grandkids doing cute things and achieving developmental milestones. It can be impossible to contribute to those babysitting-the-grandkids conversations. It can be further isolating.

I once went to a funeral for an older man. His large family attended with children and grandchildren. His adult children eulogised about 'the importance of family at such a time'. The grieving widow also expressed her gratitude for being surrounded by children and grandchildren.

Funerals are prime time for legacy talk. Prized possessions are passed to the next generation. You often see family members physically clinging to each other for mutual support.

How do childless people survive funerals?

We all need support at funerals. That is normal. I would hope one's friends and church family would be present at such a time. I would hope one would not be left alone at a funeral just because one was childless.

But I must confess, the thought of being alone at funerals leaves me cold. I have done the solo funeral thing before as a single person. Not fun. The prospect of attending increasing numbers of funerals as I get older is vaguely worrying.

There is also the worry of increasing loneliness. It is a fact of life that we lose loved ones as we outlive them. The thought of being alone in a nursing home, let alone at my own funeral, is frankly horrifying.

Funerals raise the 'Who will look after you in your old age?' question. People have used this argument to challenge people who are childless. (Presumably it will force us into magically having kids.)

Society assumes childless people will have no one to look after them in their old age, conveniently forgetting many ageing parents have children who do not or cannot care for them.

There are other options for aged care beyond one's children. Spouses, friends and services can all participate. The burden of responsibility does not need to fall on children alone. Besides, having kids primarily for aged care safety-netting purposes might be considered selfish. (Way to turn the tables on the whole 'Childless people are selfish' myth.)

As we age, we inevitably think more about ageing care requirements and who will care for us. I have seen such fears expressed on social media. But kids are not necessarily a sure solution for aged care. Perhaps we could spread the word about other options for companionship later in life.

For social situations, it can help to have a script ready for those pesky questions about grandkids.

'Actually, we never had kids.'

'We have surrogate grandchildren in our church or neighbourhood or mentoring program.'

'Mind your own business.'

Hey, use whatever works for you.

Empty nest syndrome

Parents reportedly suffer from 'empty nest syndrome' when kids leave home. It is the sudden shock and relief of no longer being needed. But what if you never had a nest, let alone an empty one?

Entering mid- or late-life phases and watching peers suffer

with empty-nest agony can prompt What-If questions from us.

What if we had succeeded in having kids?

What if they were now adults?

What if we had been able to pass on our legacies to our kids?

What if our kids now had grandkids?

These questions can be lonelifying (yes, that is a real word), as can other people's complaints of empty nests. Loneliness heightens the childless grief, reminding us of other losses we have endured.

We will not pass on family heirlooms. We will not share games and songs from our childhood with kids of our own. Our favourite books and places will not be cherished as we have cherished them. The shock and sadness of such realisations is part of lifelong grieving. It keeps bringing fresh waves of grief washing over our souls.

And that is OK. It is perfectly reasonable to grieve as we discover lost legacies, no matter how little.

And it is OK to grieve things that are not OK, things we longed for and never had.

For women

Women experience one distinct change as they move through life: menopause.

For many women, this is a liberating experience, albeit a drawn-out one. Menopause can take ten years to resolve itself. Apparently. (I cannot offer personal opinion on this. I am yet to encounter this joyous life-stage myself. But I am looking forward to it. Says the satirical woman.)

Going through menopause may trigger a mixture of emotions for childless women. There may be frequent and uncontrollable mood swings, night sweats and jubilant farewelling of menstrual cycles. Not to mention the hot flushes.

Many women are going to get hotter as they get older.

There may be grief too, at the thought of leaving the child-rearing years definitively and permanently behind. There may be a sense of closure about hope being finally laid to rest.

> There is nothing wrong with stopping when you are finished.

A few interviewees said hope kept them on the path of trying to conceive, whereas reaching a certain age helped them to stop trying and let that hope go. Hope is good, but too much hope can keep one trapped on the trying-to-conceive merry-go-round, long after the process has taken its physical, emotional and financial toll.

Giving up can be healthy. There is nothing wrong with stopping when you are finished.

Menopause can be liberating. Instead of endless wishing and wondering, menopause gives women permission to finish one chapter and start a new one.

Silver linings

One silver lining of growing older is becoming more adept at responding to unwanted questions about kids. Practise makes perfect. The answers, 'No, we do not have kids' and 'We tried but it did not work' become more convincing and effortless. Also, you can add 'No, we are too old' to your repertoire. No one ever argues with that.

Another silver lining for some—not all—is parental instincts begin to fade, like they did for Rosemary. Whether this is an effect of the biological clock, hormonal changes later in life or channelling those instincts into other pursuits, I do not know. But some notice a definite decline in these instincts.

I cannot guarantee this will happen for everyone. But it is interesting to know the longing for children can decrease with time.

Giving back

Retirement makes new things possible. (I am looking forward to this stage of life. For real.)

While grandparents become world-class babysitters, those without children have other options. You might be looking forward to your retirement plans. You might want to travel or learn a new skill like baking or woodwork. You might like to dust off an old hobby.

I know an old lady (who swallowed a fly...) in her nineties who is learning to play a musical instrument for the first time. She has been wanting to learn since she was a child. Now she is. So do not pretend you are too old. Anything is possible.

Consider how you might give back to your community and invest in children and young people. Especially if that parenting instinct never wears off for you. There are children's mentoring and support services in Australia in which you could enlist. I dare say similar services exist in other countries. You could volunteer for a charity that supports children and families.

Think about the things you would have done if you had raised children and they had now left home. What would you be doing with your new-found freedom?

Finally, think about why you wanted to be a parent. Consider the things you wanted to pass on, the difference you wanted to make in a little person's life. You could still do those things.

There may yet be ways of passing on your legacy.

The God bit

When I think of Joy's story, I remember how God restored her. She is in her sixties, childless, bereaved, alone but not alone. She has encountered much loss, but God has begun something new. He has given her a beautifully renovated home, a healing place for her. She is blessing others with hospitality in her stunning house.

God has been present, not absent, in Joy's distress. I still remember the light in her eyes, her face lifted by a sudden smile, when I asked if she has seen God at work in her life. 'Oh yes,' she breathed, her grief clearing like a passing cloud. 'Yes, he has been here. In all the pain and loss, he has been present.'

God steps into the middle of our mess and loves us through it. He does not necessarily fix us with a snap of his fingers like a divine Mary Poppins, but gradually restores us, working elegantly in our hearts for years, pulling threads of our lives together behind the scenes, softening us with the balm of his love.

We may not see it at the time, but looking back, we can see his fingerprints all over our lives. He can restore what has been lost—houses, friendships, church families, beauty, hope and meaning. He can help us survive childlessness.

When I think of Joy, I think of her face lit up by light, her heart and home lovingly restored by God. It is a stunning reminder of God's kindness.

I thank God for it.

SECTION FOUR
SURVIVAL

11

FRIENDS AND FAMILY

What Not to Say

'You will not be single forever,' my friend said cheerily. 'God has someone for you.'

We were sitting at the back of our church, indulging in conversation over a warm cup of tea.

'Really?' I said, my tone betraying cynicism. 'How can you be so sure?'

'Because,' she said, 'You are a very desirable woman. Of course God has a husband for you.'

That was over ten years ago. My friend was right. I got married.

But I must confess I did not find her reassurance helpful at the time. I knew she was being sweet. I knew she loved me.

She understood my heartache about singledom and wanted to encourage me. But her reassurances came over like false hope.

How can you possibly know that, I wanted to scream? How on earth can you know how my life will turn out?

I have fallen into this maddening trap myself, dispensing false hope and empty promises to dear friends, hoping to save them from misery. We do not like to see our loved ones in pain. We want to support them, even rescue them. If they are hurt, we want to heal them. If there is a problem, we want to solve it. But in doing so, we often promise things we cannot deliver.

'You will get better soon. People have beaten cancer before.'

'I am sure you will get that job.'

'Where there's a will, there's a way.'

'God will not deny you your heart's desire.'

'God will give you a spouse.'

'God will give you a child.'

Except we do not know the outcome. We do not know if or when the desired thing will happen. We do not know anything for sure. Unless we believe we are speaking prophetically—and prophecy should be given and received with care and wisdom—we are giving false hope.

We often feel helpless and powerless when faced with our loved ones' suffering. We need to own that. We need to accept our vulnerability. We can get better at saying, 'I don't know.' We can acknowledge our limitations. We can sit with loved ones in the silence and ambivalence of not-knowing. We can leave some problems unsolved, some questions unresolved. We do not have to fix them.

Even if we desperately want to.

False hope

My kind friend above was offering me false hope.

I am certain she had good intentions. But I am not certain it helped. My friend did not know what God had in store. Rather than saying, 'Steph, I have no idea,' she made promises on God's behalf. And I did not want her to do that. At that moment, I just needed a friend.

Many childless people have believed false hope. They were told it will happen eventually or probably when they least expect it (as though that is supposed to help). They were encouraged to keep trying. Especially by doctors and IVF clinics.

Encouraging a childless person at the start of the process can be good, especially when they are excited and hopeful about it. Telling a childless person to stay hopeful when they have clearly tried everything and are weary from the journey is not helpful.

False hope feels good at the time. It feels good to be encouraged. It feels good to give encouragement. I love encouraging others. I love it when people encourage me. All the warm fuzzies.

But if we are not careful, we can fall into the trap of encouraging the wrong thing. We can promote unhelpful hope. Hope unfulfilled can turn into despair. And childless people do not need that.

What is more helpful is to join with the childless person in their grief. Share their lament. Let them know you feel sad too. That willingness to join them in mourning can be more encouraging than any words spoken in encouragement.

Miracle baby stories are another kind of false hope.

Miracle baby stories

'My friend had a baby through IVF, you should do it.'

'Keep trying—my boss got pregnant after eight years of trying.'

'If [insert celebrity's name] had a baby in her forties, you can too!'

I did an internet search for celebrities who had babies in their forties. Heaps of results came up. There are entire websites dedicated to this topic. There are celebrities who had children into their fifties and beyond.

It seems incredible. And perhaps this is why we lap it up. The sensation of a miracle baby story is so enticing, so irresistible, we grab the slim thread of hope it offers. Even when it is false hope.

Unfortunately, for most childless people, the miracle baby story does not have its intended effect. The intended message of the story is, 'It can happen to you too, so keep the faith.' But—and this is important—this is not the message the childless person hears. What they frequently hear, wrapped up in the shiny paper of the story, is, 'It hasn't happened for me because there is something wrong with me.'

While you are storytelling, they are unfavourably comparing themselves with the successful protagonist of your story. While everyone else is having babies, the childless person is questioning their normalcy. Telling them about normal people having normal babies only rubs salt into the proverbial wound.

Want my recommendation? If you come across a juicy story of a miracle baby, do not share it with a childless person.

Resist the temptation.

'Guess who's pregnant?'

Pregnancy announcements are one of the most difficult things for a childless person to hear.

If you are not already aware of this, take my word for it. Your loved one probably finds it hard to hear someone is pregnant. It doesn't matter who it is. It just hurts.

This is not because they are uncaring or selfish. (At least, I hope not.) It is simply because anything to do with pregnancy or children can trigger the invisible grief they carry.

For some, this grief translates to jealousy of pregnant people. They probably do not hate them. They just want what pregnant people have.

Some are genuinely happy for their friends when a pregnancy announcement comes. They celebrate with them, true to Romans 12:15: 'Rejoice with those who rejoice; mourn with those who mourn'. But others are so overcome by their own grief they find this impossible.

In which case, the right response from you is not 'Get over it', 'Pull yourself together' or 'Can't you be happy for them?' No, they can't. They are in mourning. The more appropriate response is for you to 'mourn with those who mourn'.

If you must share a pregnancy announcement with your childless friend or family member, give them some advance warning. Let them know you have some news and ask if this is a good time. (Maybe mention no one has died.) Do it sensitively and respectfully.

And definitely tell them before you announce it to the whole world. Otherwise they might feel ambushed on social media.

Even if you approach it superbly, it may still be difficult for them. They may not take it well. They may need time.

If you have children

If you are a parent, I urge you to do everything in your power to keep your childless friends and loved ones in your life.

Childless people often lose friends and connections. Childlessness creates distance and difference in friendships which is sometimes insurmountable. This is part of the loss of childlessness.

Many childless people find their friendships with parent-friends become strained. Gatherings of girlfriends morph into playdates and mother's groups. And men often feel left out of social gatherings when the conversation turns to fathering.

If you witness this firsthand, you can help. You can tactfully steer the conversation back to something more inclusive.

Make the effort to see your childless friend, even if it means a lot of work getting your kids ready or having the place tidy. Invite your friend over for a meal or coffee, just like you would do with another parent. Even if your childless friend says no, I bet they will appreciate the invite.

You may worry your childless friend will not want to be around your kids. You may want to protect them from being upset. That is very thoughtful. Thank you for thinking of them. But it may not be necessary. Most childless people enjoy being around kids, especially kids they know.

I love catching up with my parent-friends and that includes catching up with their kids. I like talking to my friends' kids, playing with them, hearing about their lives. It is a privilege to share their world.

Many childless people absolutely dote on their nieces, nephews, godchildren, next-door children and children of friends. They want to be involved in your family.

This connection with children can help heal their own childlessness grief. It can give them a sense of making a difference in a child's life, even if it is not their own.

I encourage you to involve your childless friend in your family. But... make sure you do not spend the whole time talking about kid-related stuff. Talk about adult things too, like shopping, work, movies, books, projects, life aspirations, travel—the stuff you miss as a parent.

If in doubt, ask them. Tell them you want to share the latest kid-story but do not want to upset them. This gives them a chance to steer the conversation. Watch their body language. If they respond with enthusiasm about your kids, that is your green light to carry on.

And if they change the subject, take it as a sign.

Advice-giving

Childless people receive a surprising amount of advice. They are bestowed with facts, options, herbal remedies and old wives' tales that 'worked for my friend.'

Most childless people have considered every one of them.

Childless people are not ignorant. They have access to the internet. They have thought of everything: adoption, surrogacy, egg-freezing, IVF, aphrodisiacs, prayer and 'just taking it easy.' What they do not need is some helpful fairy godmother-type hovering over their shoulder, gushing, 'Have you tried...?'

So do not suggest they try adoption (unless you mean furbaby adoption. Because furbabies are awesome.) or any other instant solution. Unless they specifically request advice, refrain from giving it. Giving advice is often more about our own needs than those of a loved one. We prefer feeling helpful over feeling powerless. We want to share our knowledge. I understand this.

But.

They have already received advice from other friends and family, peers, doctors, pastors and even strangers. I guarantee it. So instead of leaping in, ask them what would be helpful. They may not have an answer but they may be able to tell you what they do not want.

Every rule has an exception. So if you discover your friend or loved one is doing something blatantly wrong, it is acceptable to step in. For example, I read about a couple who tried to conceive for four years without success. They went to their doctor who solved the mystery. Turns out it was a sex problem. They were, um, using the wrong *ahem* entrance. For four years.

As I live and breathe.

If a childless couple tell you they are having trouble falling pregnant for this kind of reason, please set them straight. Please.

Platitudes

Platitudes are well-meaning encouragements that come off sounding hollow.

'Count your blessings.'

'It will happen.'

'You still have time.'

'Just relax.'

'God is in control.'

'God is on the throne.'

Platitudes are hard to argue against because they sound true. Especially religious-sounding ones.

Take the 'Count your blessings' platitude. We absolutely should count our blessings. But telling someone to count their blessings in the midst of grief and turmoil is like telling a crazy feral cat to take a chill pill. It will not end well.

The unintended message of the platitude is: 'Your horrible situation is fine and you should be grateful for your suffering and loss.' It's like placing a band-aid over an amputated limb. It won't work.

So now what?

Real empathy

Brené Brown has a cartoon YouTube video about real empathy (2013)[69]. She says comments that start with 'At least...' are not truly empathic.

'At least you have a partner.'

'At least you have your health.'

'At least you are still alive.'

Unhelpful.

Brené says real empathy is about connection. Giving answers, advice, miracle baby stories and 'solutions' does not give us good connection with our loved one. Dispensing so-called solutions like pills causes us to disconnect from the other person. We lose sight of their pain. In order to truly empathise, we have to join with their pain, feel it, connect with it.

And that is hard.

True empathy is a position of vulnerability. We are saying, 'What you feel right now is more important than my safety, pride, joy or any other emotion I would rather feel.'

Vulnerability is open and willing. It is prepared to feel what the other person is feeling, for better or worse. It fosters true connection. It proves we are listening and not judging. It shows our willingness to mourn with them. It demonstrates our trustworthiness as confidantes.

You might fancy yourself a good listener. But if the other person is shutting down from you, pulling back or repeating themselves, it could be a sign something is missing from your listening. You might be saying unhelpful things.

Here are some truly empathic responses to childless people:

'I am really sorry to hear that.'

'I am glad you told me.'

'I don't know the answer.'

'I am here for you.'

'I am listening.'

'Is there anything you need right now?'

'I have no idea what that is like.'

'It is OK to feel that way.'

'I wish I could fix this.'

'I can only imagine what you're going through.'

'I feel so sad about that.'

'I still love you.'

Empathise in the same way you would like to be shown empathy. Listen. Really listen. Sit with those uncomfortable, vulnerable feelings.

Show them you can do it.

Do not fix it

You cannot fix another person's problems. (Unless you are the problem. In which case, knock yourself out.)

If you are anything like me, you understand the agony of doing nothing. But our best intentions are not always helpful. Sometimes the best thing is to leave it alone.

Not the person. The problem.

Let the problem sit there awhile. In the meantime, be with the person. Think of the last time you felt really stuck. How did it feel? Get familiar with that feeling. Get to know how it feels to be in a bad place without a way out. Get in touch with your own helplessness. Then you might understand them.

Even if you do not totally understand. Even if you have not experienced childlessness yourself. Even if you are unacquainted with grief. You do not need to have an identical experience in order to empathise.

Some childlessness problems cannot be fixed. Your loved one may have unexplained infertility, meaning the doctors have done everything they can. There is certainly nothing you can do to fix that.

Some childless people may be considering medical treatment or IVF or another alternative. They may be undecided about which option is best for them. You cannot fix this indecision. You certainly cannot make that decision for them. It might take months or even years to make such a complex decision.

Some are past all options. They have had enough; they are too old; they are ineligible; they have made their final decision. It is over. You cannot fix that. They may be grieving and you cannot fix that.

It is OK to acknowledge this. Admitting your own vulnerability can start a dialogue. Tell your childless friend or family member how you feel about their loss. Tell them about the helplessness you feel. You are probably feeling the frustration and powerlessness they feel every day.

It could open up doors between you. It could be worth it.

Do not ignore it

Childlessness can be taboo.

Many friends and family feel uncertain about raising the issue of childlessness. They do not know what to say and are worried about unwittingly saying the wrong thing. They do not want to upset the childless person.

So they say nothing at all.

Childless people already feel on the outer. They feel excluded by nature of their childlessness. They often wind up at family-friendly events or gatherings that isolate them further. If you stay silent, they might feel ignored.

Their problem is real. There is nothing to be gained by pretending it does not exist—except perhaps your own sense of relief. Rather than pretending it has gone or minimising their feelings, talk to them.

There is nothing wrong with a little honesty here. You could start with something tentative like, 'I want to know if you are OK but I am unsure about asking you... Do you want to talk about it? Or shall I shut up?'

People usually appreciate such respectful probing. And they will tell you if it is too painful to bring up. They will also tell you if they have been desperate to discuss it. Before you know it, conversation is flowing.

Go softly. Let them know you are happy to talk but equally happy not to talk. Tell them you are available while not pushing them. They will get the idea.

Saltwater and honey (Lowrie 2013)[70] talks about supporting your childless loved one. They recommend not only empathising but going so far as to advocate for them. Back them up in public. Help steer the conversation away from children. Challenge insensitive or clichéd responses to your loved one's childlessness.

Your loved one will know you have their back.

Special occasions

Every childless person feels differently about baby events.

Some want to be included in everything: baby showers, niece and nephew birthday celebrations and so on.

Others do not.

There is no single right answer for how to approach your loved childless one with an announcement or special occasion invite. But here are my suggestions.

Include them in invitations to family events, special occasions and celebrations. And be understanding when they say no. Their decision is one of self-care. Try not to exclude them, even if you feel frustrated with them. Let them know you understand. Even if you do not. Tell them you want to see them because you love them, however, you respect their choice.

They will appreciate your support. And they might feel a little less guilty about saying no. (Hint: do not accuse them of being selfish if they decline an invitation.)

One alternative, as discussed in Chapter 2, is to celebrate special occasions like Christmas on other days. Try negotiating a compromise. It could be worth it.

Grief can be frustrating. It is highly unpredictable. I get that. Maybe you want to stop inviting them because they always say no. I get that too. But please keep asking them. Keep the relationship alive, even if they do not come to your events. Childlessness has already taken a lot from them. It has taken the prospect of having their own family. It might have separated them from other friends or social circles. Try not to let it separate them from you as well.

When they are ready, they will say yes again.

The biblical perspective

The bible does not specifically tell us how to deal with childless loved ones. What it does offer, however, is guiding principles for loving one another. This one is a goodie:

> Love must be sincere. Hate what is evil; cling to what is good. Be devoted to one another in love. Honour one another above yourselves. Never be lacking in zeal, but keep your spiritual fervour, serving the Lord. Be joyful in hope, patient in affliction, faithful in prayer. Share with the Lord's people who are in need. Practice hospitality. Bless those who persecute you; bless and do not curse. Rejoice with those who rejoice; mourn with those who mourn.

> Live in harmony with one another. Do not be
> proud, but be willing to associate with people
> of low position. Do not be conceited. Do not
> repay anyone evil for evil. Be careful to do what
> is right in the eyes of everyone. If it is possible,
> as far as it depends on you, live at peace with
> everyone (Romans 12:9-18).

I like verse 18: 'As far as it depends on you, live at peace with everyone'.

Sometimes it is hard to live in peace with others. Authentic, messy, loving relationships require patience and tolerance. But they are important. And worthwhile.

God is deeply concerned about our relationships with others. He wants us to live in harmony with one another. Our responsibility is to live in peace as far as it depends on us. This means doing what we can. Not forcing others. And recognising our limitations.

One parent-friend of mine, whom I love dearly, recently asked me if she had ever done anything to hurt me as a childless person. My answer was an honest no. But I told her how much it meant to me to be asked. That's how you do it, folks. Check-in with your childless loved ones. And keep it real.

Childlessness can test even the strongest friendships. With courage, honesty, a dash of vulnerability and a whole lot of grace, we can keep those relationships intact.

Pray for your childless loved one. Ask God to heal them inside and out. God is just as concerned with their emotional and spiritual healing as with their physical wholeness. Ask God to comfort and care for them. He loves them just as much as you do.

It might take time for your childless friend or family member to be OK with kids or child-centric celebrations. Or they might never be OK. This might affect them for the rest of their lives. You may never truly understand their experience. But you do not need to.

Be available to them. Be supportive and listen when they need to talk. This may not sound like much. But it is probably the most helpful thing you can offer.

Many childless people find it helpful to have friends around them who understand—even if they do not understand—and who stick by them no matter what. Fiona's story emphasises how important it is to talk about childlessness. Fiona is passionate about raising childlessness awareness in her circles. So if your childless friend needs to talk, let them.

Christian interviewees told me they needed their Christian friends more than ever when they were struggling. They needed to lean on them and 'borrow' their faith.

Your presence and constancy matters. Your willingness to pray on their behalf can make a huge difference. Do not lose heart.

You do not always need to fix things or say the right words. You do not always need to say anything. Your company, even the silence of your heartfelt empathy and wordless prayer, can be the best response of all.

FIONA'S STORY
New Zealand

Fiona is childless-by-accident.

She always wanted kids and grandkids. It was a deep need and yearning, a vital part of who she was. It was her reason for being on this planet, her reason for being alive. It was non-negotiable.

Fiona dated one particular guy who was not keen on having kids because he already had two sons from a previous relationship. But she wanted to have kids with him. She ended up marrying the guy.

Her dream of parenthood looked bleak, but she held on to a little bit of hope.

They tried briefly to have kids but it did not happen naturally. Fiona then trained for foster caring. She completed the training, however, she was not approved as a foster carer. She was turned down because of her husband's extensive criminal record. Apparently, having over one hundred criminal convictions (no exaggeration) disqualifies you and your partner as foster carers.

That hit home. The realisation she would not have children, even foster children, was painful. Recovery was difficult and, to make matters worse, her depression flared up.

The turning point came in 2014 when a major earthquake hit New Zealand. It was a wake-up call. Fiona said, 'I can either give in to the pain, or find a way of living with this.' She was determined to not let the pain of childlessness destroy her.

She returned to previous passions, things she was enthusiastic about before grief took over. She remembered an old idea for a novel. She began to write and found she expressed herself better in writing. She is still working on her novel. It is a story about mothers, childlessness and vampires. She feels sheer pleasure in creating something unique. Her writing has been healing.

Funny how one idea leads to another.

While enjoying the freedom and healing power of writing, she had an epiphany: 'Could this work for other people?' She had previously worked in mental health and knew consumers benefitted from writing their experiences.

She wondered if this principle could be applied to childless women.

Spurred on by this idea, Fiona started an online program to encourage other childless women to find and pursue their passion. She wanted to help women find something to live for, as she had. Through this program, she encourages women to take the love they would have poured into their children and channel it into something else, something about which they are passionate.

'It did not make sense to me that I could not be a mother,' she reflected. 'We are all here for a purpose and some of us are fortunate to find out what that is. I thought my purpose was to be a mother. Now I know it is to help other women deal with childlessness.'

Fiona still has rough days. 'I will never be happy with childlessness,' she says candidly. 'But I have turned it into something worthwhile. This program for women gets me out of bed in the morning. It is a reason for living.'

She has a furbaby, and while this is not as good as having a child, she finds this special attachment is helpful.

It is hard to talk about, especially with her family who do not understand. Fiona thinks society in general has a hard time understanding childless people.

'We have to get comfortable talking about childlessness to help the world understand it better,' she enthused. 'Society makes us feel inferior. But parents are not questioned; why do we get questioned about childlessness?'

She believes many parents have children out of fear. They fear having no one to care for them when they are older. They fear dying alone. They fear being unable to pass on a legacy to their children.

Fiona questions this fear-based motivation, especially when having kids is no guarantee they will look after you. She knows some kids move away or refuse to help their ageing parents or even take advantage of them. This motivates her to get the message out that not everyone has children—and that is OK.

One of the hardest things is dealing with the assumptions of others. 'I was shopping for a present for a friend's child,' she recalls, 'and the sales assistant asked if I was shopping for my grandchildren. I felt bad all week after that.'

She encourages childless people not to feel guilty about being childless or about grieving. 'We are in such a hurry to move on from grief,' Fiona reflected. 'Do not try to get rid of it.'

She feels guilty for not giving her mother the gift of grandchildren, but she is working through it. She encourages others to do the same. 'Don't be so hard on yourself. Stop blaming yourself for all that has or has not happened.'

Fiona's coaching program and blog is at *www.countessdrusillasteele.com.*

MELANIE'S STORY

UK

Melanie's story is about accepting the unexpected.

She grew up wanting two kids, first a boy, then a girl. She took it for granted this would happen. There was no reason to doubt it.

When she was twenty-eight, Melanie raised the subject of children with her boyfriend. They agreed to start trying and Melanie came off the pill. They waited for it to happen.

But nothing did.

Melanie was not too concerned at first. Her mum reassured her that women have kids in their forties so she had nothing to worry about. And she was not worried. But when Melanie hit thirty-eight, ten years after first raising the topic of children, the questions about having kids became bothersome.

Then she skipped a period. The pregnancy test came back negative. When her period still did not arrive, she saw her doctor. That was when she was given the bad news. Melanie was not pregnant. She was pre-menopausal.

At thirty-eight.

Depression hit hard. The next few years were a blur. She broke up with her boyfriend and had her fallopian tubes removed. Then she found out she had a slim chance of having a child through IVF. Melanie contacted a friend who agreed to be a sperm donor. Melanie was excited at the prospect of finally having a baby. She was now forty.

She arranged an appointment with the fertility clinic. The morning of the appointment, Melanie felt a niggle in the back of her mind. She rang the clinic to confirm she was not too old for IVF.

The news came back: Melanie was indeed too old.

She was devastated. 'I gave up,' she said. 'I pushed down the feelings, the grief for something I would never have. It was hard. I felt like a failure, as a woman and a daughter.'

Menopause kicked in. Melanie had sweats, negative thoughts and mood swings. At her lowest point, she wanted to go to sleep and never wake up again.

Then something changed. She is not quite sure how, but she realised it was up to her to save herself. She enrolled in an Art of Living course, recommended by a friend. She learned about the power of meditation, mindfulness and being happy in the moment. Her mood started to lift. She felt alive again.

At this course, Melanie was introduced to the Emotional Freedom Technique (EFT), a method of freeing oneself from negative beliefs and becoming all one can be. She took a course in EFT.

It was quite an experience. She was so inspired by the trainer that she decided this was what she would do with her life: help other women believe in themselves and be free of their limitations. Melanie formally trained as an EFT practitioner.

Around this time, she had a full hysterectomy because of cancerous cells. She felt fine until a close friend became pregnant. To her surprise and horror, the old emotions came rushing to the surface. She hated herself for how she was feeling.

MELANIE'S STORY

Melanie reached out for support. She discovered the *Dovecote community* (2017)[71] and found another EFT practitioner there who encouraged her. Melanie now practises EFT and helps other women. She studied hypnotherapy and Indian head massage and integrates these into her EFT work.

She feels grateful for her struggles. 'Without them, I never would have found my strengths,' she says. She also loves her close friend's baby. 'I do not blame anyone. Blame is just giving away your personal power. I feel I have really accepted what happened to me.'

She hopes her story will inspire other women. 'There really is life without kids,' she says.

Melanie can be contacted through her website *www.melaniedrage.co.uk* or facebook at Melanie Drage Tapping into Change.

12

SANITY

A Survival Smorgasbord

There was one question I asked all my interviewees:

'How did you survive childlessness?'

People came up with touching and creative answers to my simple question. This chapter is about their answers. I present them to you as a smorgasbord of survival strategies. That way you can take the bits you like and leave the rest.

The answers pertaining to faith I have not included here, because faith gets its own chapter.

Humour

A priest, a rabbi and a childless person walked into a bar...

Sorry.

Seriously though, childlessness gives us opportunities to appreciate the funny side of life. Or just to laugh at ourselves. Everything from raunchy descriptions of IVF (because doing it into a cup is super-sexy) to sarcastic replies on kids and adoption is fuel for enjoyment.

I have a certain penchant for satire and sarcasm, so I have devised some decidedly tongue-in-cheek responses to the oft-asked, 'Why don't you have kids?':

- Because my husband and I are siblings.
- Because I am an alien.
- Well, I would, but there is so much paperwork...
- I think that's my phone.
- Sit down and I will tell you the gory details. It comes with a slideshow.
- Because I want to have a roomful of strangers staring fixedly at my vagina. It's every little girl's dream.
- Have you heard today's pop music? I just could not bring a child into that kind of world...
- I have a pet cat instead. Here, let me show you hundreds of cat photos.
- It's because my ovaries don't work properly. How about you? How are your genitals functioning?
- Sorry, I didn't realise my uterus was a matter of public concern.
- Let's make a deal. I will tell you about my reproductive organs if I can ask about your sex life.

If you think of more, drop me a line. I am always open to new survival strategies. Show me what you got.

Childless people often receive inappropriate responses to their childless stories. To even out the playing field, I present a few choice comebacks of my own:

> You don't have kids? Here, take mine!

>> OK then. *Laughs* No, really, OK then.

> You will have them when you are ready.

>> Um, I've been ready for the past twenty years.

> You are running out of time.

>> Thank goodness there are people like you to remind me of my age.

> You have plenty of time.

>> I may not have told you my true age.

> Children are not that big a deal.

>> Would you be happy to live without yours?

> You can always adopt.

>> We can't, actually, because of any of several hundred reasons why people get turned down for adoption.

> Have you considered IVF?

>> No, I never thought of that, because I have been living in a cave for the last century.

SANITY

> You should enjoy this free time while you have it.

>> Yes, I enjoy having more time to feel sad and lonely.

> A friend of mine had a kid through IVF.

>> Cool. So we're stealing her baby this Friday?

> I wish I could go to the toilet without being hounded.

>> Did I mention I have a cat?

> Just relax and let it happen.

>> Honey, if I was any more relaxed, I'd be in a coma.

> You can always freeze your eggs.

>> Awesome. With a fourteen percent success rate.

> Why don't you just adopt?

>> I did. Her name is Portia. She likes tuna, sleeping in the sun and meowing at Sam.

> You are so lucky, you get to sleep in.

>> Did I mention I have a cat?

> You have got to let it go.

>> Let what go? My car insurance? My stamp collection? My sanity?

> You're not too old. Celebrities have babies in their fifties.

> Have you tried praying?

> Yeah, they can get their babies and dentures simultaneously.

> No, I have not. I have been a Christian my whole life, but praying never occurred to me. (That was sarcasm, for people playing at home.)

And my all-time favourite:

> Who is going to look after you when you are old?

> *Pretending to ponder* How about Aged Care Services?

Please do share yours.

Humour shows others how ridiculous their responses are. And it brings relief to our weariness. It gives us an alternative to our usual auto-reply of, 'No, I don't have kids, how about you?' or the slightly less subtle, 'Get lost.' Humour is an opportunity to be creative. Or just downright weird.

Making fun of others, and ourselves, can be sanity-saving.

Too soon for jokes? The next buffet option might be more your taste.

Gratitude

In her story, Maddy wrote thank-you notes to others. It was a practise of gratitude. The purpose of her notes was not to cure her grief but shift her perspective. She wanted to know how it felt to nurture contentment rather than grief.

Not a bad idea.

Although many of us did not choose childlessness, we still get choices. Our moods and thoughts are choices. Gratitude is a choice.

For some, the possibility of contentment without children will be a revelation. But it is true. Good things exist in our lives, regardless of whether we have children or not.

It can be hard to appreciate those things when we are stressed out or struggling under the weight of grief. Even on a good day, we tend to lose sight of everyday good things. We take them for granted, becoming desensitised to them by virtue of their constancy. We no longer see what is right in front of us.

Practising gratitude can breathe new life into those good things again.

Take air, for instance. We take air for granted. We breathe on autopilot. My guess is you have been breathing while you have been reading this book, but I would hazard a guess that you have not been aware of it.

If you focused on your breathing for the next minute—not adjusting it but simply noticing it—what would you notice about it?

You might notice the air moving through your nose or mouth. You might spot a certain smell or taste in the air. You might feel the warmth or coolness of the air temperature. You might become aware of the way your body moves in response to the air, the way the lungs and diaphragm and shoulders expand and contract, the way your muscles work in tandem in this simple action of breathing.

Bet you can't stop thinking about breathing now.

(By the way, noticing our breathing is also a mindfulness technique. It is called mindful breathing. It can help with depression, anxiety, sleep problems and grief.)

Noticing our breathing is a simple way to shift in our focus. In the same way, we can shift our mentality to gratitude. Focusing on gratitude can change our perspective. Worries and concerns may move to the background. They may not go away completely, but even temporary respite may bring relief.

Making worries disappear is not the goal of gratitude. The goal is to experience thankfulness. Being thankful is not just a Christian thing. Research giants such as Brené Brown have shown gratitude to be the biggest single factor in our levels of joy (2012)[72].

> *The goal is to experience thankfulness.*

All this gratitude talk makes me want to practise it right now. I have a lot for which I am thankful. I have an amazing husband and a beautiful rescue cat. I have a rewarding job which is, blessedly, part-time. I have the capacity to write in my free time. I have resources to compose and share the music I write.

I have seen poverty overseas and in my backyard. I know firsthand how hard it can be to scratch out a living. I am glad to have enough money to buy food whenever I need it. I am profoundly grateful for small, everyday things: a reliable car that gets me to work; food in the fridge; sleeping through the night.

The more I write this, the more blessings occur to me. I have close friendships that have gone the distance. I have a supportive family. I can access doctors and medications whenever I need them. I have supermarkets, petrol stations, dentists, in fact, an abundance of essential resources at my fingertips.

Plus an iPad (mandatory for writing).

My life is absolutely filled to the brim with blessings.

Your turn.

Silver linings

Silver linings are blessings that come because of and in spite of hardship. They are mixed blessings, bittersweetness or a double-edged sword.

Many hardships are graced by a silver lining. No, silver linings are not compensation for our suffering. They do not justify the hardship we have endured. They do not make up for what we have lost. They are opportunities to shift our perspective. They can ease the pain of loss.

It is hard to find a silver lining for childlessness. But doable.

In my own situation, I am grateful I never got to that super-desperate stage for kids, because in the end, my health prevented my having children. The choice was taken away from me. I grieve that loss, but the grief would have been more profound had I tried for children and failed.

My bad health gave me an acceptance of my unique situation and saved me from a lifetime of heartache. I never thought I would thank God for lupus. But perhaps the illness is a gift from him, easing the pain of CBFC.

Odd, isn't it?

I am not the only one who is embracing their silver linings.

Joy uses her beautiful house and spare energy to provide hospitality. She regularly invites friends and children to her house to bless them.

Maddy is mentoring children as a Pyjama Angel.

John and Rachel have travelled and enjoyed other opportunities they would not have had if they had raised children.

Philippa shares her knowledge of IVF with others who need it.

Rosemary sees her friends' teenage kids going off the rails and is grateful she did not have to endure that heartache. She uses her infertility experience to advise others trying to fall pregnant.

Here's a shift in perspective: we often over-emphasise the positives of parenthood. Yes, we know parenting requires long hours and sleepless nights. But we also romanticise the positive aspects.

Each person's journey, whether it includes kids or not, involves heartache. If we had borne children, there would no doubt still be heartache in our lives in some other form.

This is not a 'count your blessings' sermon. I can't stand those. It is about how our misery can he thrown into sharp relief when we hear stories of unromantic parenting. It can remind us of the loss some parents endure. And it can, surprisingly, show us what we have as childless people.

That is a silver lining.

One frequent silver lining of suffering is the resilience it produces in us. Carmel found this out at the tender age of nine. She was diagnosed with diabetes and, just to show up her doctors, she went abseiling the following week. That is resilience—and it came in handy when Carmel faced her childnessness.

Personally, being childless has given me the opportunity to write. Yes, I appreciate the irony of childlessness giving me time to write about childlessness. But it is truly rewarding. I get to encourage other childless people. That is my silver lining.

Finding a silver lining does not necessarily fill the void or heal the enduring sadness. But it might give us a shift in perspective, like a breath of fresh air. We might find something for which we are grateful, even in the midst of pain and loss.

And that might keep us holding on.

The troublesome Shoulds

Speaking of shifting perspective, we can start challenging the Shoulds.

But what exactly are the Shoulds?

I'm so glad you asked.

The Shoulds are our personal invisible tyrants. They are the voices living in our minds and the words of others, telling us what we Should be doing—and who we Should be.

- I Should be more confident.
- I Should not feel this way.
- I Should not fail.
- I Should work harder.
- I Should do more.
- I Should feel happy.
- I Should be able to figure this out on my own.
- I Should be over this by now.

The Shoulds put unrealistic pressure on us that we were never meant to bear. It is like living with your own personal mind-bully.

The Shoulds are never satisfied. They never congratulate us for what we have accomplished. They never acknowledge our progress or limitations. They just pile on pressure to do more.

This means no matter what you do, you could always be doing more. Effectively, the Shoulds are always right. We can never win that war. Many childless people have told themselves they Should be different, their lives Should look different.

Other people give us Shoulds too. Thanks a lot.

'You Should have kids.'

'You Should relax and let it happen.'

'You Should try this magical remedy that worked for my now-pregnant friend.'

Enough already.

We put plenty of pressure on ourselves where childlessness is concerned without needing additional pressure from others or the Shoulds.

If the concept of the Shoulds resonates with you, try kicking your personal Shoulds to the kerb. Replace your Shoulds with self-talk that begins with 'I choose' or 'I will'.

- I choose to stop comparing my life with those of parents.
- I will do my best, because that is all I can do.
- I will look after myself.
- I choose to avoid child-centred events that upset me.
- I will not hide my grief.
- I choose to find life after childlessness.
- I will hold on to gratitude.

Notice the difference this makes. See if it lifts the weight from your shoulders. It might give you some breathing space. It might even help you to hold on to your sanity.

And sanity is always a plus.

Shame Resilience Theory

Developed by Brené Brown (2013)[73], *Shame Resilience Theory* is a response to the shame that silences and disempowers us. If resilience is the ability to bounce back after a rough trot, shame resilience helps us bounce back after a shame attack. It is the part of us, after insults have been hurled in our direction, that says, 'Well, I'm not going to take it personally. They don't know the real me.'

Shame resilience can help with childlessness. It can help when people ask why we have not adopted. It can come in handy when IVF does not work. It might be helpful when we are grieving what we have lost.

> One way we build resilience is by reminding ourselves who we are; our strengths, not our weaknesses; our progress, not our failures.

Resilience can be strengthened over time, like a muscle. We can practise resilience. We can build on the resilience we already have, like adding a second floor to our house. One way we build resilience is by reminding ourselves who we are; our strengths, not our weaknesses; our progress, not our failures.

We tend to focus on our mistakes: the glass is half empty. Imagine if we tried the opposite. Most of us are terrible at self-praise. I dare you to give yourself one piece of praise today.

Brené suggests we build shame resilience by telling our stories.

She says shame survives in silence, therefore it cannot survive if we speak about it. Talking about shame seems to take the power out of it.

I like that idea a lot. Because our stories matter. They are worth telling.

Try sharing your story with others, especially trustworthy people. And our stories are not just of benefit to others. The act of storytelling can be healing for us. It can chase the shame away.

Let's get talking.

Re-discovering dreams

Before childlessness hit, most of us had things we wanted out of life apart from children.

There were things we hoped to do after our children had grown up. There were goals we wanted to achieve, outside of parenthood, before we died. Those goals still matter.

What are those goals for you? What are your old dreams, things you always wanted to do with your life, apart from having children? Children were probably not your only dream. But perhaps, for a while, they were your biggest dream. Perhaps it eclipsed those other dreams. Perhaps it is time to bring those dreams out of the shadows.

It could be time to re-discover the person you always wanted to be. It might be time to figure out what that picture looks like without children in the frame. It might include old hobbies or interests that have fallen by the wayside.

Marie had not touched her guitar in years. After a whirlwind of IVF disasters, she picked it up again. Now she loves playing. It gives her a contentment and deep fulfilment she did not think was possible.

That is a re-discovered dream.

Your dream may be sporty or outdoorsy like bushwalking. It may be about travel or learning other cultures or speaking another language. It could be a bucket list.

Your dream may be about relationships. Perhaps you want to connect with your tribe (childless or otherwise). Perhaps you want to find friends who speak your language. It might involve taking risks. It might mean re-kindling old friendships that have faded over the years.

It might be fun.

Some child-related dreams may still be possible. Think about your original reasons for wanting children in the first place. Think about what you hoped to achieve.

If you wanted to mentor children, it may be possible to channel your desires into teaching or mentorship programs. If you wanted to pass on your values, there may be other ways to do that. You can help kids and role-model your values at the same time. You can share your beliefs with kids at church or in your street. You can positively influence the next generation.

These are no substitutes for having your own children. I will not pretend they are. But they might be alternatives to consider. You have gifts and skills to contribute, and you can leave a legacy despite childlessness.

Childlessness may open doors for new dreams to enter. You might discover new things about yourself, desires you want to pursue, talents you did not know you had.

You might be at the beginning of personal re-invention.

Re-invention and transformation

Deep grief and loss presents us with unique opportunities for re-invention.

When we have let go of something so closely connected with our sense of identity, we are a bit like the proverbial caterpillar entering its cocoon.

I am told by a reliable source (OK, I heard it from an acquaintance) that when caterpillars enter the cocoon, their bodies break down completely. They totally disintegrate. They turn into caterpillar soup.

Perhaps you can relate to this. You may feel your life has completely disintegrated. You may feel like soup. You may feel your sense of self has liquified.

I do not know how the caterpillar feels as it embarks upon this journey of transformation. I do not know if caterpillars possess the sentience to know what is going on. But if I were a caterpillar, I imagine I would be terrified of the cocoon.

Most of us have been devastated by childlessness. Our lives have come apart at the seams. We have been anxious and depressed. We have struggled to see the light at the end of the tunnel. We have felt life as we knew it was coming to an end.

Fortunately, our caterpillar friend re-emerges from the cocoon transformed. The caterpillar chapter of life comes to an end. The butterfly chapter begins. The butterfly has a new lease on life. Things are possible for our butterfly friend that were never possible before.

This is the transformative power of the cocoon—and grief.

You might feel like you are entering a cocoon right now. You might feel like you have been in the cocoon for years, your life turned into one big pile of goop. You might feel like it is all over, like you have nothing to live for.

You might be about to enter a period of transformation.

My interviewees talked about re-inventing themselves. It was a painful process for them. They experienced a shift in their personal identity. They grieved the closing chapter.

Fiona described the agony of entering her cocoon. Her previous identity was wrapped up in motherhood. She needed to find another purpose. Now Fiona writes in order to help people find their passion. She followed her passion and was transformed by it.

In Melanie's darkest hours, she found an Art of Living course and discovered the Emotional Freedom Technique. Now she practices EFT, using her learnings and experiences to help others find the freedom she now enjoys.

I used to write when I was younger. I never thought it would return, let alone lead to writing books. But like an old friend walking through the door, writing has returned. And I am grateful.

There are wild and varied possibilities beyond 'mother' and 'father'. We can be a mentor, teacher, coach, writer, traveller, entrepreneur, pioneer, volunteer, pastor, athlete, musician, artist, speaker or childless champion.

We can re-define who we are.

Some people think the term 'childless' is derogatory, as in child-less or less-than. We are not less-than. We are equal. We are worthy. We can find new reasons to live. Re-invention is possible. Painful? Yes. Scary? Absolutely. Well, perhaps terrifying is a more accurate word. But possible.

If you have reached rock bottom and do not know what your future holds, then perhaps, just for today, rest in the knowledge it can happen.

You might be about to enter your cocoon.

You can find meaning in your life again.

Adoption and fostering

It is easy to say, 'Just adopt' or 'Be a foster carer'. But these are not always realistic options. They are not always a 'Get out of childlessness free' card.

There are many hoops to jump through if you want to adopt or foster. You have to be assessed by the agencies and they have lots of criteria. And these differ from state to state.

When I adopted my cat Portia (insert crazy cat lady reference here), I was thoroughly assessed for my suitability as a cat mum. And that was just for a cat.

Here are a few reasons why some people get turned down for adoption in Australia (some of these were given by my interviewees so please check your own state or territory's legislation):

- Obesity or body mass index being too high;
- No backyard;
- Age gap of less than eighteen years or more than forty years between child and adoptive parent;
- Living in the wrong Australian state;
- Age (being younger than twenty-one in NSW or twenty-five in the ACT);

- Being homosexual in the NT;
- Being single in VIC (however, even if you live in another state, couples are usually prioritised over singles, and singles are only considered in 'exceptional circumstances', whatever that means);
- Being married less than three years;
- Lack of experience with children or direct parenting experience (don't ask me how a childless person overcomes that one);
- In NSW, not being a resident of NSW; or
- Not being a person of 'good repute and fit and proper to fulfil the responsibilities of parenting' in NSW (Blatchford 2017)[74].

Plus, in Australia, you have to prove you cannot have children naturally before you will be considered for adoption. (I do not know what 'prove' means, but my skin crawls just thinking about it.) So no one can put their hand up and say, 'You know what, there are too many neglected kids out there, let's adopt some'—contrary to the movie *Lion*'s depiction of easy adoption in Australia.

Even after being approved for adoption, you can wait years to receive a child, more than five years for some. Not exactly a 'quick fix'.

Some adoptions require approval from the birth parents. In NSW, children under two years in the care of the Department of Communities and Justice (our child protection agency) need approval from the birth parents before adoption (2019)[75]. That could get messy.

Fostering can be just as complicated. Foster children typically have difficult pasts and not every foster child fully recovers from it. Foster caring is a supremely demanding role, even for the most experienced carer. Some interviewees told me they do not have the right temperament, training or resources to take on potentially challenging or high-needs foster children. One interviewee suggested there ought to be special training for those intending to foster.

Not a bad idea. And I believe there is such training available for foster carers-to-be in NSW.

Adoptive children may be a little different. There are many reasons why birth parents relinquish their child. Sometimes the decision is a protective one. However, adoptive children may have bad pasts too.

> *What if adoption is not the same as having your own biological children?*

It is worth noting adoption is not necessarily a cure-all for childlessness. A childless friend of mine successfully adopted two kids and shared some unexpected insights with me.

'Adopting kids was right for my husband and me, even though it wasn't our first choice,' she confided. 'We believe God called us to adopt these children, and it offered us closure for our childlessness. But grief occasionally pops its head up—a different kind of grief, like when your child displays a temperament different to yours and you wonder what it would have been like to have biological children. Or when you feel a sense of distance with your teenager and wonder if this would have been the case otherwise.'

It was a challenge for my friend when her daughter got

pregnant and asked for her advice. My friend wished she could offer her daughter support, but she had no experience with pregnancy nor with childbirth. And later, she went through a different kind of grief watching her children grieve as they came to terms with their adoption.

The well-intended 'Why don't you just adopt?' betrays an underlying assumption that adoption solves the problems of childlessness. But what if this assumption is wrong? What if adoption is not the same as having your own biological children?

Maybe adoption does not tie up all the loose ends of childlessness, as my friend discovered. Maybe grief might shift or look different after adoption. Be prepared for that.

One more thought. The rates of adoption in Australia are appallingly low relative to the number of children awaiting adoption. Not many people are successful in adopting.

I hear the best way to adopt a child is to foster them first. I guess it proves your parenting ability, and you can bond with the child before adopting them. But becoming a foster parent is a complex process too.

Well-meaning friends and family may suggest adoption or fostering, but they are usually unaware of the hurdles and complexities involved. Christians may suggest it, preaching the merits of charity. I am not persuaded that charity in childlessness equals adopting children.

(Just imagine if it did. How many children should I adopt? Is one child sufficient to demonstrate charity? Or should I adopt as many children as I can fit into my house? Thankfully, God does not judge us by adoption-related brownie points.)

If someone suggests adoption or fostering to you, it may be helpful to explain the complications. This may help them understand why you have not jumped at the idea.

Surrogacy

I knew zip about surrogacy before writing this book. I found a website, *Surrogacy Australia* (2020)[76], and discovered each state in Australia has different legislation around it.

For example, in the NT, surrogacy is illegal. In NSW it is allowed, but there are rules: the intended parents must be over twenty-five and reside in NSW, and the surrogate mother cannot be genetically related to the couple and cannot receive payment for the surrogacy.

You cannot do surrogacy just because you want to. You must have a medical (eg. infertility) or social (eg. same-sex partner) reason for it. Even then, there are conditions. The couple seeking a surrogate and the surrogate parents must obtain legal advice and counselling first. And you have to put your surrogacy agreement in writing (Surrogacy Australia 2020)[77].

But I am not a lawyer. So I encourage you to look into the legislation in your own region.

Surrogacy may not be easy or expedient. But then, neither is IVF. Or trying to conceive, for that matter. It may be the right decision for you. If so, go for it. Get lots of support and information, and look after yourself in the process.

Freezing options

Most women are aware the number and quality of their eggs

drops off drastically with age. (By the way, I hear men experience a sperm drop-off effect as well, although whether it is to the same degree I cannot say.)

If you are considering freezing, I encourage you to do your research. Laws and regulations about egg- and sperm-freezing differ depending on the area, so make sure you are well informed.

Freezing comes with risks at each stage of the process. First, the eggs have to be defrosted (and not all eggs survive). Then the eggs have to fertilise, mature into embryos and survive the implantation process.

That is a lot of 'ifs'.

In Australia, the success rate of pregnancy from a frozen egg is between twenty and thirty-five percent (IVF Australia 2020)[78]. And the success rate drops off rapidly with age.

One woman I read about (Cha 2018)[79] froze eleven eggs. When the time came to try for a baby, only nine eggs thawed successfully. Of those nine, six eggs fertilised and developed into embryos. Of those six embryos, only one was normal. The embryo was implanted. But the pregnancy failed.

There are success stories from frozen eggs as well. So it is possible. And it can be a worthwhile option. When doing your research, some good questions to ask might be:

- How many eggs can I freeze?
- How does the freezing process affect the egg's viability?
- What is the success rate of pregnancy from frozen eggs?
- Is there a limit on how long I can store the eggs?
- Is my age a factor?

- How much will it cost?

For some, freezing may bring freedom and peace of mind.

Alternatives to parenting

There are other ways to care for children beyond adopting, fostering and surrogacy. Some alternatives, with thanks to my interviewees, include:

- Mentoring. Some organisations provide formal mentoring for kids in need, such as *Kids Hope* (2020)[80], *Big Brothers Big Sisters* (2018)[81] and the *Pyjama Foundation* (2018)[82]. You spend time with one child or young person on a regular basis, forming a long-term relationship with someone who really needs it. The experience can be incredibly rewarding and personally satisfying.
- Teaching. You can pour your parental instincts into classrooms. You can walk your students through the challenges of school and life.
- 'Surrogating.' You can be a PANK (Professional Aunt, No Kids) or PUNK (Professional Uncle, No Kids) (Notkin 2017)[83]. You can be a close family friend or neighbour to someone's children to the extent they feel like your own. They may see you as a 'surrogate' parent and call you mum or dad.
- Volunteering. You can volunteer for kids' camps or school retreats. Churches have Sunday school and youth ministries. You may have local kids groups in your area such as Scouts or sporting clubs for which you could volunteer.

- Social parenting. You can be part of a social parenting cohort. In some cultures, children are raised by the adults in the community, rather than birth parents alone. In Australian Aboriginal culture, non-parents and community elders are referred to as 'aunty' or 'uncle', a term of affection and respect. These aunties and uncles take responsibility for the children in their community.
- Sponsoring. You can be a sponsor parent. You can feed, clothe, educate and befriend a child on the other side of the world. You can make a difference.
- Spiritual parenting. Paul was childless but had spiritual children (see 1 Timothy 1:2, Titus 1:4, 1 Corinthians 4:14-15). You can connect with kids at your church or place of worship and shape the religious beliefs and values of those children. They might find faith because of you. You might pass on spiritual legacies. This could give you part of the sense of meaning and purpose you hoped for as a biological parent.

Non-children children

When I was single, I adopted a furbaby, a pet cat, rescued from death row.

I am not going to pretend a cat is anything close to my own child. (Although some days it feels that way. I mean, why does she follow me to the toilet? Why?)

In my singledom, she was dependent on me like a child. In my loneliness, she was a companion who was always there, always the same, always affectionate. Somehow she helped. She still helps. I do not dress her up in little clothes or anything (and I do not judge anyone who does), but she means a lot to me.

(Aside: many childless people, when talking to their pets, call themselves 'mummy' or 'daddy'. I have noticed I do that with my cat. Heaven knows why.)

Some childless people, including couples, adopt furbabies as a way of staving off loneliness. You would think a couple could not get lonely. After all, they have each other, right?

Wrong.

Even in a relationship, loneliness can exist. Especially in the void left by childlessness. There can be an emptiness, an aching for dreams and hopes lost. Furbabies can help fill this void, like they did for Elena. And they can give you the satisfaction of helping an animal in need.

> *You might make a difference in someone's life—someone who really needs you.*

You could even become a pet foster carer. In fact, next time someone suggests adoption, you could talk about adopting a dog.

Some like to view themselves as parents of something they have produced, such as a book or song or other project. I must admit, when I published my first book, I felt like I had birthed a baby. Just as quickly, I felt like I was giving my baby away.

Writing is a good way of leaving a legacy. And no one can say labelling yourself as a 'book mummy' or 'blog daddy' is wrong.

It may not be easy to contemplate alternatives to children. You may not want to go there. But if you do, there are options for channelling your parental instincts and making your mark on the world—something many of us longed to do through parenting.

You might create something entirely unique and right for you.

You might make a difference in someone's life—someone who really needs you.

Healthy avoidance

Being around children can be too much. Some of us need to avoid kids for the sake of survival.

Avoidance gets a bad rap. Some worry avoidance means they are not 'dealing with their issues'. They believe they should always confront and work through their problems.

I couldn't agree more. Presuming we are talking about problems that can be solved, such as doing our tax or calling the plumber or paying our bills.

For unsolvable problems, like childlessness, confrontation may not help. It can be unhealthy to be around children. Especially if it takes a month to recover. On balance, it may be healthier to avoid children. Even for a little while.

This can be temporary. One day you might be more open to it. But if the pain is raw, give yourself permission to opt out. Kick your Shoulds to the kerb. Cut yourself some slack.

That is self-care.

A strong relationship

While childlessness can impact our partner relationships, our partners can also be our saving grace. The strength and support of someone who loves us can be life-saving.

Loved ones keep us grounded. They reassure us when we feel like failures. They remind us of God's goodness. They bring us back to the here-and-now instead of living in What-Ifs. They can throw our sense of isolation into sharp relief. They can restore our gratitude.

While many believe having kids is the most important thing in life, other things can be just as important. Or more important. It can be helpful when a loved one reminds us of that.

John and Rachel's surgeon recommended against IVF for the specific purpose of protecting their relationship.

Natasha and her husband decided against IVF, preferring to trust in God. They protected their shared faith.

I am not saying everyone needs to avoid IVF in order to save their relationship. Everyone needs to choose what is right for them. For some, the chance to have children means everything. For others, the relationship comes first.

Childlessness can make you stronger as a couple. It can bring you closer together—if you keep things honest. One theme that shone through my interviews was the importance of expressing emotions. Talking frankly helps keep relationships strong.

So I encourage you to do just that. Be honest with yourself, your partner or spouse, or close trusted friends such as other childless people who get it. Tell them when you feel sad.

Some of us keep feelings bottled up in order to protect the other person. (Know anyone like that?) We try to be strong for their sake. Or we bottle it up to keep from embarrassment, say, of feeling like a sexual failure, or from guilt, say, of being infertile. Roughly translated, we fake it.

But bottling up and fakery leads to unhealthy by-products, like withdrawal, depression, irritability, anxiety, resentment and volcanic-like eruptions. Much easier to say you feel sad.

You can build your relationship by doing little things together (and I do not mean attending medical appointments). Hit the shops. See a movie. Check out a new café. Start your dating life over. Share your hopes and dreams for the future—beyond kids. Talk about places you want to see, things you want to do, what kind of person you want to be. Re-discover each other.

It might be helpful to set boundaries around kid-related conversations if you have childlessness burnout. You can get sick of life revolving around child talk. You can get sick of thinking about it.

You could set a rule like no child-talk during dinner. You can talk about anything except kids and contraception. Or maybe the weekend is a childfree zone. Or the bedroom. Do what works for you.

Take a breather. For both of your sakes.

Childlessness championing

You can be a childless champion.

Champions are fierce and public advocates for their cause. They start businesses or support groups or retreats to support childless people. They instigate events like *World Childless Week* (2020)[84], founded by childless champion Stephanie Phillips. They share their story.

You could be a less public champion. You could talk to people in your circles about childlessness. You could raise the subject at church. You could lift the profile of childlessness in your own way.

You could get the word out about the stats on fertility, ageing and real IVF success rates. Educate people on those harsh realities. You could blog or post on social media, or support people who are.

> Find a creative way you can champion childless people and get championing.

There are many ways to be a champion. Find a creative way you can champion childless people and get championing.

Professional help

Lots of interviewees recommend counselling, so I would be remiss if I did not mention it.

My interviewees sang the praises of their counsellors, even those who attended a single counselling session. Some regretted not going sooner.

There are several benefits to counselling. First, you can be completely honest about how you feel. You will not be judged for it. You can express yourself and find relief. You may better understand yourself afterwards.

Second, counselling can help you clarify what you really want. This is especially helpful if you are undecided about your next step, such as whether to do IVF again. Counselling can explore the pros and cons of such decisions.

Third, for those seeking another perspective, a counsellor can be a good sounding board. They offer unbiased, objective opinions. They can suggest alternatives.

Which brings me to my fourth and final point. A counsellor with experience in infertility or childlessness (highly recommended by my interviewees) can empathise with you. They can help you find ways to live with grief—not eradicate it from existence like a memory wipe, but co-exist with it like a roommate.

Counselling can help you find gratitude, silver linings or ways to re-invent yourself. By clarifying how you think and feel, counselling can guide you towards decisions that are right for you.

One more thing

Now for the most obvious sanity-saver in a survival book written by a Christian: God. I was just getting around to that.

The subject of faith demands and deserves a whole lot more than a passing mention. So I have dedicated a whole chapter to it.

I think you are going to enjoy it.

NATASHA'S STORY
Australia

Natasha knew she would have four kids—at least.

She grew up with one sibling. They found it hard to play outdoor games with just the two of them. So she was determined to have a minimum of four children herself.

She met her husband at university and they married when she was twenty-two. The first ten years were great. Then they felt the pressure of 'the clock'. When she was thirty-two, they began trying. They tried for a year. The following year they went to the doctor for tests.

Natasha's husband's tests came back with glowing results, so they went to a fertility clinic. The clinic decided to do an investigative laparoscopy on Natasha at thirty-four.

They prayed the whole time. Both Christians, they trusted God to go before them. They knew God could give them a child if he so chose.

The results were normal, but she was left with new unexplained pain during menstruation. They were still unable to fall pregnant, even though they were both healthy and medically able to conceive. They had 'unexplained infertility'. The fertility clinic referred them for IVF.

Here is Natasha's guide to IVF in seven easy steps:

1. Inject ovary-stimulating drugs into the woman so eggs are mass-produced. Hopefully the eggs do not burst and kill her.

2. Harvest the eggs. Put them in the fridge.

3. Collect sperm from the man. Put it in the fridge.

4. Combine eggs with sperm to make as many viable embryos as possible. Put them in the freezer.

5. Transfer embryos into the woman with a procedure 'as simple as a pap-smear'.

6. Hope and pray for success (she heard IVF in Australia has a twenty percent success rate).

7. Decide what to do with remaining frozen embryos because time is up and they need the freezer space.

They decided upfront not to pursue IVF as it raised ethical and moral dilemmas for them, especially around producing excess frozen embryos. Natasha also held a degree of self-confessed cynicism towards the fertility industry, that it promised to fulfil dreams with little success. Plus, she felt the twenty percent success rate was way too low. It was a technical 'fail'.

She was now about thirty-nine. She returned to her doctor to have final tests run, but they gave no further insight into her unexplained infertility. Natasha was officially a medical mystery.

Despite the lack of answers, she was left with the sense she had done everything possible to investigate their infertility. She knew there was nothing wrong with her or her husband. She was able—mostly—to accept her childlessness.

It was hard to tell family about the experience, especially when her father died in the middle of it all. It took Natasha five years to talk about it. Even then, she did not want to be viewed as the odd one out. She did not want to be 'that' person. She found people made assumptions about infertility, such as infertility being 'fixable' by doctors. She did not want to be subjected to that.

Her experience was difficult to articulate. She searched high and low for Christian literature on childlessness with little success. She discovered most people do not understand it.

One helpful book was *Silent Sorority* (2009)[85], a story of infertility and IVF by Pamela Tsigdinos. This book, and Pamela's blog of the same name (2020)[86], resonated with her.

Infertility had a profound effect on Natasha's faith in God. 'At times,' she said, 'my faith was the skinniest thread you can imagine, when I thought God was not hearing my pleas or had forgotten me. At other times, it was my harness or safety net to which I clung with all my might.'

She used to get questioned about kids, especially in Christian circles and early in married life. People would ask, 'Have you thought about IVF?' Sometimes Natasha said no, just to see what they said.

Now forty-three, those questions do not come up anymore. People assume she is past having kids. This is OK with her. If the subject does arise, she quickly turns the question around. 'No, and you?' This allows her to find out about other people's kids, something in which she is genuinely interested.

New paths have opened up for Natasha and her husband because of childlessness. They have participated in youth camps. They have financially supported Christian ministries. They have helped family members. They have even built their own house, a mammoth ten-year task. This marathon endeavour was hard work but rewarding.

They do not know what the future holds but they trust God's direction. 'I know God has a plan for me and his plan is good,' says Natasha. 'I am just not sure what it is.'

When I asked Natasha how she survived childlessness, she said she has not survived. Childlessness has forever changed her.

She still feels sad.

She feels left out with friends who have kids.

She sometimes cries and asks herself, 'Why me?'

It still does not make sense.

In spite of this, there are moments when the old, happy Natasha re-surfaces, when she can relax and enjoy things and be herself again.

For others travelling the childlessness highway, her advice is to stay away from difficult events like Mother's Days and baby shower celebrations.

She cautions against IVF because of the low success rate. She believes a lot of IVF disappointment comes from built-up expectations, hence she thinks it is better not to hope for too much. Or not try IVF at all. Her recommendation is to try to conceive naturally and trust God with the outcome.

Natasha is particularly grateful for her husband. 'He was supportive and comforting. He reminded me of God's sovereignty,' she recalls. 'I could have blamed him and ruined the relationship. I have seen it happen with other couples. But I thank God for my husband. For others in similar situations, I definitely advise you to hold on tight to your husband or wife.'

She has a special encouragement for Christians. 'God is in control. He has a plan for you and his plan is good. Trust him and he will get you through.'

13

FAITH

The Meaning of it All

I got really excited about this chapter.

Then I got scared.

What do I know about faith? What makes me think I can offer solutions to the great faith mysteries of the universe? Who do I think I am?

Thankfully, I realised two things. First, it takes faith to write about faith. Ironic, I know. Second, I cannot offer answers or solutions to the great faith mysteries of the universe. Because I do not have them. So I have decided not to try.

Phew.

If you hoped to find tidy answers to the problematic questions of faith, you will not find them here. I am not a theologian. I am just me. And my faith is messy.

And my magic wand is broken.

And I am fresh out of fairy dust.

And my supermarket will not be stocking unicorns for another year.

All I can offer is what I have learned about faith so far. Plus the experiences of my interviewees. So here is what I know.

(This could be a very short chapter.)

Faith is not a smooth bitumen road. It is a quagmire, a swampy jungle filled with quicksand traps and false trails and fog. Sometimes there is very little light by which to navigate.

At times we have travelling companions. Often we are alone. It is a hard quest, one that does not necessarily get easier with time or age or experience. So we will not pretend to have the faith route all mapped out.

We will take it one baby step at a time.

Forgive the pun.

The problem with faith

Yes, I am going to start by talking about the problem with faith. This is happening.

Those of us who have been Christians for more than five minutes know that faith presents special difficulties. We know following Jesus is not all puppies and rainbows. We understand faith means believing in things unseen. Hard things. Impossible things.

We have good days when anything seems possible. We have bad days that are devastating and we would like to give up, thanks very much.

When I have had a good night's sleep and am enjoying work and am not too sick and have been out for a walk in the fresh air, it is dead easy for me to believe God can do anything.

When I have not slept and the pain is debilitating and my job is falling apart and I am at my wits end, believing that God can do the impossible seems impossible.

> *Without opportunity to develop, faith stagnates.*

On those bad days, I have no energy left to fight the doubts. I wonder if God hears my prayers. I begin to question my faith. My health, my stress levels and my mood affect my faith.

The paradox of faith is it takes faith just to keep faith alive. It builds on itself. When faith is hard to find, we need even more faith. When you are starving, you need a feast, not a snack.

Occasionally Christians get this crazy idea that being Christian means you never have doubts. (No one reading this book, of course.)

Imagine that. Imagine a life where you never question anything, never have doubts about what you are doing, never wonder if you are following God or whether your Christian walk sucks out loud.

Such faith would be devoid of reflection. A faith without room to question, explore or wonder would lack depth. Doubt can give our faith gravitas. It's counterintuitive but true.

Questions and doubts clarify what we really believe. Not what we say we believe. Not what we are supposed to believe. What we actually believe deep down in our bones.

Questioning our faith can lead to stronger faith. Faith that just sits there, inactive, like a trophy on a shelf, is useless. It is simply a reminder of something we once did. Without opportunity to develop, faith stagnates. It is not a one-off achievement, unlike our metaphorical trophy. Faith is organic. It is constantly either growing or withering.

Let's switch metaphors for a second. I have a lemon tree in my backyard. I can see it right now. It has produced a number of lemons. It is a good lemon tree. But right now, there is something wrong with it. The leaves are fading from green to yellow. They are curling up. The flowers, plentiful a week ago, are withering and dropping off the tree.

It is not looking healthy at all.

There are a few possible explanations. We have had some rough weather lately. It has been a dry season. Without rain, the tree is suffering. Lemon trees need rain in order to thrive. I am guessing here. I am not a gardener. I am terrible with plants. (Hence the dying tree.)

Perhaps there is another issue underlying my tree's demise. Perhaps it is low on nutrients. Perhaps it has an infestation. The soil could need fertilising or ploughing. Perhaps the tree is asking to be replanted. Without asking it myself, I cannot be sure.

Perhaps you know what my tree needs.

If faith is anything like my lemon tree, it requires care and nurturing and attention. It needs good soil so the roots can go down deep. It sometimes needs pruning and replanting, a painful process, but necessary for the tree's sake.

Our faith needs certain things to grow.

Here is the paradox. Many think their faith will grow by attending church, reading the bible, praying and doing the normal Christian stuff. And that stuff is good. That stuff can definitely help us get to know God.

But faith does not grow out of the good stuff. Faith grows out of hardship. Like our lemon tree, sometimes our faith grows out of a big pile of poo.

> Many Christians suffer more when they follow Christ, not less.

We need suffering and difficulty in order to find our trust in God. Without trials, we never get a chance to test-drive our faith, as it were. We never find out how deep or strong it is.

So how is your faith?

Some Christians do not like this stuff. They want an easy life. They want to be happy, follow their dreams and receive God's blessings. They want to do the church thing on Sundays and tick the religious boxes.

That would be lovely. Except suffering is a reality of life and Christians do not get special treatment. There is no spiritual 'Get out of jail free' card. Indeed, many Christians suffer more when they follow Christ, not less. So we are misguided if we believe Christianity inoculates us against problems and suffering.

Of course, you already know this. You are probably reading this book because you are already acquainted with hardship, AKA childlessness. You know firsthand that faith does not always seem to grow during times of suffering.

But it can. And does.

Refining gold

What if suffering refines our faith?

1 Peter talks about this:

> These [trials] have come so that the proven genuineness of your faith—of greater worth than gold, which perishes even though refined by fire—may result in praise, glory and honour when Jesus Christ is revealed (1 Peter 1:7).

Peter compared our trials of faith to refining gold in fire.

The analogy is clear. We get a picture of our faith digging deep to endure suffering, just like genuine gold comes forth under extreme heat. The heat is a necessary part of the process.

I am curious about why anybody refines gold. I wonder what would drive someone to take that time and effort to burn away its impurities. I conclude it is because of the value and preciousness of gold.

Do we thus conclude that God sees us as valuable and precious? Is that the reason he purifies our faith? That is one possible conclusion. If you come up with another, let me know.

The book of James talks about this refining process in the first chapter:

> Consider it pure joy, my brothers and sisters, whenever you face trials of many kinds, because you know that the testing of your faith produces perseverance. Let perseverance

finish its work so that you may be mature and
complete, not lacking anything (James 1:2-4).

Suffering enhances our faith by forcing us to persevere, and perseverance is linked to our maturity. Thus faith-testing is necessary for our growth and maturity.

The best way for a runner to get good at running marathons is to run marathons. Deep, I know. But it is the only way to properly train a marathon runner. Sure, they can practise on the treadmill, but eventually they have to go outside and run the real thing. There is no substitute, no shortcut, for learning endurance.

God cares about our spiritual endurance.

James goes on: 'Blessed is the one who perseveres under trial because, having stood the test, that person will receive the crown of life that the Lord has promised to those who love him' (James 1:12).

Our suffering is not for nothing. God sees it and rewards it if we endure.

Best get our running shoes on.

A glance at the king of suffering (nope, not Jesus this time), Job, gives us further insight. He went through appalling suffering and loss. His life fell apart in one day. Everyone else turned away from God and urged Job to do the same. But he refused. In Job 23:10, he declared: 'But [God] knows the way that I take; when he has tested me, I will come forth as gold.'

Job got it. He saw the long-term outcome of the refining process. He was surrounded by utter devastation, yet he understood his inner 'gold' was being refined at that very instant. His lemon tree roots were going down deep.

He trusted God to bring him out the other side.

While refinement is painful, it can help to remember the goal of the Christian life is not avoiding pain. It is becoming more like Christ. Even in suffering.

It takes real courage and a whole lot of grace.

If Job did it, we can do it too.

Distance from God

When we suffer, we often look for someone to blame. We may believe God is the source of our suffering. We may question him, get angry with him, hold him responsible for our sorrow.

Especially if we believe God promised us children.

Being angry with God is not a crime in itself. I think anger is quite healthy. It helps us speak up about wrongdoing. It drives us to action, to protect ourselves or someone else. God himself gets angry from time to time.

It is what we do with our anger that can be helpful or harmful.

Sometimes anger has nowhere to go. Some anger is hard to express. Some anger can be guilt-inducing. It is common to feel these kinds of anger with God. And that in itself can be frustrating.

How do you get angry with someone who is perfect? How do you tell them they got it wrong, messed up your life, caused you pain? That is not exactly a 'Christian' thing to do.

> *Sometimes we are so preoccupied with being nice that we lose our honesty.*

Or so we believe.

We Christians have this terrible habit of being polite. We think we are supposed to be nice all the time. This is a good thing. Mostly. But sometimes we are so preoccupied with being nice that we lose our honesty. We pretend things are great when they are not. We put on a happy face when we are dying inside. And we do the same with God.

We might feel bad for feeling angry with him. We might believe we are bad Christians. We might feel ashamed. So we bottle it up. We are caught between the proverbial rock and hard place.

Bottling emotions creates distance. Anger unreleased will fester inside us. It gives birth to bitterness, cynicism and despair. We lose our hope. We lose our trust. We lose our faith in God.

Some interviewees developed distance between themselves and God. They had a sense of wanting to love God but pulling away from him, a simultaneous dance of drawing near and running away. They felt torn. They were in a spiritual tug-of-war.

Imagine the chaos of loving someone you no longer trusted. Imagine going to church, listening to songs about God's faithfulness, trying to pray, but believing deep down God has betrayed you. The simple act of talking to God can bring sunken anger and blame and despair rushing back to the surface.

This is a sign that your faith has been damaged. Recovery will take time. I do not know how long. There may never be a satisfactory resolution in this lifetime. But I believe healing is possible. I have seen people recover from terrible and traumatic blows to their faith, and I have travelled that road of recovery myself.

It is possible to heal the distance between you and God.

There is no formula to cure this. But neither is there a deadline. So take your time. Don't pressure yourself to be a certain type of Christian. Just be you. There is no pressure to even turn to him. But know that God is still moving towards you, even if you move away for a while.

Healing is not something you can hurry. God knows this. He will not force you to get close to him. He might invite you, beckon you, wait for you. But he will not make you. He will leave the choice up to you.

Childlessness can impact our relationships and the same goes for God. Being apart from him can hurt. But God has fields of mercy and grace waiting for us. For problems big or small, there is grace for us all.

You may think God will not wait for you. You may worry God will get fed up and walk away. I know how that feels. I have been there. We usually fear God's rejection because that is what we would do if we were God.

Thankfully, God is way more patient with us than we are with ourselves. And he is kinder than we think.

Ways to pray

In times like these it can be hard to pray.

When I have trouble praying, there are a few go-to scriptures that ground me. Some of my favourite entry-to-prayer passages come from the Psalms.

I love the Psalms. They are boisterous and bursting with joy, as well as being super-melancholy and bordering on despair. But whether uplifting or depressing, they are always honest. No matter what the psalmist goes through, they do not avoid God. They do not bottle things up. They come right out and tell God how they are feeling. They ask the hard questions. They blame God.

Whether right or wrong, they start the conversation. That is the main thing.

When we avoid the honest stuff, we shut down any chance of an open dialogue with God. If we start the conversation, it gives us a chance to go somewhere with it. It gives God a chance to respond.

Psalm 60:1-5 is a real picker-upper:

> You have rejected us, O God,
> And burst forth upon us;
> You have been angry—now restore us!
>
> You have shaken the land and torn it open;
> Mend its fractures,
> For it is quaking.
>
> You have shown your people desperate times;
> You have given us wine
> That makes us stagger.
>
> But for those who fear you,
> You have raised a banner
> To be unfurled against the bow.
>
> Save us and help us with your right hand,
> That those you love may be delivered.

Notice how this psalm moves. It starts with God's rejection. The psalmist, David, makes his case, explaining in detail the hurt and damage done.

There is a moment. A pause. You can almost hear him take a breath. Then comes the 'but' bit. David starts talking about God's banner being a sign of salvation for those who fear God.

It is almost like he says, 'Hang on. I am furious with God, but I have just remembered he has done good things for me before.' Before we know it, he is pleading with God for salvation and deliverance. Within five verses, David moves from blatant accusation to a cry for help. The conversation has shifted. It is a beginning.

Lamentations is chock-full of high-quality melancholia. It was written at a time of devastation for God's people. The first few chapters are dedicated to mourning and despair. Then, in Chapter 3, things take an interesting turn.

> I remember my affliction and my wandering,
> The bitterness and the gall.
>
> I well remember them,
> And my soul is downcast within me.
>
> Yet this I call to mind,
> And therefore I have hope:
> Because of the Lord's great love
> We are not consumed,
> For his compassions never fail.
>
> They are new every morning;
> Great is your faithfulness.
>
> I say to myself,
> 'The Lord is my portion;
> Therefore I will wait for him'.
>
> The Lord is good to those

> Whose hope is in him,
> To the one who seeks him;
> It is good to wait quietly
> For the salvation of the Lord.
>
> It is good for a man to bear the yoke
> While he is young.
>
> Let him sit alone in silence,
> For the Lord has laid it on him.
>
> Let him bury his face in the dust—
> There may yet be hope (Lamentations 3:19-29).

Check out the last two verses, this time in The Message:

> When life is heavy and hard to take,
> Go off by yourself.
>
> Enter the silence.
>
> Bow in prayer.
>
> Don't ask questions;
> Wait for hope to appear (Lamentations 3:28-29).

I love that. It's like a recipe for prayer. I am not into formulas, but we have been handed a beautiful formula right here.

Find a quiet place. Be there with God. Bow in prayer. Show respect to God. You can bow literally or in your heart, showing God you put him first and he is Lord. Then, rather than asking burning questions, wait for the appearance of hope.

It takes the pressure off us for a change. We do not have to do all the talking. (Good news for some of us.) We can wait in the silence, in an attitude of bowing, without making demands. We can wait for the Holy Spirit to bring us hope.

Where there is turmoil, the Holy Spirit brings peace. Where there is mourning, he brings joy. When our hearts are swept away by bitterness and anger, the Holy Spirit catches us

> *There is no need to 'perform' prayer.*

and restores us with his love. He brings these gifts to us, gifts we cannot buy or earn with any amount of striving. They are true gifts. And they come when we wait.

Next is my favourite verse about prayer (I have shared this one before). Jesus is preaching to the multitudes and he says:

> And when you come before God, don't turn that into a theatrical production either. All these people making a regular show of their prayers, hoping for stardom! Do you think God sits in a box seat?
>
> Here's what I want you to do: Find a quiet, secluded place so you won't be tempted to role-play before God. Just be there as simply and honestly as you can manage. The focus will shift from you to God, and you will begin to sense his grace.
>
> The world is full of so-called prayer warriors who are prayer-ignorant. They're full of formulas and programs and advice, peddling techniques

> for getting what you want from God. Don't fall
> for that nonsense. This is your Father you are
> dealing with, and he knows better than you
> what you need. With a God like this loving you,
> you can pray very simply (Matthew 6:5-8).

I hope you saw that bit in verse 6 about finding a quiet, secluded place. (Sounds familiar.)

There is a theme emerging here. Be yourself before God. Be honest. Ask for what you need. Remember he is your Father who loves you. There is no need to 'perform' prayer. I love that. We don't need a script. We can talk naturally, as to a friend who knows and loves us. Such a relief.

Imagine God smiling as you talk, hanging on your every word. I think that is how he really sees us.

Encouragement in suffering

In *The Problem of Pain* (1940)[87], C. S. Lewis suggests suffering tells us about our future home. According to Lewis, suffering demonstrates that this planet, this life, is a poor fit. Our eternal home is the place that really fits.

And our current suffering is nothing compared to that place.

It is like getting braces. When I was a teenager, I endured two years of braces-induced agony. It shredded the inside of my mouth. It gave me jaw-ache. It stopped me from eating toffee.

Hardship, right?

But the joy of removing those braces was incredible. I was elated. I ate toffee and apples and toffee-apples. I indulged in all manner of chewy goodies. Even better, my teeth were straightened. It was a short-term investment for a long-term gain.

I think this is what Lewis is saying. What we are going through now is bad, but it is nothing compared to the future joy and elation that awaits us. Judging by our suffering, our future home is going to be freaking incredible.

In the meantime, suffering can be difficult and isolating. We do not always want to talk about it, even when we should. We can think we are the only ones going through this. The bible is filled with reassurance on this point. It tells of saints gone before us who persevered despite their suffering.

Check out Hebrews 11 (the entire chapter) for a list of fine examples.

In Isaiah 30:18-19, we glimpse how God sees us in suffering:

> Yet the Lord longs to be gracious to you;
> He rises to show you compassion.
>
> For the Lord is a God of justice.
>
> Blessed are all who wait for him!
>
> O people of Zion, who love in Jerusalem, you will weep no more. How gracious he will be when you cry for help! As soon as he hears, he will answer you (NIV).

Hebrews 12:4-11 suggests what feels like punishment is actually a form of discipline from God. And not because we have been naughty. (I used to think God's discipline was accompanied by holy eye-rolling and long-suffering sighs because we are so rotten, but no.) It is because discipline helps us grow into full maturity. It means God, our Father, is deeply concerned about our maturity.

In 1 Peter 4:12-19 we find encouragement for those who suffer for doing good. Some of our childlessness suffering could be included in this. I do not mean being childless counts as 'doing good', but those of us who faithfully serve God might encounter suffering along the way, and this might include childlessness.

Maddy railed at God about her childlessness. She objected to the injustice of being childless when unfit and abusive parents were falling pregnant with ease. 'Why,' she pleaded, 'are evil people getting pregnant when I am not?' Sometimes when we are doing good, we suffer more.

Sarah grieved the loss of her faith and unfulfilled prophecies. She told God exactly how she felt, that she did not know who he was anymore, and that he had caused her tremendous pain. She questioned the meaning and purpose behind her suffering. Her anger towards God died down—eventually.

There is good news for those who mourn. Jesus gives blessings to those who endure hard times. He does not promise we will have children, but here is what he does promise:

> Blessed are you who are poor,
> For yours is the kingdom of God.
>
> Blessed are you who hunger now,
> For you will be satisfied.
>
> Blessed are you who weep now,

For you will laugh (Luke 6:20-21).

If you need further good news about mourning, Psalm 51 is pretty hard to beat:

> My sacrifice, O God, is a broken spirit;
> A broken and contrite heart you, God,
> Will not despise (Psalm 51:17).

Here is a similar sentiment in Psalm 34:

> The Lord is close to the brokenhearted
> And saves those who are crushed in spirit
> (Psalm 34:18).

This is echoed by Isaiah the prophet:

> These are the ones I look on with favour:
> Those who are humble and contrite in spirit,
> And who tremble at my word (Isaiah 66:2).

God feels compassion for our suffering. He offers us comfort. He is especially close to the brokenhearted.

When we feel most alone, he is most near.

Forgiveness

Forgiveness can be a touchy subject.

Many Christians associate forgiveness with forgetting, as in the old adage, 'Forgive and forget'. It infers we should forget the harm anyone has ever done to us, like some kind of spiritual amnesia.

I do not agree with this. Any more.

I used to practise this religious-sounding amnesia. It landed me in trouble. I kept putting myself in vulnerable situations with people who abused, bullied or otherwise took advantage of me.

I do not think this is what Jesus had in mind when he preached forgiveness.

Jesus forgave the people who put him on the cross. It did not make his situation any better. It did not let those soldiers off the hook. It was an act of grace on his part, releasing any hatred or ill-feeling towards them.

Forgiveness does not mean others are released from consequences. For those who have truly done the wrong thing, their actions should be addressed. Forgiveness is more about being at peace with something or someone who has done you wrong. It is accepting you cannot control others. It is yielding to God's sovereignty in all things. It is deciding not to be ruled by bitterness.

It can be tough to do. And it is not necessarily a one-off action. It might be a daily decision to not let the actions of others rule our lives. It can involve ongoing prayer for the other person and for ourselves.

It is hard to truly love our enemies.

In childlessness, there are usually three kinds of forgiveness that apply.

First, there is the forgiveness of others. We need to forgive others for how they treated us. We need to forgive friends and family for their thoughtless comments or insensitive questions or pressure for us to have kids.

We need to forgive doctors and medical staff for their unhelpful 'assistance'. We need to forgive IVF clinics and the health system for failing us.

We need to forgive society for the pressure they place on minority childless people to become majority-type parents. We need to forgive their pronatalism.

We need to forgive those who are able to have children—including bad parents.

We need to forgive exes for abandoning us to chidlessness-by-singledom.

We need to forgive the entire universe of social media.

We need to forgive the church for not understanding or including us.

We need to forgive those who gave us prophecies about having children that never came true.

Second, there is God. I know he counts as an 'other', but there is something unique about forgiving an all-perfect supernatural being.

Just how do you forgive a deity?

And if you forgive God, does that mean he was in the wrong?

It helps to understand the true meaning of forgiveness. Forgiving someone is not about assigning blame to them. In fact, in forgiving someone, you are saying, 'I am prepared to stop blaming you.'

Many Christians blame God for their troubles, even if they do not really think God is to blame. The anger and disappointment of childlessness can tempt us to find someone, anyone, to blame. God is a convenient choice. After all, he is all-powerful. He could have helped us, couldn't he?

It is easy to blame an omnipotent, omniscient God. And he can take it. He is so wonderful that he does not even get upset or offended when we are upset or offended with him. He just keeps loving us anyway.

Forgiving God is a big deal. The good news is he can help with forgiveness. He has enough grace to consume our bitterness. He can show us the way. Even when it comes to forgiving him.

That's our God.

Third, some of us need to forgive ourselves. We need to forgive our health issues. We need to forgive our infertility. We need to realise our circumstances made it impossible for us to have children. We need to accept it was not our fault.

We need to forgive ourselves for not giving our parents grandchildren.

We need to forgive ourselves for not giving our partners the gift of being a mother or father.

We need to forgive ourselves for giving up hope.

We need to forgive ourselves for calling an end to the madness of trying to conceive or IVF or applying for adoption, because enough was enough.

We need to forgive ourselves for opting out of unhealthy, child-centric situations and friendships because they take such an enormous toll on us.

Time to cut ourselves some slack. Let's show ourselves a tiny bit of kindness, the kindness we would readily show a friend if they were in our shoes. Forgive yourself as fully and freely as you would forgive a loved one.

> *He can show us the way. Even when it comes to forgiving him.*

Forgiveness is not easy. It might not happen all at once. It might be something at which we chip away, bit by bit, year by year. But forgiveness is one of the bravest, most hard-core, most courageous things we do.

And I think it makes us more like Jesus.

Getting real

I do not have a lot of time for clichés.

We Christians are good at spouting religious-sounding phrases that do nothing for our pain. They come across as empty and provide little comfort. Christianese does not help.

Here are Christian clichés I have heard and used myself over the years:

- God is in charge.
- It's all good. (If you say this in breathless tones, it actually sounds spiritual.)
- I am praying for you. (Often spoken 'in faith', that is, before you have started praying.)
- Let go and let God. (Let him what?)
- You need to surrender everything to God.
- You need to pray more.
- You need to have more faith.

In summary, we need to pray more and believe more while letting go of everything. Oh, and never doubt God.

And people wonder why we go crazy.

Clichés, beyond triggering my cringe reflex, might sound religious through overuse of words like 'faith' and 'prayer' and 'God', but they lack compassion. They lack nuance. They lack an honest acknowledgement and expression of real emotion. In fact, most clichés act to silence our emotions.

'Keep quiet,' they whisper. 'Keep your doubts and negative emotions to yourself, or else it will look like you don't trust God. You will look like a bad Christian. And then what will people say?'

So-called negative emotions, like stress and worry and frustration, do not negate the presence of faith. The two are not mutually exclusive. One may express significant doubt and confusion while at the same time hanging on to God with all the rigour of a cat hanging on to a tree branch.

> *Most clichés act to silence our emotions.*

Clichés minimise suffering. They turn agony into inconvenience, heartache into nuisance, tears into tokens. Clichés have no time to truly listen or empathise with pain.

I have low tolerance for clichés. Anything that sounds remotely fake or removed from human reality grinds in my brain.

Job also had zero tolerance for clichés. And he hung on to God for dear life. This is highlighted in Eugene Peterson's introduction to Job in The Message:

> Job suffered. His name is synonymous with suffering. He asked, 'Why?' He asked, 'Why not?' And he put his questions to God. He asked his questions persistently, passionately, and eloquently. He refused to take silence for an answer. He refused to take clichés for an answer. He refused to let God off the hook.
>
> Job did not take his sufferings quietly or piously.

He disdained going for a second opinion to outside physicians or philosophers. Job took his stance before *God*, and there he protested his suffering, protested mightily...

Job gives voice to his sufferings so well, so accurately and honestly, that anyone who has ever suffered—which includes every last one of us—can recognise his or her personal pain in the voice of Job. Job says boldly what some of us are too timid to say. He makes poetry out of what in many of us is only a tangle of confused whispers. He shouts out to God what a lot of us mutter behind our sleeves. He refuses to accept the role of a defeated victim.

It is also important to note what Job does *not* do, lest we expect something from him that he does not intend. Job does not curse God as his wife suggests he should do, getting rid of the problem by getting rid of God. But neither does Job *explain* suffering. He does not instruct us in how to live so that we can avoid suffering. Suffering is a mystery, and Job comes to respect the mystery.

In the course of facing, questioning, and respecting suffering, Job finds himself in an even larger mystery—the mystery of God...

The ironic fact of the matter is that more often

than not, people do not suffer *less* when they are committed to following God, but *more*. When these people go through suffering, their lives are often transformed, deepened, marked with beauty and holiness, in remarkable ways that could never have been anticipated before the suffering.

Job provides us with a model for suffering differently. He is vocal. He does not try to avoid suffering, and his suffering continues for a time. God does not magically deliver him from his sorry state. But Job never stops talking to God about it.

Many of us ignore or suppress our emotions. We are taught to do this from childhood. We are raised to believe certain emotions are bad, even harmful.

No one told us as children about the consequences of hiding our true selves. No one warned us these things can fester inside us, accumulating over time, simmering away until they reach boiling point.

I think we have hidden our feelings long enough.

I think it could be time to let them out.

I think we can learn a lot from Job.

The main thing

Children are not the main thing in life.

It might sound like an odd thing to say in a book on childlessness. But for those who belong to God, the bottom line in life is serving God, whether life is good or bad.

This throws any social comparison into sharp relief. We do not have to be like anyone else. We do not have to live up to social norms or expectations. We cannot criticise others for how they live and they cannot criticise us.

Paul makes this explicit in Romans 14:

> None of us are permitted to insist on our own way in these matters. It's God we are answerable to—all the way from life to death and everything in between—not each other. That's why Jesus lived and died and then lived again: so that he could be our Master across the entire range of life and death, and free us from the petty tyrannies of each other.
>
> So where does that leave you when you criticise a brother? And where does that leave you when you condescend to a sister? I'd say it leaves you looking pretty silly—or worse. Eventually, we're all going to end up kneeling side by side in the place of judgment, facing God. Your critical and condescending ways aren't going to improve your position there one bit (Romans 14:7-10 MSG).

I like that bit in verse 8. 'It's God we are answerable to... not each other.' Take that, advice-givers.

If there is a scriptural opinion here, I think it is this: wherever life takes you, including childlessness, keep your eyes fixed on Christ. As long as we live with clear consciences, following God to the best of our ability, we are on the right track. Let us walk that track without regret.

The eternal perspective reminds us everything on earth is temporary. I don't know about you, but I intend to live for God—yes, even in heartache, even without children.

Let your passion for God light a fire in your soul.

In life, in death, in childlessness, in great joy and deep sorrow, let us pursue God above all.

> Wherever life takes you, including childlessness, keep your eyes fixed on Christ.

Embracing suffering

Suffering has the capacity to deepen and beautify our souls.

Many of us want to be beautiful on the inside. Many of us ask God to make us holy. What if the best way to do that is to embrace suffering?

When I think of suffering, I think of Jesus, bowed low in the garden of Gethsemane, praying for God to remove the upcoming crucifixion from him. Jesus did not want to go there. He asked God repeatedly to be delivered. Then, in what I can only imagine was the smallest voice possible, he said, 'Yet not as I will, but as you will' (Matthew 26:39b NIV).

There is such bravery in that prayer. The willingness to surrender, even when the path ahead leads to places we do not want to go, is a beautiful thing. And it marks us with holiness and maturity.

God is more concerned with our holiness than our happiness. He wants us to grow and reach full maturity more than anything else, more than we want children.

I do not know why we are childless when we do not want to be. But maybe God has a way of using this to make us more faithful, more holy, more reliant on him. Maybe God will use this to make us more like him.

Christ suffered when he lived on earth, perhaps more than any other living soul. God honoured him for it. In our suffering we have the opportunity to join Christ in his suffering and show the same obedience he showed.

We tend to shy away from suffering. But maybe we have this suffering thing all backwards. Maybe suffering is an honour in God's kingdom, not a handicap or mark of shame. Maybe we should not be running from it. Maybe we can accept, even embrace, the suffering God allows into our lives. Maybe, instead of praying for deliverance from suffering, we could start praying for more suffering, more refinement in God's fire, until we are holy. Like him.

That is the scariest prayer I could ever pray.

We badly need God's grace in this marathon. Thank God he is faithful to help when suffering abounds. He helps us even while we are trying to live for him.

God does not promise us children. But he does promise the comfort and wisdom of the Holy Spirit. He promises us peace in the midst of our trials. He promises to turn our mourning into joy.

These are the promises he keeps. Promises of joy, peace and comfort.

May God grant us grace to hold on to these promises.

14

INCONCLUSIONS

Now What?

The best way to end a self-help book is to finish with a strong conclusion. It should be bold, a call to action, a tour de force.

So I guess we're screwed.

There is no simple conclusion to childlessness. There is no straightforward answer to suffering and grief and loss. There is certainly no one-size-fits-all formula.

Since I am lacking a definitive conclusion, let's see what kinds of inconclusions we can draw from our learnings so far.

Society, you are the problem

The language of childlessness is problem-saturated.

Terms like 'childless', 'non-parent' and 'infertile' are defined by their opposites: those who have children, those who are parents, those who are fertile.

But what if childlessness is not the problem?

I think a lot of our problems arise from the isolation and stigma surrounding childlessness. We are not invited to friends' houses or events or conversations because of our childlessness. We feel like the odd one out at churches, workplaces and family-friendly celebrations.

News flash: it is not completely our fault.

The structure and culture of society supports child-rearing. Perhaps that is the problem. Instead of blaming ourselves for being abnormal, it is high time we located some of the blame with others. Such as our pronatalist society.

I do not mean we should go around confronting every insensitive comment we hear (we have other things to do, after all). But we can recognise when the outrage and insensitivity of others contributes to our suffering.

Imagine how different life could be if we lifted a little guilt from our shoulders.

Society expects a lot from childless people. It sees us as different, selfish, subhuman. It is OK to mentally give that back once in a while and free ourselves from self-blame. It might help us breathe a little easier.

Sometimes society is the problem.

Opting in, opting out

There is wisdom in giving oneself permission to opt out.

Whether it be baby showers, child-centric conversations,

happy-family movies or the world of social media, opting out gives us a little control in our crazy and unpredictable grief.

Grief can bamboozle us. Some days it is like little ripples of water around our ankles. Other days it hits us like a tsunami. On the ripply days, you can opt in without a problem. It might be a refreshing change. On the tsunami days, however, give yourself permission to opt out.

Our bodies and emotions are designed to raise flags when something is wrong. Pay attention to those warning flags. Find out what they are trying to tell you. And look after yourself.

I have found it helpful to opt out of Christmas carols. It is one of my current survival tools. Being around so many kids running around madly or sitting on their picnic blankets with their families is just too much.

I usually opt out of Mother's and Father's Day church services. I empathise with churches on those days, because they are tough gigs. Some churches do great sermons about God's fatherly and motherly traits, and this is greatly appreciated. But even so, such days can be painful. It is usually easier to opt out.

Opting out is better for my mental health. It is better for my relationship. It is better for my faith, rather than sitting through church doing the mental gymnastics required to stay in the room.

I try to be wise about my sanity. I encourage you to do the same.

Social essentials

It is powerful when someone understands our struggles. It is refreshing to discover they have similar struggles. We get that reassuring moment of, 'Thank goodness it's not just me'.

I regularly meet with childless friends. It breaks down the sense of isolation. It affirms my belief that life can continue, even be normal, despite childlessness. When I complain to them, it is enough for my friends to say, 'Oh, I know. Tell me about it.' They get it. They understand.

Many childless people benefit from having supportive people, especially other childless people, in their corner. For some, this connection and support can be found in counselling. (Disclaimer: I am a counsellor, so I am biased.) I encourage you to consider it. What is the worst that could happen?

While church support can be life-saving, some churches struggle to give the right kind of support. There are many ways the church can improve its care of childless members, especially in terms of embracing honesty, inclusivity and vulnerability.

I love the church. It is because I love the church that I want it to be better. I speak about church issues because I want us, the church, to be more welcoming, more empathic, more like Jesus. If this means speaking up about childlessness, I will.

When it comes to relationships, I encourage you to opt in where possible. That includes church relationships. We may opt out of certain services, avoid the family-oriented Sunday mornings and keep carols at arm's length, but we still need people. Where church relationships are meaningful and honest, try to keep them intact.

I am on the lookout for good news childlessness stories. So if you have one, especially about your church, reach out to me. I would love to hear about your positive experiences. Like the one I had with my new pastor.

Given how many of us lose friendships through childlessness, it's vital to hold on to those friendships when you can. All of us (even introverts) need relationships with others.

I hope we can find a sense of connection through sharing our stories.

Which brings me (rather neatly I think) to my next point.

Stories worth telling

During my interviews for this book, I realised how much we have in common.

Sure, our stories are unique in circumstance, impact and survival. But they also share common threads of circumstance, impact and survival.

About halfway through my interviews I remember thinking, 'Wow. These are stories worth telling'. I was captivated. I was enthralled. I became increasingly convinced of the power of story to connect us and break down isolation, shame and silence.

Stories can highlight the struggles and triumphs of childlessness. And every single one of our precious stories is worth telling.

I am persuaded sharing our stories is powerful both for ourselves and those who listen, whether we share with a select few or the whole world. Sharing our stories empowers us to speak

> *In that void of missing relationship, only relationships will heal.*

truthfully about childlessness. It gives us back a slice of control from the pie of grief. And it gives us the opportunity to connect with others who have similar stories.

Solidarity can be healing. It may not eliminate the pain we feel, but it may give us a buffer against the worst of it.

Grief is about lost connection. For childlessness, the loss is about the connection we hoped to have with our children. It is an absence of relationship. In that void of missing relationship, only relationships will heal.

Which brings me to the most powerful healing relationship of all.

The God bit

I call it a 'bit' when it is really the centre of it all.

In suffering we find ourselves grappling with the mysteries of the universe. We are filled with unknowns and whys and inconclusions. And there, in the vast ocean of loss, we find the largest mystery of all: God.

God is full of mystery. He himself is mystery.

He designed the universe in ways we cannot fathom. He gave us a planet filled with beauty and flaws and brokenness. He has given us a single life in which to experience love and loss, joy and heartbreak, closure and irresolution.

He designed us with questioning minds that seek meaning for the suffering we experience. And he has not always provided answers. Some answers may elude us all our lives.

I do not know why God allows hardship in our lives. I do not know why some prayers go unanswered. I do not understand the way God works behind the scenes. I do not perceive his purposes and intentions behind our suffering. There are some things I really do not get about God.

Because yeah, he is a mystery.

But two things I know, and these are my anchors in the storm of childlessness.

God does not always answer my prayer (at least, not in the way I would like), but he hears every word, every frightened whisper, every groan, every beat of the heart turned towards him.

He sees every tear we shed in profound loss. He hears the ripping and shredding of our hearts. He see us, he knows us, even when we think he has forgotten us.

Through every storm in my life, God's matchless companionship has never faltered. He has often withheld answers from me, especially when he knew I could not stand to hear them. But he has always been near. Even when I thought he had left.

I do not know how or why he keeps working in my life. But I know that he does.

The other thing I know is I often meet God in new, unexpected and faith-deepening ways when I suffer. I do not meet God in these ways when I am happy and content. Only when I am desperately digging deep in my faith do I discover new realms of closeness with God. Happiness breeds comfort and contentment. Suffering breeds determination and endurance. Both have a place.

If God had never allowed my worst life experiences, I would not have known his faithfulness firsthand. I would not have discovered how he is most faithful when I am least faithful. I would not have felt the moment-by-moment fear he would leave, only to find he stayed with me.

I would not have met his kindness full-faced. I would not have felt his grief alongside my own. I would have failed to look up and see the tears brimming in his eyes as I wept. I would not have learned he was just as grief-stricken by my loss as I was. I would not have witnessed God's vulnerability.

I would not have realised his grace really is all-sufficient. He took the worst pieces of my life, the trauma and life-altering doubt and mistrust, and wrapped it up in a blanket of compassion.

Like an anchor for the soul (Hebrews 6:19), he has been sure and true. Like a sunrise, his grace has risen upon me again and again. Because of his ever-renewing grace, I can turn to him when I need him most.

Suffering does more than put us to the test. It puts God's grace to the test. I know it sounds strange to test God, but our suffering proves God is as pure as gold, just like our suffering continually refines us like gold.

This is the paradox and mystery of suffering. It demonstrates our faith and God's grace like nothing else can. It forces our faith to put down roots firmly in God. It beckons us towards holiness. It invites us to trust him like children.

C. S. Lewis (1940) said, 'Suffering is not good in itself. What is good in any painful experience is, for the sufferer, his submission to the will of God, and, for the spectators, the compassion aroused and the acts of mercy to which it leads[88].'

Compassion and acts of mercy are silver linings to our suffering. To surrender all to God, without understanding, without certainty, takes true courage. It is the act of one with an anchor.

God is my single biggest anchor in the sea of childlessness.

Find your anchor

How does one survive childlessness? By finding one's anchor. The anchor grounds us, transforms us, turns our suffering into purpose and meaning. The anchor gives us something for which we can reach and strive and live. It is a reason to get up in the morning. It makes us come alive.

My interviewees shared their anchors in stories of holidays, writing novels and picking up an old guitar. They have stories of travel, career re-training, bucket list-writing and self-discovery.

There are tales of non-parenting parenting, including teaching, mentoring, aunting and uncling (hey, they are real words), adopting furbabies, passing on legacies and re-shaping identities. One of these might be your anchor.

Your anchor might be supportive people: partners, families, friends, counsellors, ministers, online forums and other childless people. And furbabies.

You might find an anchor in using your childlessness for good. Childlessness might ignite a passion in you to help other childless people, like it did for several interviewees. The same was true for me.

Perhaps these stories will be an anchor of solidarity for you, knowing you are not alone. Your story could be an anchor for someone else. Maybe one day you can share your story. Because your story is worth telling.

Faith could be your anchor. Maybe it used to be your anchor but the rope has been severed. Maybe it can be re-attached. Maybe it needs time to settle down and re-anchor.

When my faith anchor came loose once, I found certain parts of my faith were still anchored. Prayer was impossible. Talking to other Christians was no help. Being at church was at times torturous. These bits of my faith had come loose, drifting in the tide.

But one thing stayed anchored: worship. I found I was able to sing to God, despite my misgivings about him. I sang old worship tunes, playing the keyboard when words were too hard, returning to the songs I used to sing as a child. My worship anchor stayed in place amidst the driftwood.

Faith may look different during suffering. It might look like reading one bible verse instead of a whole chunk of scripture. It might look like playing heavy metal worship instead of the sweet stuff. It might appear quiet on the outside while your insides are shouting to God in protest, like Job. It might consist of tears. It might have no words.

Look for your anchor when your faith is adrift and God seems distant. Find it in a song, a bible verse, a friend. Find it in a different church. Find it in hope, even if it is only hanging by a thread.

> How does one survive childlessness? By finding one's anchor.

The tiniest thread can keep you hanging in there.

Whether you are childless-by-choice, childless-by-circumstance, single and childless, undertaking infertility treatment, applying for adoption, childless-by-forced-choice like me or inventing your own brand of childlessness, I pray you find your anchor. I pray you find meaning in childlessness.

I pray God transforms you in and through your suffering.

No matter what, I pray you live for Christ. I pray you cling to God even when the cost is high. In doing so you will have the noblest honour of joining Christ in his suffering, being refined like gold, becoming more like Jesus every minute.

I can think of no higher goal.

HELPFUL RESOURCES

Access: *access.org.au*.

BeyondBlue: 24/7 free counselling helpline, forums and online chat. Phone: 1300 224 636 (in Australia). Website: *beyondblue.org.au*.

BeyondNow: BeyondBlue's suicide prevention app.

Big Brothers Big Sisters: *bigbrothersbigsisters.org.au*.

Dovecote Community: *thedovecoteorg.wordpress.com*.

DV Line: 24/7 counselling and assistance. Phone: 1800 63 64 65 (in Australia).

DV/Sexual Assault Line: 24/7 counselling and assistance. Phone: 1800 737 732 (in Australia).

Fertility Network: *fertilitynetworkuk.org*.

Fiona's blog: *countessdrusillasteele.com*.

Gateway Women: *gateway-women.com*.

Kids Hope: *kidshope.org.au*.

Lifeline: 24/7 free counselling helpline. Phone: 13 11 14 (in Australia). Text: 0477 13 1114 (between 12pm-12am).

Melanie Drage Tapping into Change (in England and on facebook): *melaniedrage.co.uk*.

Pink Elephants Support Network: *pinkelephants.org.au* or *miscarriagesupport.org.au*.

Pyjama Foundation: *thepyjamafoundation.com*.

Rhythm of Hope: *rhythmofhope.co.uk*.

Saltwater and Honey: *saltwaterandhoney.org*.

Sands: *sands.org.au*.

World Childless Week: *worldchildlessweek.net*.

ABOUT THE AUTHOR

STEPH PENNY is a writer and composer, passionate about having countercultural conversations and challenging the status quo. *Surviving Childlessness* is the second book in the *Survival* Series; it follows Steph's debut book, *Surviving Singledom*.

Steph's weekly blogs can be found at **www.stephpenny.com.au**. You can subscribe to her blog and contact her through her blog page. You can also email Steph directly at steph@stephpenny.com.au.

Steph's songs can be found at her website **www.stephpenny.com.au** and on YouTube (just search for Steph Penny) and don't forget to subscribe to her YouTube channel!

Follow Steph on [f] and [t] for the latest on her books, blogs and songs.

If you have enjoyed Steph's writing, why not let her know? She would love to hear from you!

REFERENCES

1 Voysey, S 2013, *Resurrection Year*, Thomas Nelson, Nashville, Tennessee, United States of America.

2 Access Australia 2020, Access Australia, Silverwater, New South Wales, Australia, viewed 13 October 2020, http://www.access.org.au

3 Access Australia n.d., *The immune system and infertility factsheet,* Access Australia, viewed 13 October 2020, http://www.access.org.au/wp-content/uploads/2010/01/2-immune-system-and-infertility.pdf

4 'Antiphospholipid antibodies are reliable predictors of adverse outcome in pregnancy, and are associated with early and late foetal loss, pregnancy induced hypertension, intrauterine growth retardation, prematurity, and both venous and arterial thrombosis occurring during pregnancy. It must, however, be firmly emphasised that these associations are not observed in every woman, nor in every pregnancy.' Access Australia n.d., Access Australia, Silverwater, New South Wales, Australia, viewed 13 October 2020, http://www.access.org.au/wp-content/uploads/2010/01/2-immune-system-and-infertility.pdf

5 Day, J 2017, *The lost tribe of childless women,* online video, 2

June, viewed 13 October 2020, https://www.youtube.com/watch?v=uufXWTHT60Y&feature=youtu.be

6   Lynch, B 2018, 'Male childlessness: "You think, If I'm not reproducing–then what am I?"', *The Guardian*, viewed 13 October 2020, https://www.theguardian.com/lifeandstyle/2018/nov/17/male-childlessness-not-reproducing-what-am-i

7   Endometriosis Australia 2020, Endometriosis Australia, North Sydney, New South Wales, Australia, viewed 13 October 2020, https://www.endometriosisaustralia.org

8   Marsh, S 2017, '"It's the breaking of a taboo": The parents who regret having children', *The Guardian*, viewed 13 October 2020, https://www.theguardian.com/lifeandstyle/2017/feb/11/breaking-taboo-parents-who-regret-having-children?CMP=share_btn_tw

9   Hanna, E, Gough, B & Coan, S 2017, *Men's experiences of infertility: Findings from a qualitative questionnaire study,* Fertility Network UK, United Kingdom, viewed 13 October 2020, https://fertilitynetworkuk.org/wp-content/uploads/2017/11/Report-on-Male-Fertility-Survey.pdf

10 Gorman, G 2016, 'The untold grief of childless men', *Nationwide news,* viewed 13 October 2020, https://www.news.com.au/lifestyle/parenting/kids/the-untold-grief-of-childless-men/news-story/afd12390a8e450d5b9c04e7db6e9d88b?pg=1

11 Corsetti, S 2017, 'Childless couples "on track to be Australia's most common family type"', *ABC News,* viewed 13 October 2020, https://www.abc.net.au/news/2017-05-15/childless-households-on-the-rise/8528546

12 Adams, R, Fung, H, Scheller, A & Shifflett, S 2015, '270 reasons women choose not to have children', *The Huffington Post*, viewed 13 October 2020, http://data.huffingtonpost.com/2015/07/choosing-childfree

13 Marcotte, A 2017, 'Childfree and OK with it—but still dealing with moral scolding and social disapproval', *Salon,* viewed 13 October 2020, http://www.salon.com/2017/03/06/child-free-and-ok-with-it-mdash-but-still-dealing-with-moral-scolding-and-social-disapproval/

14 Keizer, R, Dykstra, PA & Poortman, AR 2011, 'Childlessness and norms of familial responsibility in the Netherlands', in *Journal of Comparative Family Studies*, vol. 42, issue 4, pp. 421-438.

15 African Feminism 2017, 'Living childfree: A conversation with Nina Steele', *African Feminism*, viewed 13 October 2020, http://africanfeminism.com/living-childfree-a-conversation-with-nina-steele/

16 Access Australia n.d., *Coping with Christmas and other religious festivals and special days factsheet,* Access Australia, viewed 13 October 2020, http://www.access.org.au/wp-content/uploads/2010/01/5-coping-w-ChristmasMothers-Day.pdf

17. Frost, M 2017, 'Why should women have all the fun smashing the patriarchy!', *Mike Frost,* web log post, 20 October, viewed 13 October 2020, https://mikefrost.net/women-fun-smashing-patriarchy/

18. Kirchgaessner, S 2015, 'Pope Francis: "Not having children is selfish"', *The Guardian,* viewed 13 October 2020, https://www.theguardian.com/world/2015/feb/11/pope-francis-the-choice-to-not-have-children-is-selfish

19. Lowrie, D 2015, 'Supporting a friend struggling with childlessness', *Saltwater and Honey,* web log post, 23 April, viewed 13 October 2020, http://saltwaterandhoney.org/supporting-a-friend-struggling-with-childlessness

20. Saltwater and Honey 2020, Saltwater and Honey, viewed 13 October 2020, http://saltwaterandhoney.org

21. Fertility Network UK 2020, Fertility Network UK, United Kingdom, viewed 13 October 2020, https://fertilitynetworkuk.org

22. Rhythm of Hope 2020, Rhythm of Hope, Gloucestershire, United Kingdom, viewed 13 October 2020, https://www.rhythmofhope.co.uk

23. Fertility Solutions 2020, *Infertility statistics and facts for Australian couples*, Fertility Solutions, Buderim, Queensland, Australia, viewed 13 October 2020, https://fertilitysolutions.com.au/infertility-statistics/

24 Fertility Solutions 2020, *Infertility statistics and facts for Australian couples*, Fertility Solutions, Buderim, Queensland, Australia, viewed 13 October 2020, https://fertilitysolutions.com.au/infertility-statistics/

25 Fertility Solutions 2020, *Infertility statistics and facts for Australian couples*, Fertility Solutions, Buderim, Queensland, Australia, viewed 13 October 2020, https://fertilitysolutions.com.au/infertility-statistics/

26 Health Engine 2008, *Infertility,* Health Engine, viewed 13 October 2020, https://www.myvmc.com/diseases/infertility/

27 Health Engine 2008, *Infertility,* Health Engine, viewed 13 October 2020, https://www.myvmc.com/diseases/infertility/

28 Endometriosis Australia 2020, Endometriosis Australia, North Sydney, New South Wales, Australia, viewed 13 October 2020, https://www.endometriosisaustralia.org

29 McArthur, S 2007, *Fact file: Infertility,* ABC Health and Wellbeing, Australia, viewed 13 October 2020, http://www.abc.net.au/health/library/stories/2007/05/30/1919840.htm

30 Hadley, RA 2018, 'The lived experience of older involuntary childless men', in AC Sparkes (ed.), *The annual journal of the british sociological association study group on auto/biography,* BSA Auto/Biography Group, Durham, United Kingdom.

31 McArthur, S 2007, *Fact file: Infertility,* ABC Health and

Wellbeing, Australia, viewed 13 October 2020, http://www.abc.net.au/health/library/stories/2007/05/30/1919840.htm

32 Fertility Solutions 2020, *Infertility statistics and facts for Australian couples*, Fertility Solutions, Buderim, Queensland, Australia, viewed 13 October 2020, https://fertilitysolutions.com.au/infertility-statistics/

33 Chambers, G 2017, 'Women now have clearer statistics on whether IVF is likely to work', *The Conversation*, viewed 13 October 2020, https://theconversation.com/women-now-have-clearer-statistics-on-whether-ivf-is-likely-to-work-81256

34 McArthur, S 2007, *Fact file: Infertility,* ABC Health and Wellbeing, Australia, viewed 13 October 2020, http://www.abc.net.au/health/library/stories/2007/05/30/1919840.htm

35 EHSRE 2020, *ART fact sheet,* EHSRE, viewed 22 November 2020, https://www.eshre.eu/-/media/sitecore-files/Pressroom/ART-fact-sheet-2020-data-2016.pdf

36 McArthur, S 2007, *Fact file: Infertility,* ABC Health and Wellbeing, Australia, viewed 13 October 2020, http://www.abc.net.au/health/library/stories/2007/05/30/1919840.htm

37 Cuthbert, H 2017, *IVF glossary: Fertility treatment terms explained*, Manchester Fertility, Manchester, England, viewed 13 October 2020, https://www.manchesterfertility.com/blog/ivf-glossary-fertility-treatment-terms-explained-/

38 Best, M 2012, *Fearfully and wonderfully made*, Matthias Media, Kingsford, New South Wales, Australia.

39 Campbell, L 2017, 'When I donated my eggs 10 years ago, I wish I'd known these things', *ABC News,* viewed 13 October 2020, https://abcnews.go.com/Lifestyle/donated-eggs-10-years-ago-things/story?id=48477302

40 Access Australia n.d., *When is enough, enough? factsheet,* Access Australia, viewed 14 October 2020, http://www.access.org.au/wp-content/uploads/2010/01/39-when-is-enough.pdf

41 Penny, S 2016, *Surviving singledom: Or hang in there!*, Christianity Works, India.

42 Gateway Women 2020, Gateway Women, viewed 22 November 2020, http://www.gateway-women.com

43 Day, J 2013, '50 ways not to be a mother...', *Gateway Women*, web log post, 6 September, viewed 13 October 2020, http://gateway-women.com/50-ways-not-to-be-a-mother-with-apologies-to-paul-simon/

44 Day, J 2017, *The lost tribe of childless women,* online video, 2 June, viewed 13 October 2020, https://www.youtube.com/watch?v=uufXWTHT60Y&feature=youtu.be

45 Keizer, R 2014, 'Childlessness', in AC Michalos (ed.) *Encyclopedia of quality of life and wellbeing research*,

Springer, Dordrecht, Netherlands.

46 Notkin, M 2017, *Welcome to the otherhood,* online video, 24 March, viewed 13 October 2020, https://m.youtube.com/watch?v=75RFZb7c33M

47 Penny, S 2016, *Surviving singledom: Or hang in there!*, Christianity Works, India.

48 Piper, J 2014, 'How are women saved through childbearing?', *Desiring God,* viewed 13 October 2020, https://www.desiringgod.org/articles/how-are-women-saved-through-childbearing

49 Eagleson, H 2013, 'Jazz up your baby-making sex', *Parents.com,* viewed 13 October 2020, http://www.parents.com/getting-pregnant/fertility/boost/make-trying-to-get-pregnant-more-fun/

50 Pepper, L 2008, 'How to keep sex smokin' when trying to conceive', *Baby Center,* viewed 13 October 2020, http://www.babycenter.com/0_how-to-keep-sex-smokin-when-trying-to-conceive_10317251.bc

51 Access Australia n.d., *Infertility and sexuality factsheet,* Access Australia, viewed 13 October 2020, http://www.access.org.au/wp-content/uploads/2010/01/16-infertility-sexuality.pdf

52 Australian Bureau of Statistics 2017, *Personal safety,* Australia, Australian Bureau of Statistics, New South Wales, Australia, viewed 13 October 2020, https://www.abs.gov.au/ausstats/

abs@.nsf/Lookup/by%20Subject/4906.0~2016~Main%20Features~Experience%20of%20Abuse%20before%20the%20age%20of%2015~27

53 Felitti, VJ, Anda, RF, Nordenberg, D, Edwards, V, Koss, MP & Marks, JS 1998, 'Relationship of childhood abuse and adult dysfunction to many of the leading causes of death in adults', in *American Journal of Preventative Medicine,* vol. 14, issue 4, pp. 245-258. https://www.ajpmonline.org/article/S0749-3797(98)00017-8/abstract

54 Harris, NB 2014, *How childhood trauma affects health across a lifetime,* online video, September, viewed 13 October 2020, https://www.ted.com/talks/nadine_burke_harris_how_childhood_trauma_affects_health_across_a_lifetime?language=en

55 Kimmel, MS 2002, 'Male victims of domestic violence: A substantive and methodological research review', *Violence against women,* viewed 14 October 2020, http://www.ncdsv.org/images/male_DV_victims1.pdf

56 Australian Institute of Health and Welfare 2020, *Family, domestic and sexual violence,* Australian Institute of Health and Welfare, viewed 14 October 2020, https://www.aihw.gov.au/reports-data/behaviours-risk-factors/domestic-violence/overview

57 Huecker, MR & Smock, W 2020, *Domestic violence,*

StatPearls, Bethesda, Maryland, United States of America, viewed 14 October 2020, https://www.ncbi.nlm.nih.gov/books/NBK499891/

58 Department of Communities and Justice 2019, *The effects of domestic and family violence on children and young people,* DCJ, New South Wales, Australia, viewed 14 October 2020, https://www.facs.nsw.gov.au/domestic-violence/about/effects-of-dv-on-children

59 The Pyjama Foundation 2018, The Pyjama Foundation, Albion, Queensland, Australia, viewed 14 October 2020, https://thepyjamafoundation.com

60 Brown, B 2010, *The power of vulnerability,* online video, June, viewed 14 October 2020, https://www.ted.com/talks/brene_brown_the_power_of_vulnerability?language=en#t-7197

61 Franks, R 2018, 'The taboo topic affecting 282 Aussie women a day that can cause longlasting grief and mental health problems', *Nationwide news,* viewed 14 October 2020, https://www.news.com.au/lifestyle/parenting/pregnancy/the-taboo-topic-affecting-282-aussie-women-a-day-that-can-cause-longlasting-grief-and-mental-health-problems/news-story/6868aa0b01cefe7496e342ef5b75a9b8

62 Doka, KJ 1989, *Disenfranchised grief: Recognising hidden sorrow,* Lexington Books, Lanham, Maryland, United States of America.

63 Lifeline, n.d., *Text service information,* Lifeline, Australia,

viewed 14 October 2020, https://www.lifeline.org.au/projects/lifeline-text

64 Beyond Blue 2020, Beyond Blue, Australia, viewed 14 October 2020, https://www.beyondblue.org.au

65 Sands 2020, Sands, Surrey Hills, Victoria, Australia, viewed 14 October 2020, https://www.sands.org.au

66 The Pink Elephants Support Network 2020, The Pink Elephants Support Network, Botany, New South Wales, Australia, viewed 14 October 2020, https://www.pinkelephants.org.au

67 Joy 1995, 'Never to be a mother', in *Poems from the heart: Personal experiences of infertility,* Australia.

68 Hadley, RA 2018, '"I'm missing out and I think I have something to give": experiences of older involuntarily childless men', *Emerald insight,* viewed 14 October 2020, http://www.emeraldinsight.com/doi/abs/10.1108/WWOP-09-2017-0025?af=R&

69 Brown, B 2013, *Brené Brown on empathy,* online video, 10 December, viewed 14 October 2020, https://m.youtube.com/watch?v=1Evwgu369Jw

70 Lowrie, D 2015, 'Supporting a friend struggling with childlessness', *Saltwater and Honey,* web log post, 23 April, viewed 13 October 2020, http://saltwaterandhoney.org/supporting-a-friend-struggling-with-childlessness

71 The Dovecote 2017, The Dovecote, United Kingdom, viewed 14 October 2020, https://thedovecoteorg.wordpress.com

72 Brown, B 2012, *Brené Brown on joy and gratitude,* online video, 28 November, viewed 14 October 2020, https://m.youtube.com/watch?v=2IjSHUc7TXM

73 Brown, B 2013, *Brené Brown: 3 things you can do to stop a shame spiral,* online video, 6 October, viewed 14 October 2020, https://m.youtube.com/watch?v=TdtabNt4S7E

74 Blatchford, E 2017, 'Adoption in Australia: Everything you need to know', *The Huffington Post,* viewed 14 October 2020, https://www.huffingtonpost.com.au/2017/09/11/adoption-in-australia-everything-you-need-to-know_a_23203810/

75 Department of Communities and Justice 2019, *Adopting locally,* DCJ, New South Wales, Australia, viewed 14 October 2020, http://www.community.nsw.gov.au/parents,-carers-and-families/fostering,-guardianship-and-adoption/adoption/want-to-adopt/local-adoption

76 Surrogacy Australia 2020, Surrogacy Australia, Crows Nest, New South Wales, Australia, viewed 14 October 2020, www.surrogacyaustralia.org

77 Surrogacy Australia 2020, *New South Wales,* Surrogacy Australia, Crows Nest, New South Wales, Australia, viewed 14 October 2020, https://www.surrogacyaustralia.org/australian-surrogacy-legislation/new-south-wales/

78 IVF Australia 2020, *Egg freezing,* IVF Australia, viewed 14 October 2020, https://www.ivf.com.au/treatments/fertility-preservation/egg-freezing

79 Cha, AE 2018, 'The struggle to conceive with frozen eggs', *Chicago Tribune,* viewed 14 October 2020, https://www.chicagotribune.com/lifestyles/health/ct-struggle-to-conceive-with-frozen-eggs-20180129-story.html

80 Kids Hope Australia 2020, Kids Hope Australia, Scoresby, Victoria, Australia, viewed 14 October 2020, https://kidshope.org.au

81 Big Brothers Big Sisters Australia 2018, Big Brothers Big Sisters Australia, Bentleigh East, Victoria, Australia, viewed 14 October 2020, https://www.bigbrothersbigsisters.org.au

82 The Pyjama Foundation 2018, The Pyjama Foundation, Albion, Queensland, Australia, viewed 14 October 2020, https://thepyjamafoundation.com

83 Notkin, M 2017, *Welcome to the otherhood,* online video, 24 March, viewed 13 October 2020, https://youtu.be/75RFZb7c33M

84 World Childless Week 2020, Hello Lovely, United Kingdom, viewed 14 October 2020, www.worldchildlessweek.net

85 Tsigdinos, PM 2009, *Silent sorority: A barren woman gets busy, angry, lost and found,* BookSurge Publishing, Charleston, South Carolina, United States of America.

86 Tsigdinos, PM 2020, *Silent Sorority,* viewed 14 October 2020, https://blog.silentsorority.com

87 Lewis, CS 1940, *The Problem of Pain,* Collins Clear-Type Press, London and Glasgow, Great Britain.

88 Lewis, CS 1940, *The Problem of Pain,* Collins Clear-Type Press, London and Glasgow, Great Britain.

www.ingramcontent.com/pod-product-compliance
Lightning Source LLC
Chambersburg PA
CBHW022027290426
44109CB00014B/776